Anonymous

The Return Excerpts

Anonymous

The Return Excerpts

ISBN/EAN: 9783744651417

Printed in Europe, USA, Canada, Australia, Japan

Cover: Foto ©ninafisch / pixelio.de

More available books at **www.hansebooks.com**

partakers, equally with Jesus Christ, in the glories of eternal life, can it be presumed for a moment that we can attain to that glory, and treat lightly, or disregard those principles which it was necessary for him to observe in order to obtain that high and exalted privilege? (for he says himself. "I came not to do my own will, but the will of him who hath sent me," which clearly shows that whatever be done or taught was agreeable to the will of God, and consequently the law of heaven.) We think not. Let us, therefore, fellow travellers to the unseen world, examine carefully, and see if those principles which are required to govern us in order to constitute us heirs of God, are dwelling in our bosoms, and we actuated thereby; if so, happy are we: Knowing that if the spirit of him that raised up Jesus from the dead dwell in us, he that raised up Christ from the dead will also quicken our mortal bodies, and we shall have a part in the first resurrection, upon whom the second death hath no power.—E. R.

PALESTINE.

"Since I came here, where a large proportion of Jews know Hebrew well, and some can even converse in it, I have given away a good many Hebrew Testaments. I only give them to those that can read Hebrew, and who expresses a desire to possess copies and promise to give them a careful perusal. I could not afford to do otherwise, for it is easy enough for a Missionary to part with books, but not so very easy to procure fresh supplies. He must, therefore, husband his resources; and, moreover, I am not favorable to indiscriminate distribution—my experience forbids it.

It is pleasant to witness the readiness, and at times even eagerness, with which the Jews receive Salkinson's Version *when told that it is the translation of a Hebrew brother,* a great master of the sacred tongue, revised by another Hebrew brother, a no less talented, erudite scholar; and that the work is, therefore, thoroughly idiomatic; more so than any previous Version.

During the forty years of my Missionary career in Morocco, Algeria, Tunisia, Turkey in Europe and Asia Minor, Gibraltar, Spain, Italy, and other lands, I have been instrumental in disseminating thousands of Hebrew New Testaments, with my own hands, by the agency of colporteurs, and in Scripture Depots, and I do not think there ever was so generally an inclination to receive and read the New Testament, or a more favorable disposition to listen to the message of redeeming love, among the Jews as there is now-a-days. Formerly, it was no rare thing for a Jew to say, no, thank you; it is sinful to read that book. Now I seldom meet with any such objection, *specially when it is explained that it was written by brother Jews,* who sacrificed their lives for the truths they taught; nor is the spirit to controvert and quibble over the facts and doctrines of the Gospel so prevalent as formerly. Speaking generally, I think I may say that never, since Apostolic times, was there a more propitious time for proclaiming the gospel to the Jews. It is indubitably evident that they are getting weary waiting for the promised Messiah; and learning more fully than ever before to distinguish between Protestant or Evangelical Christianity and Popery and other spurious forms of it. It is unquestionably one of the important fruits of missions to them. And if this be so, should not the Church in all its branches be more active and devoted in the work amongst God's ancient people? In the case of the Jews, more than any other people on earth, it is not only winning souls capable of immortality, but also turning active adversaries of the Gospel into friends and fellow-workers, as is abundantly demonstrated by the large proportion of Hebrew converts, who become earnest preachers of the Gospel of the Grace of God." A. BEN-OLIEL.

THE RETURN.

PUBLISHED MONTHLY AT $1.00 A YEAR.

E. ROBINSON, EDITOR AND PROPRIETOR.

DAVIS CITY, IOWA, APRIL, 1869.

THE ELDERS OF THE CHURCH OF CHRIST will please bear in mind that our conference convenes at Richmond, Mo., on Friday evening, the 5th of April, inst., at 7 o'clock. Provision will be made for the accommodation of visiting brethren.

———o———

"WE wish our Subscribers to bear in mind that the only advantage or satisfaction there is in registering a letter, is the fact that a receipt is signed by the party to whom the letter is sent, providing it reaches its destination, and the receipt is forwarded back, to the sender. In case of a Mail robbery, or if the letter should get lost any other way, the government is not responsible for the loss. A Post office order is the safest, for if the letter gets stolen or lost, the government is responsible for the loss, and the cost on a small amount, is only five cents, one half that of a registered letter.

———o———

WE WOULD URGE upon the brethren and sisters, members of the church of Christ, to be humble, and cultivate a meek and quiet spirit, which, in "the sight of God is of great price," and to let nothing draw you away from your steadfastness in Christ, knowing that God cannot look upon sin with any degree of allowance. Do not suffer yourselves to be drawn into a *contentious* argument or debate, for Jesus hath said, he that hath the spirit of contention is of the devil, and almost as certain as you suffer yourselves to enter into such a controversy, you partake of that spirit which brings leanness and barrenness of soul. Remember the words of Jesus where he says: "Blessed are ye when men shall revile you, and persecute you, and say all manner of evil against you falsely for my sake. Rejoice and be exceeding glad: for great is your reward in heaven."

Let us strive to conduct ourselves in such a way as to be worthy to attain unto the heavenly reward, which we cannot do if we render railing for railing; but let us bear patiently all things through which we may be called to pass, that we may become the children of our "Father who is in heaven."

———o———

ITEMS OF PERSONAL HISTORY OF THE EDITOR.

IT IS SAID, "There is one thing you cannot cheat a person out of, and that is, their experience." This we are sure is true. What a person passes through, that they know for themselves. You need not tell them they never experienced such and such things, when you know nothing about it, neither knew them, or their surroundings.

We commenced to learn the art of printing with Mr. E. A. Maynard, in the "Observer" office, in the city of Utica, New York; in the spring of 1832; afterwards worked under instruction, with Mr. L. L. Rice, in the "Ohio Star" office in Ravenna, Portage Co. Ohio. Remained with Mr. Rice until he sold out his printing establishment to Lauren Dewey, in December, 1833. Mr. Rice afterwards purchased a printing establishment from E. D. Howe, of Painesville, Ohio, among the papers of which, he unwittingly, became in possession, and custodian, of the noted "Spaulding Manuscript Found," which, with other papers, was put away in a trunk and not examined for some fifty years, until Dr. McKosh, President of the Oberlin College of Ohio, was visiting him when they thought they would look over his old abolition papers, and found this Spaulding manuscript, properly certified to.

Mr. Rice was a very amiable christian gentleman, and had a very interesting, pleasant family.

Mr. Rice sold out to Mr. Dewey, we went to Hudson, Ohio, and worked in the "Hudson Observer" office, a Presbyterian paper, published in the interest of the Hudson College in that place.

In May, 1835, went to Kirtland, Ohio, and obtained a situation in the Latter Day Saints' church printing office, which was conducted under the firm name, of F. G. Williams & Co.. The firm consisted of Joseph Smith, jr. F. G. Williams and Oliver Cowdery. We engaged to work by the month and be boarded by our employers, when we went there we had no faith in their religion, as it was everywhere spoken against, but as we wrote to one of our sisters residing in the state of New York, we considered "Mormon money as good as anybody's money," and were very glad to secure the situation. We boarded the first two months in the family of Oliver Cowdery, the second two months in the family of F. G. Williams, and the third two months in the family of Joseph Smith jr.. We found them all very pious, good christian people, asked a blessing at the table and all attended to family worship morning and evening. This we was glad to see, as we had been accustomed to it from our earliest childhood in our father's home.

We had made a profession of religion when about fifteen years of age, but had not joined any church, as we could not find any that taught the gospel as we read it in the new testament scriptures, and had so stated to our friends when importuned to join their church. We had been raised a baptist of the strictest order of the sect, both parents belonging to that church, and a brother and two sisters having recently united with it, and one brother united with the Methodist church. We had also been importuned by a young friend belonging to the Presbyterian church, to join that church, our reply was, "they all had some parts of the gospel, but none had it all, and we would not join any church until we found one that had it all." We believed in faith and repentance and baptism by immersion, and the enjoyment of the gifts and blessings promised by our Savior as recorded in the last chapter of Mark; and a consistant christian daily walk as portrayed by our Savior in his Sermon on the Mount. We found a people there who, to our surprise, taught them all; and, to our understanding, practiced them.

The members of the church there in that day all seemed to love one another, and take a deep interest in each others welfare, and it was a pleasure to be with them. It seemed to us that if they met several times a day they would always greet each other with a hearty shake of the hand, and a "God bless you," and all seemed anxious to live according to the teachings of Christ.

All the other hands in the printing office were members of the church, but none of them ever made any attempt at proselyting us. On one occasion when boarding at Joseph Smith's, he said to us, "when you are baptized I want to baptize you," on another occasion, as we were walking together after dinner, from his house to the printing office, he said to us, "you will help me build Zion, wont you?" do not recollect of making any reply at either time.

Our prejudices were such when we first went there, that when the Elders coming into the office and speaking of their success in the ministry which they attributed to the power of truth, as presented by them, we remember to have momentarily stopped from our work, and of mentally saying: "Truth, what do you know about truth." It was not long however, until we became satisfied we were with a people who not only taught, but more perfectly practiced the gospel lessons, than any people we had ever before known, and we began earnestly to look into the matter. Then for a short time, felt an anxiety to believe the old Calvinistic doctrine of election and reprobation in which we had been reared; reasoning thus, if that doctrine be true, and we should lead ever so pious, self denying a life and be a reprobate, we would be consigned to the pit; whereas, on the other hand, if we were re-elected if be saved we could lead ever so free and easy a life and yet have salvation. But our heart revolted at the thought, and we dismissed it from our mind.

(TO BE CONTINUED.)

CORRESPONDENCE.

Hornick Woodbury Co., Iowa.

BROTHER ROBINSON:—Please find enclosed one dollar for the subscription of the RETURN, for one year, and if you can, please send me the back numbers. I am a member of the church of Christ. Myself and wife were baptized over a year ago, at Hillsdale, Iowa, by Elder Solomon Thomas, and we have never regreted our adoption in the same. God has greatly blessed us with his spirit when we live worthy to receive the same.

I am one of a family of 12 children now living. They all belong to the Reorganization with the exception of the two younger brothers. I never joined that church it being shown me, in a night vision, that there was a greater light that I should accept some time in the future. I was then but a youth, but when that light dawned upon me, I accepted it, and I feel that I have found a "pearl of great price." The church of Christ is now advocating the same principles which I have believed for a long time past, which are according to the everlasting covenant of our Lord and Savior Jesus Christ.

I have read, and re-read, Bro. David's address, and how any one can read that address and reject it, is more than I can understand. I can read that address with the same spirit that I read Nephi, Alma, and Mormon's writings, also the writings of the Apostles of the Lamb. The spirits seem to agree, and it seems to be the selfsame spirit of Jesus Christ himself.

Some time in the future, if I feel so impressed, I may write some for your paper (THE RETURN,) and if you think it worthy of a place in your paper, all right and if not all right. I have read the first No., and I like the spirit of it:

May God bless you with his spirit while endeavoring to spread the gospel of Christ, through the columns of THE RETURN, is my prayer.—From your Brother in Christ. W. S. ROBERTS.

EXTRACTS FROM LETTERS.

A friend in Arkansas, writes:

"Dear Brother.—I was made glad a few days since by the receipt of your letter. I feel that you have begun in the right way. The great sin of Latter Day Saints has been "Priestcraft," and "Organization;" whereas, in former times, the church of God was wherever a number of baptized believers were, with the necessary Elders and helps, and each body was responsible to itself and God alone for its acts, both temporal and spiritual, but the ambition of men have run into "Popery" in every age, through so called "organization," making the Kingdom of God "*with* observation," contrary to the teaching of Jesus.

May the Lord bless and prosper his work and people, and give us grace and strength to overcome, and endure to the end. And may the church of Christ never again, set up a censor over the thoughts and conscience of men; but having learned that no two men think just alike, be content to obey the gospel, and let each learn his own duty in the fear of God. May the Lord bless you in your effort, and give you wisdom for this important work."

A Friend in New York City, writes:

"I have been greatly interested in your new publication, also in the pamphlet, "An address to all believers in Christ," which you so kindly sent me.

I think you are at work in the right direction, and are doing much to enlighten us respecting Mormonism. The prevailing opinion regarding the Mormons is, that the one and inseparable thing with them, is *polygamy.*"

A friend in San Francisco, writes:

"Inclosed, find P. O. order for THE RETURN for one year.

May blessings in abundance flow
From Heaven above, from earth below
On you and yours, sincerely prays
Your humble friend in Gospel grace."

THE RETURN.

"Truth, crushed to earth, shall rise again; The eternal years of God are hers."

Vol. 1. No. 4.   DAVIS CITY, IOWA, APRIL, 1889.   Whole No. 4.

The Return.

PUBLISHED MONTHLY AT $1,00 A YEAR,

Entered at the Post Office at Davis City, Iowa, as second class matter.

DIVINE AUTHENTICITY OF THE BIBLE.

In the investigation of this subject, we shall necessarily make numerous quotations from the bible, some of which may be of considerable length, containing prophecies and promises to Israel, and also to all the gentile nations of the earth; as the destiny of *all nations* is inseperably interwoven and linked in with the destiny and history of Israel. And shall endeavor to show the literal fulfillment of prophecy in many cases in the past, and speak of some which are now being fulfilled in a marvellous manner, and also of some yet in the future.

And also call the attention of the reader to the marvellous manner in which the Lord has preserved the children of Israel, as a separate and distinct race of people from all others, notwithstanding they have been scattered among all nations, for nearly two thousand years, as *living witnesses*, for him, that there is ONE LIVING AND TRUE GOD. This, evidently, was one of the prime reasons of his entering into covenant with Abraham; and as a sure means to accomplish this end, gave him the covenant of circumscision, with a commandment that: "Every man child among you shall be circumscised, ** and it shall be a token of the covenant betwixt me and you, **** and my covenant shall be in your flesh for an *everlasting* covenant."

This ordinance of circumscision has been religiously kept by the Jews, according to the commandment given to Abraham, to this day, as their history abundantly proves.

In our former article we briefly traced the history of Israel down to the days of Moses, and left him in the land of Midian, where he married the daughter of the priest of Midian. While Moses was thus sojourning in Midian, the Lord appeared unto him and gave him directions to go down into Egypt and deliver Israel from the cruel bondage and oppression put upon them by the Egyptians, as will be seen by the following quotation from the 3rd chap. of Exodus, from the 1st to the 15th verses inclusive:

"Now Moses kept the flock of Jethro his father-in-law, the priest of Midian: and he led the flock to the back side of the desert, and came to the mountain of God, even to Horeb. And the angel of the LORD appeared unto him in a flame of fire, out of the midst of a bush: and he looked, and, behold, the bush burned with fire, and the bush *was* not consumed. And Moses said, I will now turn aside, and see this great sight, why the bush is not burnt. And when the LORD saw that he turned aside to see, God called unto him out of the midst of the bush, and said, Moses, Moses. And he said, here *am* I. And he said, Draw not nigh hither; put off thy shoes from off thy feet; for the place whereon thou standest *is* holy ground. Moreover he said, I *am* the God of thy father, the God of Abraham, the God of Isaac, and the God of Jacob. And Moses hid his face, for he was afraid to look upon God. And the LORD said, I have surely seen the affliction of my people which *are* in Egypt, and have heard their cry by reason of their task-masters; for I know their sorrows: And I am come down to deliver them out of the hand of the Egyp-

This resolution places the responsibility of every person's conduct where it belongs, upon themselves.

---o---

ITEMS OF PERSONAL HISTORY OF THE EDITOR.

(Continued from page 59.)

After having conclusively settled in our mind that the Calvinistic doctrine of election was not a safe one to risk the salvation of our soul upon, we then went to work in earnest, searching the scriptures, and praying fervently to our Heavenly Father to be pleased to show us the truth as it was with him, as it was the truth, and the truth only, that we wanted.

It was not long until our Heavenly Father condescended to manifest to us clearly, by his peaceful spirit, that the gospel, as set forth in the New Testament Scriptures and Book of Mormon, which was taught by this people, was true. Straight-way upon receiving this testimony, we felt an intense desire to be baptized, but told no one our feelings.

At dinner that day, (Oct. 16, 1835,) Joseph Smith, jr. finished his meal a little before the others at the table, and went and stood in the door-way, (the door being open, it being a warm pleasant day,) with his back to the door jamb, when we arose and went and stood before him, and looking him in the face said, "do you know what I want?" when he replied, "No, without it is to go into the waters of Jordan." We told him that was what we wanted, when he said he would attend to it that afternoon. We then went to the printing office together, he to his council room which adjoined the printing room where we worked, and we to our work in the printing office. We worked until well on to the evening, feeling very anxious all the time, for it seemed that we could not live over night without being baptized; after enduring it as long as we could, went to the door of their room, and gently opened it, (a thing we had never presumed to do before.) As soon as Mr. Smith saw us he said, "yes, yes, brethren, Brother Robinson wishes to be baptized, we will adjourn and attend to that."

We repaired to the water, (the Chagrin river which flows through Kirtland,) and, after a season of prayer, Brother Joseph Smith, jr. baptized us by immersion, and as we arose from the water it seemed that everything we had on left us, and we came up a new creature, when we shouted aloud, "Glory to God," Our heart was full to overflowing, and we felt that we had been born again in very deed, both of water and of the spirit.

In going up from the water Brother Joseph Smith said to the brethren, "I am not afraid of Brother Robinson ever denying the faith." We thank our Heavenly Father that a doubt of the truth of the glorious gospel of our Lord and Savior, Jesus Christ, which we then obeyed, has never found lodgement in this poor heart from that day to this, (April 25, 1889,) for one single moment Our soul rejoices in it still, and we trust it will, by his grace assisting us, while our Heavenly Father gives us breath.

The principles of the gospel, as presented to our understanding, and which we received and obeyed, were, faith on the Lord Jesus Christ

the gifts and blessings promised by our Savior in the last chapter of Mark's gospel, where he says:

"Go ye into all the world, and preach the gospel to every creature. He that believeth and is baptized, shall be saved; but he that believeth not, shall be damned. And these signs shall follow them that believe; In my name shall they cast out devils; they shall speak with new tongues; They shall take up serpents; and if they drink any deadly thing it shall not hurt them; they shall lay hands on the sick, and they shall recover."

We were taught by that people that all these precious gifts and blessings can be enjoyed by the believers in this age of the world, as in former ages, we believed these things with all our heart, and after more than fifty years experience we can certify to the truth of the same.

It is by virtue of teaching this gospel, with the signs and blessings following, which gives the Elders of *all the factions* of the church their success.

These signs and blessings have followed, and been enjoyed by the honest hearted, pure minded members of the Brighamite, or Utah church, of whom we verily believe there are thousands. Several very remarkable, well authenticated cases of healing are on record in their public journals, where the parties have followed the instuction given by the apostle James, in the 5th chapter and 14th and 15th verses of his Epistle, where he says: "Is any sick among you? let him call for the elders of the church; and let them pray over him, annointing him with oil in the name of the Lord: and the prayer of faith shall save the sick, and the Lord shall raise him up:"

We can testify, in truth, that these gifts and blessings were enjoyed by members of the church in Elder Rigdon's organization; and he used to take it as a righteousness is accepted of him;" and that these things are individual matters, for Jesus says: "*He* that believeth and is baptized shall be saved. * * and these signs shall follow *them that believe*. This was, and is our faith.

We are credibly informed that these signs and blessings were enjoyed by members of Elder J. J. Strang's organization, and we believe the testimony.

We also believe the same is true of the members of Wm. Bickerton's, Granville Hederick's, Lyman Wight's, and other organizations.

But to return to Kirtland.

The first Sunday after our baptism, were confirmed a member of the church by the laying on of the hands of the elders, and for the gift of the Holy Ghost, as anciently practiced, as recorded in the 8th and 19th chapters of the Acts of the Apostles, but experienced no perceptible change at the time, having received the birth of the spirit at baptism.

Not long after this an incident occured which caused us to go to our heavenly Father for his protection and guidance. Brother Oliver Cowdery called us into his office, (the council room of the first presidency, spoken of before,) and said they would settle with us, and that they could get along without our services longer; however, if we would stay for eleven dollars per month we could do so. This surprised us very much, as it was the first intimation we had received that our services were not needed. The first thought was to leave and go to Columbus, Ohio, where printers were in demand and wages far greater than at Kirtland, but we did not wish to go where we would be deprived of church privileges. We told Brother Cowdery we would let him know, and returned to our work setting type as before, but our heart was full, and we looked to our heavenly Father with all the feelings of our soul, and, dropping our face upon our hands, as we stood at the case, said: "*Father what shall I do?*" In an instant the answer came in words clear and distinct, "*Stay and be happy.*" We went directly to Brother Cowdery and told him we would stay.

Not long after this, another incident occurred which tested the truthfulness of the teachings of Jesus, and the happy effect of obedience to the gospel had upon our own heart.

James Carrell, foreman in the printing office, became exceedingly angry at us, and charged us with having told something about him which we had not told, and was innocent of the charge as a babe, but could not make him believe it. The more we protested our innocence the more angry he seemed to get, until, as we were walking by the side of the imposing stone in the middle of the room, and he behind us, something said to us, "he is striking at you," when we instantly dodged our head forward just in time to save the force of the blow, but he struck us in the back of the neck with sufficient force to knock our hat off, when we turned and smiled at him. We did not feel one particle of anger. He turned and walked the other way. We went to our work as usual. Just before sundown he came to us and said he wished we would take a walk with him. We went together to a field not far away, when he told us he "dare not let the sun go down on his wrath," and that when he struck us and we turned and smiled at him, it whipped him the most severely he ever was whipped in his life, and begged us to forgive him, with tears and weeping. We cheerfully forgave him all, and was thankful at the result. It gave us a practical demonstration of the truthfulness of the teachings of our Savior where he commands us to render good for evil, and it should be like "heaping coals of fire upon their heads."

(To be continued.)

———o———

WE trust the members of our church will not be so vain as to think we are the only people in all the earth who are entitled to the consideration and blessings of the Lord.

It took Peter some time to learn the great truth that "he that feared God and worked righteousness was accepted of him." Notwithstanding our Savior had given him his charge to go "into *all* the world and preach the gospel to *every creature*," yet he clung to his Jewish tradition that none but Israel could be favored with the glad tidings of the gospel, until the Lord impressed it upon him by an open vision, repeated three times, and an outpouring of the Holy Ghost upon Cornelius and his household.

———o———

RELIC LIBRARY.

We have received the first No. of the "*Relic Library*," published by John K. Sheen, of York, Neb.

This No. contains a reprint of the life of Joseph Smith from his early childhood up to May 1829, written by himself. Also a brief preface and a few short foot notes. It seems to be the intention of the publisher to embody in one volume all the writings of Joseph Smith, a work which we have wished, for several years past, to see done by some one.

Mr. Sheen is the son of the late Elder Isaac Sheen, who was the first Editor of the "*Saints' Herald*." He furnishes 24 Nos. of 32 double column pages each, for two dollars.

———o———

(*From the Messenger and Advocate, of 1845.*)

Is it true that we have given us in the person of Jesus of Nazareth, a perfect example of obedience to the principles of eternal salvation? By imitating the pattern which he has left us by treading the path which his footsteps have hallowed, who was the way, the truth, and the life, we can enter the holiest of all whither the forerunner hath for us entered.

Although it is necessary we should make our ingress by the door, "into the sheepfold, that we may be constituted legal heirs according to the promise—that is not *all* which is requisite to secure the "inheritance of the saints in light." It is not enough that we yield obedience to the first principles of the doctrine of Christ, unless we go on unto perfection, "by patient continuance in well doing unto the end."

The standard of excellence which is erected by the Savior, is nothing short of the perfection of Deity. "Be ye perfect, even as your Father who is in heaven is perfect." This implies the renunciation of all evil, and the advocacy and practice of all good. We are at once directed to God as the source of unmixed good. "The works that I do," remarkable declaration, "are the works which I have seen my Father do." In acting then upon the principles which you see do govern me in my life you can become perfect even as your Father who is in heaven is perfect, and this is the only road that leads thereto.

It is recorded of Jesus Christ, that "he was tempted in all points like as we are, yet without sin." Do we ask by what principle did he overcome? Hear his answer, "resist the Devil, and he will flee from you." There is one principle which we must think, more than any other means in our power, conduces to our victory over the Devil, and all his works—watching, unto fasting and prayer. In what condition did the Son of God encounter that memorable onset of Satan, in the wilderness? And how gloriously did he triumph on that principle. How remarkably he admonished his disciples to the performance of this duty or means of victory.

To those who have diligently perused the sacred records, we would ask, in what condition, and under what circumstances, do we find men in every age, and in every clime, seeking and obtaining power with God and power with man, by the out-pouring of the Spirit of God; so that no power save that of God, could withstand them?

Go thou and do likewise.

---o---

EXTRACTS FROM LETTERS.

A friend in western Iowa writes, "Dear Brother.—I received THE RETURN, For which I am thankful; it has been the means of opening my eyes so I can see the true plan of redemption, and the many 'Isms' that have been taught since the rise of the church of Christ. I am satisfied if we are ever to become one it is through the teachings of the two Books. I send you the subscription for THE RETURN as I do not wish it stopped." I remain as ever in the bonds of peace.

---o---

Rogers, Ark., March 23rd, 1889.
ELDER E. ROBINSON,

Dear Brother,—THE RETURN is before me, and two or three extra copies for this month. I will try to place them to good use. I would not do without it for many times its price. I believe it will be the means of doing great good, if it continues in the same spirit in which it has started.

I also believe that the small beginning which has been made is destined to grow and spread over the earth until every nation shall hear the pure gospel preached by the Elders of the Church of Christ, devoid of all the "machinery" and "system" which mark the churches of men, and which bind the soul, and blind the eyes, until men lose sight of the worship of God in their admiration for, and devotion to their "system" or "Organization." All this is contrary to Christ. In Him all are equal, and each one is responsible to Him, for the way he performs what *Christ*, (*not his superior brother*) tells him to do.

I notice the conference appointment for Richmond. I should be glad to meet with the brethren, but my affairs will not permit it. May the Spirit of peace meet with you all, and may all clearly understand the danger of attempting to enact laws, or placing fixed construction upon laws given in the scriptures, for the governing of the members of the church. The scriptures are plain on all points on which Christ desires unalternble rules, and those which he has left without positive statement, may

The Return.

PUBLISHED MONTHLY AT $1.00 A YEAR,

Entered at the Post Office at Davis City, Iowa, as second class matter.

DIVINE AUTHENTICITY OF THE BIBLE.

(CONTINUED FROM PAGE 51.)

We are told in the 6th verse of the 6th chapter of Exodus, that the Lord would bring the children of Israel out from under the burdens of the Egyptians with *great judgments*, and in the 7th and 8th verses he said: "And I will take you to me for a people, and I will be to you a God; *and ye shall know that I am the Lord your God*, which bringeth you out from under the burdens of the Egyptians. And I will bring you in into the land, concerning the which I did swear to give it to Abraham, to Isaac, and to Jacob; and I will give it you for a heritage: I am the Lord."

When Moses spake these words to the children of Israel they hearkened not to Moses for anguish of spirit, and for cruel bondage.

The Lord then sent Moses and Aaron in unto Pharaoh again to demand the release of the children of Israel, but told them before they went, saying:

"But Pharaoh shall not hearken unto you, that I may lay my hand upon Egypt, and bring forth mine armies, and my people the children of Israel, out of the land of Egypt by great judgments. And the *Egyptians shall know that I am the Lord*, when I stretch forth mine hand upon Egypt, and bring out the children of Israel from among them." Ex. vii: 4, 5.

Moses and Aaron went as commanded, when they found it as the Lord had told them, for when Aaron threw down his rod and it became a serpent, the magicians of Egypt cast down their rods and they became serpents also, but Aaron's rod swallowed up their rods. Pharaoh's heart was hardened and he would not let the people go.

Again, when Aaron smote the waters, and they were turned to blood; so also did the magicians. And again when Aaron smote the waters and frogs came forth, so also did the magicians. But when Aaron smote the dust of the earth and lice came forth, the magicians tried their enchantments but could not bring forth lice. "Then the magicians said to Pharaoh, *This is the finger of God*, and Pharaoh's heart was hardened, and he hearkened not unto them as the Lord had said." After this we have no further account of the magicians making any effort to compete with the miracles wrought by the hands of Moses and Aaron.

The next plague in order was bringing forth innumerable swarms of flies upon all the Egyptians, but in the land of Goshen, upon the Hebrews, were no flies, as the Lord said to Pharaoh, "And I will sever in that day the land of Goshen, in which my people dwell, that no swarms of flies shall be there; to the end thou *mayest know that I am the Lord* in the midst of the earth."

After the flies came the plague of the murrain. "And all the cattle of Egypt died; but of the cattle of the children of Israel died not one."

After the murrain was the plague

THE RETURN.

PUBLISHED MONTHLY AT $1.00 A YEAR.
E. ROBINSON, EDITOR AND PROPRIETOR.

DAVIS CITY, IOWA, JUNE, 1889.

—Some kind friend in California sent us a list of over 400 names to whom we will send sample copies of THE RETURN. Wish the friend had furnished us their own name, so we could have sent them a personal note of thanks. Presume it was one of our several subscribers in that state. Whoever it is we thank them kindly, and trust their generous act will be instrumental in saving some honest souls from error.

—We purpose to take up the subject of high priests, priests, tithing, the order of Enoch, polygamy, baptism for the dead, and other important subjects, in due course of time, the Lord willing. We wish to be in his hands as clay in the hands of the Potter, and hope to do according to his will.

—We notice in the minutes of the general conference of the Reorganized church held in St. Joseph, Mo., commencing April 6, 1889, the statement that Ebenezer Robinson had been expelled from the branch of the church to which he belonged.

Seeing that notice in the *Saints' Herald* was the first intimation we had ever received that we had been *expelled* from the church. No officer, or member of the Davis City branch of the church have ever notified or told us that such was the case. One thing is certain, there never has been *one legal step* taken in that direction, according to the law of the church in the New Testament scriptures, or Book of Covenants, as we read them, we therefore pronounce the statement incorrect.

—We wish our subscribers to give us notice whenever THE RETURN fails to reach them, and we will mail them another with pleasure, as we wish them to have a full set. We have back numbers which can be furnished to old or new subscribers.

—We have on hand several lengthy articles sent us for publication, which our limited space precludes our publishing.

ITEMS OF PERSONAL HISTORY OF THE EDITOR.

(Continued from page 76.)

In addition to the papers and hymn book which were being printed in the office, there were also being printed the first edition of the book of Doctrine and Covenants, having on its title page these words, which we copy from one of the books printed at that time, now lying before us.

"Doctrine and Covenants of the church of LATTER DAY SAINTS: carefully selected from the revelations of God, and compiled by Joseph Smith junior, Oliver Cowdery, Sidney Rigdon, Fredrick G. Williams, (*Presiding Elders of said church*,) Proprietors. Kirtland, Ohio. Printed by F. G. Williams & Co. for the Proprietors. 1835."

On the 17th day of August, 1835, a general assembly of the church convened in the lower part of the temple, to hear the report of the compiling committee of said book, and determine, by vote, whether they "accepted and acknowledged it as the doctrine and covenants of their faith.

After the only two members of the committee, who were present, viz: Oliver Cowdery and Sidney Rigdon, had reported, several official members of the church, Presidents of quorums, arose, one after another, and testified to the truth of the book, and they and their quorums "accepted and acknowledged it as the doctrine and covenants of their faith."
Afterwards the question was put to the whole assembly and carried, unanimously.

We attended that meeting, and

noticed that a majority of those voting did so upon the testimony of those who bore record to the truth of the book, as they had neither time or opportunity to examine it for themselves. They had no means of knowing whether any alterations had been made in any of the revelations or not.

Neither Joseph Smith jr. or Fredrick G. Williams, were present at this general assembly, as they had gone to Michigan.

The church had been engaged for nearly two years in building a temple, and were making great efforts to complete it sufficient to have it dedicated, as upon that occasion they believed a great endowment from the Lord would be conferred upon them, having so understood some of the revelations upon the subject. Several official members of the church residing in Missouri, had been called to Kirtland to be present on that occasion, to wit; David Whitmer,—John Whitmer, Edward Partridge, W. W. Phelps, George M. Hinkle, Elisha H. Groves, George Morey, and others. These brethren were frequently in the printing office, which gave us an opportunity to get acquainted with them.

On the 13th day of December, 1835, we were united in wedlock with Miss Angeline Eliza Works, a member of the church. We immediately commenced house-keeping, when we commenced family prayer morning and evening, and asking a blessing at meals, which practice has been continued in our family to this day. Our companion was a spiritually minded woman, and one of great faith, which was a great help to us. We were taught these duties by the Elders of the church, as well as our own promptings, and were blessed and prospered of the Lord.

As the time drew near for the dedication of the temple, the brethren and sisters seemed anxious to humble themselves, and have their hearts prepared to receive the rich and choice blessings of heaven, the anxiously looked for endowment.

On Sunday the 27th day of March, 1836, previous notice having been given, the members of the church began to assemble in the temple before 8 o'clock a. m. and by 9 o'clock the house was crowded full, so that the doors were ordered closed. It was estimated there were 1,000 people present. Services commenced by reading the 96th and 24th Psalms, and singing hymn "Ere long the vail will rend in twain," and prayer by President Sidney Rigdon, after which he delivered a powerful sermon of two hours and a half duration, from the 20th verse of the 8th chapter of Matthew.

The exercises lasted until past four o'clock p. m. with a short intermission of about 15 minutes at noon.

We now quote from the March, (1836) No. of the "Latter Day Saints Messenger and Advocate" giving an account of the proceedings of the meeting.

"The P. M. services commenced by singing a hymn. President J. Smith jr. then rose, and after a few preliminary remarks, presented the several Presidents of the church, then present, to the several quorums respectively, and then to the church as being *equal with himself*, acknowledging them to be *Prophets* and *Seers*. The vote was unanimous in the affirmative in every instance. Each of the different quorums was presented in its turn to all the rest, and then to the church, and received and acknowledged by all the rest, in their several stations without a manifest dissenting sentiment. President J. Smith jr. then addressed the congregation in a manner calculated to instruct the understanding, rather than please the ear, and at or about the close of his remarks, he prophesied to all, that inasmuch as they would uphold these men in their several stations, alluding to the different quorums in the church the Lord would bless them: yea, in the name of Christ, the blessings of Heaven shall be yours. And when the Lord's anointed go forth to proclaim the word, bearing testimony to this generation, if they receive it, they shall be blessed, but if not, the judgments of God will follow close upon them, until *that* city or *that* house, that rejects them, shall be left desolate."

He then offered the dedication prayer, which occupies over seven columns of the "Messenger and Advocate.

"President Smith then asked the several quorums separately and then the congregation, if they accepted the prayer. The vote was, in every instance, unanimous in the affirmative.

The Eucharist was administered. D. C. Smith blessed the bread and wine and they were distributed by several Elders present, to the church.

President J. Smith jr. then arose and bore record of his mission. D. C. Smith bore record of the truth of the work of the Lord in which we are engaged.

President O. Cowdery spoke and testified of the truth of the book of Mormon, and of the work of the Lord in these last days.

President F. G. Williams bore record that a Holy Angel of God, came and sat between him and J. Smith sen. while the house was being dedicated."

We did not see the angel, but the impression has evidently obtained with some, that we did see the angel, from the fact that different persons, strangers from abroad, have called upon us and expressed gratification at meeting with a person who had seen an angel, refering to the above circumstance. We told them they were mistaken, that we did not see the angel, but that President F. G. Williams testified as above stated. We believed his testimony, and have often spoke of it both publicly and privately.

"President Hyrum Smith, (one of the building committee) made some appropriate remarks concerning the house, congratulating those who had endured so many toils and privations to erect it. That it was the Lord's house built by his commandment and He would bless them.

President S. Rigdon then made a few appropriate closing remarks; and a short prayer which was ended with loud acclamation of Hosanna! Hosanna! Hosanna! to God and the Lamb, Amen. Amen and Amen! Three times. Elder B. Young, one of the Twelve, gave a short address in tongues; Elder D. W. Patten interpreted and gave a short exhortation in tongues himself; after which, President J. Smith jr. blessed the congregation in the name of the Lord, and at a little past four P. M. the whole exercise closed and the congregation dispersed."

Elder J. M. Grant, prophesied there would be a railroad built from Kirtland to Jackson county, Missouri within ten years. There is no railroad to Kirtland to this day.

The official members of the church met in the temple and attended to the ordinance of washing and anointing each other with oil in the name of the Lord, and washing each others' feet. The number of official members were so great that several days and nights were occupied in these exercises. But not having yet been ordained, we were not present at any of them.

April 6, it being the sixth anniversary of the organization of the church, "agreeable to the laws of our country," in commemoration of which the church in Kirtland met in the temple and held a prayer meeting.

On the 30th of April we were ordained an elder in the church, and enrolled in the first quorum of 70, several others were ordained at the same time. The next forenoon, May 1, those elders who had been ordained the day previous, and several others, met in the temple to attend to the ordinance of anointing and washing of feet, after which we waited upon the Lord in prayer and fasting until evening, when we partook of consecrated bread and wine, and tarried all night still waiting upon the Lord, and rejoicing in him. Some testified of having the visions of heaven opened to their view, others enjoyed the spirit of prophecy, and prophesied of many great any glorious things which were yet in the future, all of which have not yet come to pass. For our part we did not have any of those gifts bestowed upon us on that occasion, but we rejoiced greatly, and felt to "praise the name of the Lord of hosts, because he was restoring to the children of men in these days the ancient order of things, and opening the way for the gathering of Israel." Thus we wrote in our journal at the time.

Some brethren expressed themselves as being disappointed at not receiving more and greater manifestations of the power of God, but for our part, we had found the pearl of great price, and our soul was happy and contented, and we rejoiced greatly in the Lord. And we wish now to say to our friends and all the world, after these years of experience, that the PEARL OF GREAT PRICE *is in this Mormon problem*, and notwithstanding Satan has sought to overwhelm it with his machinations and corruptions, yet it will shine forth gloriously in a day to come, and prove a blessing to the pure and the good.

In the latter part of May began to make preparations to go on a mission to preach the gospel to our fellow men, feeling the great importance of the salvation of precious souls.

On the 2nd day of June, 1836, took leave of wife and home, and with valise in hand, started out on foot, without purse or scrip, (leaving the last penny at home,) being only twenty years and eight days old, trusting solely on the Lord. Went to Richland county Ohio, was absent from home five weeks.. Held some twenty meetings and baptized four persons.

A remarkable case of healing which occurred on that mission is worthy of mention.

There was a brother in the church by the name of Kelley, who had a son some ten or twelve years old, who had been subject to fits from early childhood. They would seize him at any moment, and were as apt to throw him into the fire or into the water, as any other place, so that it was unsafe to leave him alone. His parents wished to have him administered to according to the instruction given in the New Testament, by James, where he says, "Is any sick among you? let him call for the elders of the church; and let them pray over him, anointing with oil in the name of the Lord: and the prayer of faith shall save the sick." James v: 14, 15.

Elder George A. Smith, Joseph Smith's cousin, had come and was with us a few days, and we were together at the time. Before attending to the ordinance of anointing, we went by ourselves into a solitary place and had a season of solemn fervent prayer. We returned to the house, and calling the family to order, knelt before the Lord and had another season of prayer, when we arose and anointed the lad with olive oil, which had been consecrated and set apart for the purpose of anointing the sick, after which we laid our hands upon his head and asked our heavenly Father, in the name of the Lord Jesus Christ, to be pleased to rebuke the evil spirit, and heal the lad, according to the promise of our Savior, in Mark 16: 18, and left him in the hands of the Lord. He was perfectly restored from that very hour, and troubled no more with that sore affliction. We saw his father over forty years later, who told us his son never had another fit after he was administered to that time, whereas, before they were of such frequent occurrence that it was unsafe to leave him alone. That he was now residing in Nebraska the head of a family.

(To be continued.)

CORRESPONDENCE.

Hillsdale, Iowa, March 17, 89.

BRO. ROBINSON; I want to write you a dream that I had about 16 years ago. I dreamed I was in a very large vessel, it seemed we were going to start to cross the ocean, but it seemed we lost our course and were going up a dirty slough; we finally got into the mud so it was difficult for the vessel to move. A

The Return.

PUBLISHED MONTHLY AT $1,00 A YEAR.

Entered at the Post Office at Davis City, Iowa, as second class matter.

DIVINE AUTHENTICITY OF THE BIBLE.

(CONTINUED FROM PAGE 68.)

In our last article we brought the account of the dealings of God with the Egyptians down to the eve of the departure of the children of Israel out of Egypt. That event was so memorable as to be the commencement of a new era with the Hebrews, as the Lord said to Moses, "This month shall be unto you the beginning of months, it shall be the first month of the year to you."

On the evening before the departure, "Moses called for all the elders of Israel, and said unto them, draw out and take unto you a lamb according to your families, and kill the passover. And ye shall take a bunch of hysop and dip it in the blood that is in the basin, and strike the lintel and the two side posts with the blood that is in the basin; and none of you shall go out at the door of his house until the morning. * * And the children of Israel went away, and did as the Lord had commanded Moses and Aaron, so did they." Ex. xii: 21, 22 and 28.

That night "at midnight the Lord smote all the first born of Egypt," so that "there was not a house where there was not one dead."

"And Pharaoh rose up in the night" and called for Moses and Aaron, and said, "Rise up and get you forth from among my people, both ye and the children of Israel; and go and serve the Lord as you have said. Also take your flocks and your herds, as ye have said, and be gone; and bless me also. And the Egyptians were urgent upon the people, that they might send them out of the land in haste; for they said, we be all dead men. And the people took their dough before it was leavened, their kneading troughs being bound up in their clothes upon their shoulders." Ex. xii: 31-34.

Thus were they thrust out of Egypt in great haste. They had gone down to Egypt a small handful, seventy and three souls, including Joseph and his two sons, where they had sojourned four hundred and thirty years, and now they came out a mighty host, "about six hundred thousand on foot, that were men, beside children. "Evidently not less than one million five hundred thousand, including men, women and children, notwithstanding the Egyptians had sought their destruction by ordering their male infants to be killed at their birth.

By this we see with what care our heavenly Father watches over his people, and fulfills the promise made to Abraham, that his seed should become innumerable for multitude.

When they started on their journey out of Egypt, towards the promised land, the Lord went before them by a cloud by day and a pillar of fire by night. They had not proceeded far on their journey until the Lord notified Moses that Pharaoh's heart was hardened, and that he would pursue them with his army, which he did. And when he "drew nigh, the children of Israel were sore afraid, and said unto Moses. Because

THE RETURN.

PUBLISHED MONTHLY AT $1.00 A YEAR.

E. ROBINSON, EDITOR AND PROPRIETOR.

DAVIS CITY, IOWA, JULY, 1889.

::o::

ADMONITION.

We wish to say to the writers for THE RETURN, that it is important we be careful what we say, and how we say it, for words are powerful things, and we are writing as for eternity. Words when printed, remain for men to look upon when we are gone. Words when spoken, are indelibly recorded, for Jesus says: "all things are written by the Father," and, "by thy words thou shalt be justified, and by thy words thou shalt be condemned. for every idle word that men do utter, they shall give an account thereof in the day of judgment."

Words spoken or written, are the cause of all the wars and contentions there are in the world. And Jesus says, "he that hath the spirit of contention is not of me, but is of the devil, who is the father of contention;" therefore, as we do not wish to be numbered with the children of the wicked one, let us be careful that we do not give place to his spirit in our hearts, for "out of the abundance of the heart the mouth speaketh."

The admonition given by the angel of the Lord to Joseph Smith, jr., in the commencement of the coming forth of the marvellous work of the Lord in these last days, when he told him that "unless he labored with an eye single to the glory of God, he would not accomplish the work assigned him," is just as obligatory upon us to-day, as it was upon Joseph at that day, for we are told "no one can assist in this work, except he shall be humble, and full of love, having faith, hope and charity, being temperate in all things, whatsoever shall be entrusted to his care."—Doc. and Cov. Sec. xi:4.

:o:

As this number commences the second half of the first volume of our paper, we would call the attention of those subscribers who have paid for six months, to the fact that the time of their subscription has expired, but we hope they will be willing to continue on our list. We will try and make our little sheet as interesting as possible, and trust, as one correspondent expresses it, that it "will improve" as it progresses.

ITEMS OF PERSONAL HISTORY OF THE EDITOR.

No. 4.

INCLUDING SOME ITEMS OF CHURCH HISTORY NOT GENERALLY KNOWN.

Immediately upon our return home from the mission spoken of in our last article, we discovered a great change had taken place in the church, especially with many of its leading official members. A spirit of speculation was poured out, and instead of that meek and lowly spirit which we felt had heretofore prevailed, a spirit of worldly ambition, and grasping after the things of the world, took its place. Some farms adjacent to Kirtland, were purchased by some of the heads of the church, mostly on credit, and laid out into city lots, until a large city was laid out on paper, and the price of the lots put up to an unreasonable amount, ranging from $100 to $200 each, according to location.

We were sorry to see this order of things, as we felt it would tend to evil instead of good. But having received an assurance of the truth of the gospel, and having an anxiety to warn our fellow men to flee from the wrath to come, and make their calling and election sure, through obedience to the gospel, we therefore, made arrangements to take a second mission.

When at home we worked in the printing office as usual. The hands in the office were the same as formerly, to wit: James Carrell, foreman, Don Carlos Smith, (Joseph Smith's youngest brother, who was president of the Quorum of high priests,) Solomon Wilber Denton, who was a member of the high priest's Quorum, and Samuel Brannan, who has since figured so extensively in San Francisco, California. We may have occasion to make mention of each of these hereafter.

church, by the name
me to Kirtland and
amount of money had
the cellar of a cer-
lem, Massachusetts,
d to a widow, and he
only person now liv-
ledge of it, or to the
se. We saw the broth-
a Carlos Smith told us
hidden treasure. His
lited by the brethren,
en to try and secure
which we will speak
her place.
of the 25th of July, 1836
o go on a mission to
Y. (our native county)
of Mormon, the restor-
latives and friends in
were accompanied by
ar as Cayuga county,
ther resided, near the
here she remained vis-
nts and friends, while
east to prosecute our

with our companion
hat money we had, as
ere then starting out
d, and that it was our
just as Jesus had com-
urse or scrip, having
e Lord would provide,
hearts of the people
h necessary food and
e are happy to say,

pon our youngest sis-
was nearly two years
riter being the young-
en, ten of whom were
was married to a Mr.
ving in Vienna town.
They were pleased to
ee or four days with
ng in the School house
od. Conversed freely
r neighbors upon the
he Book of Mormon,
of the last days, un-
y, our sister expresed

om our journal kept

"Tuesday, Aug. 9, in the afternoon left there to go to Charles E. Tinker's my brother-in-law, who married my sister Mary. They lived in West Leyden, Lewis Co. * * Found them in good health, but who expressed themselves as feeling very badly because I had joined the Mormons, as they called them. Remained with them until Friday noon. They continued very much prejudiced, and really bitter in their feelings all the time, which so marred my enjoyment with them that I concluded I would go and see my brother Joseph, who lived in the township of Boonville, Oneida Co. some five miles from my sister's, and if he should express the same bitterness of feeling, I would leave my testimony with them, and turn to strangers."

"Friday afternoon, Aug. 12, 1836, went to my brother, Joseph's. They seemed pleased to see me; we soon had a pleasant conversation on the subject of religion, in which he manifested a deep intrest. In the evening, before retiring, he asked me to pray with them, which I did, and enjoyed a good degree of the Holy Spirit. After I finished my prayer he commenced praying, and thanked the Lord for the privilege of meeting with me once more, and above all, that the Lord had called me to preach the gospel. When he came to touch upon that, his soul seemed to be filled with the love of God, and he broke out with the exclamation: "*I believe, yea I do believe* thou hast called my youngest brother to preach the gospel," and it seemed as though language was too feeble to express the gratitude of his heart. The Spirit of the Lord rested upon us with power, and we had a joyful time together.

A VISION.

"While my brother was thus at prayer I had an open vision. I saw a beautiful female, perfect in form and features, who seemed to be a little taller than the average female, standing erect, upon a platform elevated some eight or ten inches above the floor, but notwithstanding her beauty and perfect symetry in form, she was full of sores from the crown of her head to the soles of her feet. I marvlled and wondered within myself, is it possible the church is so corrupted."

THE RETURN.

remained on this mission some ten weeks, during which time we baptized our brother, Joseph L. Robinson, and our sister Asenath Brown, and three others, and returned to our home in Kirtland, O. in October.

On our return home we went to work in the printing office as heretofore.

We soon learned that <u>four of</u> the leading men of the church had been to Salem, Massachusetts in search of the hidden treasure spoken of by Brother Burgess, viz: <u>Joseph Smith, jr. Hyrum Smith, Sidney Rigdon and Oliver Cowdery</u>. They left home on the 25th of July, and returned in September. They were at Salem, when we had that vision of the woman full of sores, on the evening of the 12th of August, at my brother Joseph's.

Joseph Smith jr. in his history, as published in the 15th vol. of the "*Millennial Star*," pages 821, & 822 says:

"On Monday afternoon, July 25th, in company with Sidney Rigdon, brother Hyrum Smith, and Oliver Cowdery, I left Kirtland, and at seven o'clock the same evening, we took passage on board the steamer *Charles Townsend*, S. Fox, master, at Fairport, and the next evening, about ten o'clock, we arrived at Buffalo, New York, and took lodgings at the "Farmer's Hotel." * *

From New York we continued our journey to Providence, on board a steamer; from thence to Boston, by steam cars, and arrived at Salem, Mass. early in August, where we hired a house, and occupied the same during the month, teaching the people from house to house, and preaching publicly, as opportunity presented; visiting, occasionally, sections of the surrounding country, which are rich in the history of the Pilgrim Fathers of New England, in Indian warfare, Religious superstition, bigotry, persecution, and learned ignorance.

I received the following—

<u>Revelation, given at Salem, Massachusetts, August 6th, 1836.</u>

I, the Lord your God, am not displeased with your coming this journey; notwithstanding your follies; I have much treasure in this city for you, for the benefit of Zion; and many people in this city whom I will gather out in due time for the benefit of Zion, through your instrumentality! therefore it is expedient that you should form acquaintance with men in this city, as you shall be led; and as it shall be given you; and it shall come to pass in due time, that I will give this city into your hands, that you shall have power over it, insomuch that they shall not discover your secret parts; and its wealth pertaining to gold and silver shall be yours. Concern not yourselves about your debts, for I will give you power to pay them. Concern not yourselves about Zion, for I will deal mercifully with her. Tarry in this place, and in the regions round about; and the place where it is my will that you should tarry, for the main, shall be signalized unto you by the peace and power of my Spirit, that shall flow unto you. This place you may obtain by hire, &c. And inquire diligently concerning the more ancient inhabitants and founders of this city; for there are more treasures than one for you in this city; therefore be ye as wise as serpents and yet without sin, and I will order all things for your good, as fast as ye are able to receive them. Amen.

Thus I continued in Salem ann vicinity, until I returned to Kirtland, some time in the month of September."

We were informed that Brother Burgess met them in Salem, evidently according to appointment, but time had wrought such a change that he could not, for a certainty point out the house, and soon left. They however, found a house which they felt was the right one, and hired it. It is needless to say they failed to find that treasure, or the other gold and silver spoken of in the revelation.

We speak of these things with regret, but inasmuch as they occured we feel it our duty to relate them, as also some of those things which transpired under our personal observation, soon after.

ments. To this end a Banking Institution was organized, called the "Kirtland Safety Society" as we see by the following quotation from the history of Joseph Smith jr. as published on the 823rd page of the "Millennial Star:"

"On the 2nd of November the brethren at Kirtland drew up certain articles of agreement, preparatory to the organization of a Banking Institution, to be called the "Kirtland Safety Society."

President O. Cowdery, was delegated to Philadelphia to procure plates for the Institution; and Elder O. Hyde, to repair to Columbus, with a petition to the Legislature of Ohio, for an act of incorporation, which was presented at an early period of their session, but because we were "Mormons," the Legislature raised some frivolous excuse on which they refused to grant us those banking privileges they so freely granted to others. Thus Elder Hyde was compelled to return without accomplishing the object of his mission, while Elder Cowdery succeeded at a great expense in procuring the plates, and bringing them to Kirtland."

As stated above, Orson Hyde failed in securing a Bank Charter, but Oliver Cowdery returned with Kirtland bank bills printed to the amount it was said, of *two hundred thousand dollars*, which would be worthless unless some way could be devised by which they could be used. To meet this emergency, the following action was had, which we quote from Joseph Smith's history, as found on page 843, "Millennial Star."

"*Minutes of a Meeting of the Members of the "Kirtland Safety Society," held on the 2nd day of January, 1837.*

At a Special Meeting of the Kirtland Safety Society, two-thirds of the members being present, S. Rigdon was called to the Chair, and W. Parrish chosen Secretary.

was, on motion, by voice of the meeting, a to adopt articles of which the "Kirtland S are to be governed.

After much discussi gation, the following Articles of Agreement by the unanimous voi ing.

We, the undersigne for the promotion of interests, and for the l ment of our differen which consist in agricu ical arts, and merchand by form ourselves into pany for the before-: jects, by the name of Safety Society Anti-] pany," and for the p ment of said Firm, w and jointly enter into following articles of

Here followed 16 ar ment, of which the 14th follows:

Art. 14th. "All n said Society, shall be Treasurer and Secreta we, the individual in firm, hereby hold of for the redemption of

At the conclusion of agreement, Joseph Smit say:

"In connexion with cles of agreement of Safety Society." I pu lowing remarks, to preparing themselves ing their wise men, f of building up Zion in the January numbe *enger and Advocate—*

"It is wisdom, ac mind of the Holy S should call at Kirtlan

counsel and instruction upon those principles that are necessary to further the great work of the Lord, and to establish the children of the kingdom, according to the oracles of God, as they are had among us; and further, we invite the brethren from abroad, to call on us, and take stock in our "Safety Society;" and we would remind them also of the sayings of Isaiah, contained in the 60th chapter, and more particularly the 9th and 17th verses, which are as follows—"Surely the isles shall wait for me, and the ships of Tarshish first, and to bring thy sons from far, their silver and their gold (not their bank notes,) with them, unto the name of the Lord thy God, and to the Holy one of Israel, because he hath glorified thee. For brass I will bring gold, and for iron I will bring silver, and for wood, brass; and for stones, iron. I will also make thy officers peace, and thine exactors righteousness." Also 62nd chapter, 1st verse—"For Zion's sake I will not hold my peace, and for Jerusalem's sake I will not rest, until the righteousness thereof go forth as brightness, and the salvation thereof as a lamp that burneth. J. SMITH, jr."

Joseph Smith, jr. was elected Treasurer, and Sidney Rigdon was elected Secretary.

In accordance with the foregoing arrangements, quite a large number of the bills were brought into the printing office, and the word *anti*, in very fine type, was printed before the word Bank, and the sylable, *ing*, also in fine type, was printed after the word Bank, thus making it read, "Kirtland Safety Society Anti Banking Co.," in which form the bills were signed by Joseph Smith jr., Treasurer, and Sidney Rigdon, Secretary, and put into circulation as bank bills.

<u>We wish our readers to bear in mind that these things have nothing to do with the gospel, but they seem to show us the weakness of poor human nature, and how easily men can be led astray when they cease to listen to the counsel of God, but are left to follow the dictates of their own will and carnal desires."</u> The fruit of such conduct is exceedingly bitter, and the results most disastrous, as we will see further on.

We do not believe the members of the church generally knew the object of those brethren visiting Salem, and <u>we did not know of the Revelation given at Salem until recently, when we saw it in the *Millennial Star*.</u>

(To be continued.)

———:o:———

From the San Francisco Herald.

DISCOVERY OF RUINED CITIES IN CALIFORNIA.

The great basin between the Colorado and the Rio Grand is an immense table-land, broken towards the Gila and the Rio Grande by detached sierras. Almost all the streams run through deep canyons. The country is barren and desolate, and entirely uninhabited. But though now so bleak and forbidding, strewn all around may be seen the evidence that it was once peopled by a civilized and thickly settled population. They have long since disappeared, but their handiwork still remains to attest their former greatness. Captain Walker assures us that the country from the Colorado to the Rio Grande, between the Gila and San Juan, is full of ruined habitations and cities, most of which are on the tableland. Altho' he had frequently met with crumbling masses of masonry, and numberless specimens of antique pottery, such as have been noticed in the immigrant trail south of the Gila, it was not until his last trip across that he ever saw a structure standing. On that occasion he had penetrated about midway from the Colorado into the wilderness, and had encamped near the Little Red River, with the Sierra Blanca looming up to the south, when he noticed at a little distance an object that induced him to examine further. As he approached, he found it to be a kind of citadel, around which lay the ruins of a city more

...ut all had been re-
...y the action of some
...r had evidently pas-
...le country. It was
... conflagration, but
some fierce furnace-
, similar to that issu-
cano, as the stones
some of them almost
glazed as if melted.
. was visible in every
. storm of fire seemed
ver the whole face of
the inhabitants must
re it. In the centre
efer to rose abrupt-
30 feet high, upon
i stood a portion of
at had once been an
ig. The outline of
s still distinct, altho'
n angle, with walls
ig, and 10 feet high,
These walls were
:one, well built. All
the building seemed
rut to cinders, and
a mere pile of rub-
rock on which it
ared to have been
y the heat. Captain
me time in examin-
ing spot. He traced
eets and the outlines
it could find no other
As often as he had
is character, he had
occasion discovered
if the ancient people.
a number of hand-
) those still used by
Mexicans for grind-
They were made of
:k, and consisted of
t two feet long, and
:, the one hollowed
er made convex like
e concavity. They
:ticles that had resis-

had seen antique potte:
of the country, fron
the Gila.

Captain Walker con
ney, and noticed sev
a little off his route ne
could not stop to exa:
this side of the Colora
er seen any remains,
present races. The l
traditions relative to t
ple once thickly sett
gion. They look wit
these remains, but kn
their origin. Captai
we may remark, is a r
and close observer, 1
the generality of ol
with a wonderfully re
ry, is of opinion that
so barren, was once a c
try, sustaining millio
and that its present
been wrought by the
canic fires. The n
proves that the anci
farmed; the country,
pears, never could be
is inferred it must ha
ent in early days. T
had sheep, too, for the
of that useful animal
ved upon a piece of p

The description given
larly concerning the c
truction of the cities and
the desolations of the cc
most remarkably with
the Book of Mormon,
fearful destructions, by
wind, earthquake, whic
people and the land at t
the Lord Jesus Christ. (
by fire from heaven, an
of the country was chan
derfully this agrees with
given by Captain Walk
an ordinary conflagratio
been some fierce furnace
similar to that issuing
as the stones were all

HE RETURN.

to earth, shall rise again; The eternal years of God are hers.

DAVIS CITY, IOWA, JULY, 1889. Whole No. 7.

Return.

...Y AT $1.00 A YEAR,

...Office at Davis City, ...nd class matter.

...HENTICITY OF ...BIBLE.

(FROM PAGE 83.)

...o. 5.

...icle we spoke brief-
...meral way, of the
...urses pronounced
...rael, and stated that
...us were interested
...e think it will be
...e explicit on this
...ct, inasmuch as the
...are to receive the
...h have been endured
...it not for the same
...of the Lord has said
...vork short in right-

...have a faint idea of
...ses which are to be
...e gentiles, we will
...which Moses predic-
...upon the children
...should become dis-
...egarding the com-
...e Lord.
...ou be in the city, and
...e in the field. Cursed
...and thy store. Cursed
...of thy body, and the
...the increase of thy
...s of thy sheep. Cursed
...n thou comest in, and
...be when thou goest
...hall send upon thee
...and rebuke, in all that
...hand unto for to do,
...royed, and until thou
...ause of the wickedness
...reby thou hast forsak-
...shall make the pesti-
...thee, until he hath

consumed thee from off the land, whither thou goest to possess it. The LORD shall smite thee with a consumption, and with a fever, and with an inflamation, and with an extreme burning, and with the sword, and with blasting, and with mildew, and they shall pursue thee until thou perish. And the heaven that is over thy head shall be brass, and the earth that is under thee shall be iron. The LORD shall make the rain of thy land powder and dust: from heaven shall it come down upon thee, until thou be destroyed."

"And the LORD shall scatter thee among all the people, from the one end of the earth even unto the other: and there thou shalt serve other gods, which neither thou nor thy fathers have known, even wood and stone. And among the nations shalt thou find no ease, neither shall the sole of thy foot have rest: but the LORD shall give thee there a trembling heart, and failing of eyes, and sorrow of mind. And thy life shall hang in doubt before thee: and thou shalt fear day and night, and shalt have none assurance of thy life: In the morning thou shalt say, Would God it were even! and at even thou shalt say, Would God it were morning! for the fear of thine heart wherewith thou shalt fear; and for the sight of thine eyes which thou shalt see." Deut. xxviii:

Both the blessings and the curses, predicted by Moses, have been fulfilled to the very letter upon Israel, up to the present time.

It is a matter of astonishment, to see with what brevity, and yet with what clearness, and accuracy, Moses foretold, and wrote the future history of Israel for more than three thousand years from his day; which shows conclusively, that the spirit which dictated the matter for him was divine, as he had no power to bring to pass either the blessings or curses which have come upon them, according to their history, which has been kept from his day to the present.

This being true, it stands us in hand, as gentiles, to note carefully

taught in the New Testament and the Book of Mormon. They have departed in a great measure from the faith of the CHURCH OF CHRIST as it was first established, by heeding revelations given through Joseph Smith, who, after being called of God to translate his sacred word, the Book of Mormon, drifted into many errors and gave many revelations to introduce doctrines, ordinances and offices in the church, which are in conflict with Christ's teachings. They also changed the name of the church. Their departure from the faith is also according to prophecy. *"Now the spirit speaketh expressly that in* THE LATTER TIMES *some shall depart from the faith, giving heed to seducing spirits and doctrines of devils."* (1 Tim. iv;1.) On account of God giving to Joseph Smith the gift to translate the plates on which was engraven the Nephite scriptures, the people of the church put too much trust in him—in the *man*— and believed his words as if they were from God's own mouth. They have trusted in an arm of flesh. (Jeremiah xvii;5) *"Thus saith the Lord: Cursed be the man that trusteth in man, and maketh flesh his arm, and whose heart departeth from the Lord."* They looked to Joseph Smith as lawgiver; we look to *Christ alone*, and believe only in the religion of Jesus Christ and not in the religion of any man.

The doctrine of polygamy was not introduced until about 14 [11 ED.] years after the church was established; but other doctrines of error were introduced earlier than this. I left the body in June, 1838, being 5 [3] years before polygamy was introduced.

Joseph Smith drifting into errors after translating the Book of Mormon, is a stumbling block to many, but only those of very weak faith would stumble on this account. Greater abominations are recorded of David in the Bible, than is recorded to-day of Joseph Smith; but do you reject the Psalms on this account? Do you reject the Proverbs because Solomon was a polygamist? Stop and think, you who are hasty to condemn. If you desire to know whether or not the Book of Mormon is true, read the book and investigate it, for Christ has promised that he who seeks in the right way shall find the truth of all things. We are commanded to *"Prove all things; hold fast that which is good."* (1 Thes. v:21.)

The Reorganized Church of Jesus Christ of Latter Day Saints, believe that Joseph Smith was a true prophet up to his death, and accept his revelations in their Book of Doctrine and Covenants. The revelation to practice polygamy is not printed in their Doctrine and Covenants. They do not believe in the doctrine of polygamy. The Church of Jesus Christ of Latter Day Saints (the church at Salt Lake City) believe that Joseph Smith was a true prophet up to the time of his death, and accept his revelations which they have published in their Book of Doctrine and Covenants. In this book is the revelation on polygamy.

It is also a stumbling-block to those who desire to investigate as to the truth of the Book of Mormon, to see the believers in that book divided; but the divisons have been brought about by the revelations of Joseph Smith. We, the Church of Christ, who accept only the Bible and the Book of Mormon as the rule and guide to our faith, agree on the doctrine and gospel of Christ. The Book of Mormon comes forth claiming to be the scriptures of the tribe of Joseph, written by holy men of God, which record has been kept pure. It claims that when the Bible was written by the tribe of Judah (the Jews,) it was plain to the understanding of men; and that many plain and precious things have been taken from it by a great and abominable church; and that on this account the Gentiles stumble over the true doctrine of Christ. The

Book of Mormon comes forth claiming to make plain the doctrine of Christ as taught in the New Testament; and it does make it so plain that a child can understand it. To all who are without prejudice, the Book of Mormon is the key to the understanding of the Bible. As I have stated, all who take it and the Bible alone as the guide to their faith, agree on the doctrine of Christ.

---:o:---

ITEMS OF PERSONAL HISTORY OF THE EDITOR.

No. 5.

INCLUDING SOME ITEMS OF CHURCH HISTORY NOT GENERALLY KNOWN.

While these temporal matters, spoken of in our last article, were being attended to by some, others did not neglect the spiritual things of the church.

There was a family by the name of Newcombe, residing about one mile south of the temple in Kirtland. His wife's brother, (a man we should judge about thirty years of age,) was a raving maniac of the most violent kind. He had to be kept chained in an out house by himself, and clothed with strong coarse clothing, for when he could, he would tear his clothing from him. He would also rave and rage exceedingly whenever any person came near him excepting his sister, Mrs. Newcombe, she had control over him. We saw him different times, but it was a distressing sight.

In the latter part of November or in December, 1836, several brethren took his case in hand, and went to brother Newcombe's and commenced to fast and pray for power over the evil spirit, and deliverance for the man from his power. Joseph Smith Sen. (father of Joseph Smith, jr., the translator of the Book of Mormon,) had charge, assisted by brethren John P. Green, Oliver Granger, and others. They continued in fasting and prayer for three days and nights, with occasionally, one at a time, taking a little respite, when brother Smith, sen. told them to bring the man into the room where they were, which they did.

They laid their hands upon him in the name of the Lord Jesus Christ, and rebuked the evil spirit by which he had been bound, when the man wilted down, and became as a little child. Brother Joseph Smith, sen. ordered them to take the chains from off him. He was healed, to the great joy of all, and they felt to render thanksgiving and praise to our heavenly Father, to whom be glory and honor forever and ever, Amen.

The man continued sane and well, and during the winter attended church with the family at different times. It was customary in the church in those days to give an invitation and opportunity for any one who wished to unite with the church by baptism, to make it manifest by rising to their feet. This invitation was given at the close of the morning sermon each Sunday. One Sunday in March, 1837, this man who had been healed, sat next to me at my right hand in the same pew with me, in the temple in meeting, and when the invitation for baptism was given out, he arose, and was afterwards baptized.

During the winter we assisted in printing the second edition of the Book of Mormon.

In the early spring, a singular circumstance transpired. A brother from Canada, who was stopping at brother Truman O. Angel's, became very much exercised, spiritually, and fasted and prayed, as we were told, for several days, when one morning, just after daylight he came out of the house and passed along near where we lived, hallooing at the top of his voice, warning the people and the nations to repent and prepare for the things which were coming upon the earth. The people came running together to see what was the matter, thinking perhaps there might be a house on fire. We remember of seeing brother Joseph Smith, jr. come in haste with a water bucket in his hand, and when he learned the cause of the outcry, turned back, and walking with his head down, seemed to be in deep thought, and have a heavy heart, but Brigham Young came with a raw-hide whip, and whipped the man back into the house.

Heretofore there had been some individual church trials, which would naturally occur among a people as numerous as the church had become, and some individuals had denied the faith. There had not been any general dissension however,

of the leading Elders of the church. Frederick G. Williams, one of the first Presidency, Martin Harris, David Whitmer, Luke and Lyman E. Johnson, Parley P. Pratt, Wm. E. McLellin, John F. Boynton, (the five last named were members of the Quorum of the twelve apostles,) Roger Orton, one of the seventy, and a number of others, including S. Wilbur Denton, printer, a high priest, who testified of having seen a great vison, during the time of the washings and annointings the preceeding March; these all objected to the course being pursued by brother Joseph Smith, jr. and the church, but we asked no particulars with regard to the matter, thinking that all things would be reconciled in a short time, and church matters move along as heretofore. One thing we felt sure of; the gospel was true, and that truth and righteousness would ultimately prevail, the saints be gathered, Zion redeemed and established in everlasting strength; and we believed the church was the medium through which this glorious result would be brought about; therefore looked upon all who opposed or who did not agree with Joseph Smith and the church, as weak in the faith, or dissenters from the faith. But the disaffection continued and, if anything, grew stronger.

Early in April we began to settle our affairs preparatory to moving to Far West, Caldwell county, Missouri, where the members of the church were gathering.

On the morning of the 17th of April, 1837, we took leave of our friends at Kirtland, Ohio, and started on our journey for Missouri. Travelled by team to Wellsville, a town on the Ohio river, where we took passage on a steamer for St. Louis, where we changed to a Missouri river steamer and landed at Camden, Ray Co. Mo. which is the nearest landing to Far West, forty miles distant.

Arrived at Far West about the 7th of May, where we found several of our about nine months old, yet it already contained several hundred inhabitants. It was settled almost exclusively by members of the church.

The division in the church extended to Missouri. Several of the brethren who were disaffected with brother Joseph Smith jr. were living in Far West, but we adhered to him, feeling that it was necessary to do so in order to retain a standing in the church, and knowing the gospel to be true; we prized a standing in the church as above price, besides, we had a dream soon after reaching Far West which helped settle the matter in our mind.

We dreamed we saw a long piece of hewed timber apparently about 14 inches square, elevated upon blocks the right height for the master workman to lay off the frame work, and brother Joseph Smith, jr., standing by it with a square and scratch awl in his hands laying out the work. After receiving this dream we felt confirmed in our desire to remain with and work for the church, notwithstanding our better judgment taught us the city lot speculation and Bank business was contrary to the spirit of the gospel. Darkness and confusion followed these transactions as will be seen by the following proceedings of the High Council, which we copy from the history of Joseph Smith, as published in the "Millennial Star," vol. 16, page 10, as follows:

"*Minutes of a High Council held in the Lord's House, in Kirtland, Monday, May 29th, 1837. ten o'clock A. M.*

Isaac Rogers, Artemas Millet, Abel Lamb, and Harlow Redfield, appeared as complainants against Presidents F. G. Williams and David Whitmer, and Elders Parley P. Pratt, Lyman Johnson, and Warren Parrish. Sidney Rigdon presiding.

COUNSELLORS.

John Smith,   John Johnson,
Jared Carter,   John P. Green,
Noah Packard,   Oliver Granger,
Joseph Kingsbury, Samuel H. Smith,
Joseph Coe,   Martin Harris,
Gideon Carter,   W. Woodstock.

President Rigdon then read the following complaint—

"To the Presidency of the Church of Latter Day Saints—We, the undersigned, feeling ourselves aggrieved with the conduct of Presidents David Whitmer and F. G. Williams, and also with Elders Lyman Johnson, Parley P. Pratt, and Warren Parrish, believing that their course for some time past has been injurious to the Church of God, in which they are high officers, we therefore desire that the High Council should be assembled, and we should have an investigation of their behaviour, believing it to be unworthy of their high calling—all of which we respectfully submit.

"ABEL LAMB,
"NATHAN HASKINS,
"HARLOW REDFIELD,
"ARTEMAS MILLET,
"ISAAC ROGERS.

"Kirtland, May, 1837."

Elder W. Parrish then stated that the declaration just read was not in accordance with the copy which they received, of the charge preferred against them.

A resolution was then offered and carried, that three speak on a side.

The Council was then opened by prayer, by President Rigdon.

After a short address to the Counsellors, by President Rigdon, President F. G. Williams arose, and wished to know by what authority he was called before the present Council; that according to the Book of Covenants, he ought to be tried before the Bishop's court.

After some discussion between Presidents Rigdon and Williams, President Rigdon gave his decision that President Williams should be tried before the present council.

President David Whitmer also objected to being tried before the present Council.

President Williams then expressed a willingness to be tried for his conduct, and if this was the proper tribunal, he would be tried before it, but still thought it was not.

President David Whitmer objected to being tried before the present Council stating that he thought the instructions in the Book of Covenants, showed that this was not the proper authority to try him.

Counsellor Green gave it as his opinion that the present Council was not the proper authority to try Presidents Williams and Whitmer.

President Rigdon then submitted the case to the Counsellors.

Counsellor John Smith then put the question to the Council for a decision, in substance as follows—Have the present Council authority, from the Book of Covenants, to try Presidents Williams and Whitmer? A majority of the Council decided that they could not conscientiously proceed to try Presidents Williams and Whitmer, and they were accordingly discharged.

After one hour's adjournment, the Council sat again at one o'clock, P. M. Sidney Rigdon and Oliver Cowdery presiding.

Counsellor John Smith stated that he had selected three High Priests to sit in the Council to fill vacancies, and asked the Council if they accepted the selection he had made. Council decided in the affirmative.

On motion of Warren Parrish, the Counsellors were directed to sit as they were originally chosen, or according to the form in the Book of Doctrine and Covenants as far as possible.

Resolved, that three speak on each side.

Counsellor Martin Harris motioned that President F. G. Williams take a seat with the Presidents.

After much discussion as to the propriety of his sitting, motion carried, and President Williams took his seat.

Elder P. P. Pratt then arose and objected to being tried by President Rigdon, or Joseph Smith, junior, in consequence of their having previously expressed their opinion against him, stating also that he could bring evidence to prove what he then said.

President Rigdon then stated that he had previously expressed his mind respecting the conduct of Elder Pratt, and that he had felt and said that Elder Pratt had done wrong, and he still thought so, and left it with the Council to decide whether, under such circumstances, he should proceed to try the case.

After much discussion between the Counsellors and parties, President Rigdon said that, under the present circumstances, he could not conscientiously proceed to try the case, and after a few remarks left the stand.

President Oliver Cowdery then said, that although he might not be called upon to preside, yet if he should be, he should be unfit to judge in the case, as he had previously expressed his opinion respecting the conduct of Elder Pratt and others, and left the stand.

President Williams then arose and said, that as he had been implicated with the accused, he should be unwilling to preside in the case, and left the stand.

The Council and assembly then dispersed in confusion.

W. F. COWDERY, Clerk.

These proceedings were had in a little over one month after we left Kirtland.

We present these things to show that the course pursued by Joseph Smith jr. and some of the heads of the church was contrary to the clear and express command of the Lord, and that David Whitmer and others had good reason for entering their protest, and withholding their influence from such an order of things.

The foregoing action of the High Council at Kirtland, clearly shows that they were devoid of the spirit of the Lord, consequently any act of theirs, while in that condition, could not affect the spiritual standing of any person whom they might profess to deal with.

The High Council at Far West seemed to be in a similar condition, judging from the following proceedings had by them.

We quote from the history of Joseph Smith as published in the 16th volume "Millennial Star," commencing on the 115th page.

Minutes of the proceedings of the Committee of the whole Church in Zion, in General Assembly, at the following places, to wit: At Far West, February 5th, 1838, Thomas B. Marsh, Moderator, John Cleminson, Clerk.

After Prayer, the Moderator stated the object of the meeting, giving a relation of the recent organization of the Church here and in Kirtland. He also read a certain revelation given in Kirtland, September 3rd, 1837, which made known that John Whitmer, and W. W. Phelps, were in transgression, and if they repented not, they should be removed out of their places; also read a certain clause contained in the appeal published in the old *Star*, on the 183rd page as follows: "And to sell our lands would amount to a denial of our faith, as that is the place where the Zion of God shall stand, according to our faith and belief in the Revelations of God."

Elder John Murdock then took the stand and showed to the congregation, why the High Council proceeded thus, was, that the Church might have a voice in the matter; and that he considered it perfectly legal according to the instructions of President Joseph Smith, junior.

Elder G. M. Hinkle then set forth the way in which the Presidency of Far West had been labored with, that a committee of three, of whom he was one, had labored with them. He then read a written document, containing a number of accusations against the three Presidents. He spoke many things against them, setting forth in a plain and energetic manner the iniquity of Phelps and Whitmer, in using the monies which were loaned to the Church. Also David Whitmer's wrong in persisting in the use of tea, coffee, and tobacco.

Bishop Partridge then arose and endeavoured to rectify some mistakes of minor importance, made by Elder Hinkle; also the Bishop spoke against the proceedings of the meeting, as being hasty and illegal, for he thought they ought to be had before the Common Council, and said that he could not lift his hand against the Presidency at present, He then read a letter from President Joseph Smith, junior.

A letter was then read by T. B. Marsh, from William Smith, who made some comments on the same, and also on the letter read by Bishop Partridge.

Elder George Morey, who was one of the committee sent to labour with the Presidency, spoke, setting forth in a very energetic manner, the proceedings of the Presidency, as being iniquitous.

Elder Grover, also, being one of the Committee, spoke against the conduct of the Presidency and Oliver Cowdery, on their visit to labour with them.

Elder D. W. Patten then spoke with much zeal against the Presidency, and in favour of Joseph Smith, junior, and that the wolf alluded to, in his letter, were the dissenters in Kirtland.

Elder Lyman Wight stated that he considered all other accusations of minor importance compared to their selling their lands in Jackson county; that they (Phelps and Whitmer) had set an example which all the Saints were liable to follow. He said that it was a hellish principle, and that they had flatly denied the faith in so doing.

Elder Elias Higbee sanctioned what had been done by the Council, speaking against the Presidency.

Elder Murdock stated that sufficient had been said to substantiate the accusations against them.

Elder Solomon Hancock pleaded in favour of the Presidency, stating that he could not raise his hand against them.

Elder John Corrill then spake against the proceedings of the High Council, and laboured hard to show that the meeting was illegal, and that the Presidency ought to be had before a proper tribunal, which he considered to be a Bishop and twelve High Priests. He laboured in favor of the Presidency, and said that he should not raise his hands against them at present, although he did not uphold the Presidents in their iniquity.

Simeon Carter spoke against the meeting as being hasty.

Elder Grover followed brother Carter in like observations.

Elder Patten again took the stand in vindication of the cause of the meeting.

Elder Morley spoke against the Presidency, at the same time pleading mercy.

Titus Billings said he could not vote until they had a hearing in the Common Council.

Elder Marsh said that the meeting was according to the direction of brother Joseph, he therefore considered it legal.

Elder Moses Martin spoke in favor of the legality of the meeting, and against the conduct of the Presidency, with great energy, alleging that the present corruptions of the Church here, were owing to the wickedness and mis-management of her leaders.

The Moderator then called the vote in favor of the present Presidency; the negative was then called, and the vote against David Whitmer, John Whitmer, and William W. Phelps, was unanimous, excepting eight or ten, and this minority only wished them to continue in office a little longer, or until Joseph Smith, junior, came up. * * * *

The High Council of Zion met in Far West, on Saturday, March 10th, 1838, agreeable to adjournment; * *

A charge was then prefered against William W. Phelps, and John Whitmer, for persisting in unchristian-like conduct.

Six Counsellors were appointed to speak, viz., Simeon Carter, Isaac Higbee, and Levi Jackson, on the part of the accuser; and Jared Carter, Thomas Grover, and Samuel Bent, on the part of the accused; when the following letter was read by brother Marcellus Cowdery, bearer of the same, belonging to Thomas B. Marsh, previous to giving it to its rightful owner—

"Far west, March 10, 1838.

"Sir—It is contrary to the principles of the Revelations of Jesus Christ, and his Gospel, and the laws of the land, to try a person for an offence by an illegal tribunal, or by men prejudiced against him, or by authority that has given an opinion or decision before hand, or in his absence.

"Very respectfully we have the honor to be

"DAVID WHITMER, ⎫ Presidents of
"W. W. PHELPS,   ⎬ the church of
"JOHN WHITMER, ⎭ Christ in Mo.

"To T. B. Marsh, one of the travelling counsellors.

"Attested, OLIVER COWDERY, clerk of the High council of the church of Christ in Missouri.

"I certify the foregoing to be a true copy from the original.

OLIVER COWDERY, ⎱ clerk of the
                ⎰ High c'ne'l."

All the effect the above letter had upon the council, was, to convince them more of the wickedness of those men by endeavoring to palm themselves upon the church as her Presidents, after the church had by a united voice, removed them from their presidential office, for their ungodly conduct; and the letter was considered no more nor less than a direct insult or contempt cast upon the authorities of God, and the church of Jesus Christ; therefore the council proceeded to business.

A number of charges were sustained against these men, the principal of which was for claiming $2000 church funds, which they had subscribed for building an house to the Lord in this place, when they held in their possession the city plot, and were sitting in the presidential chair; which subscription they were intending to pay from the avails of the town lots; but when the town plot was transfered into the hands of the Bishop for the benefit of the church, it was agreed that the church should take this subscription from off the hands of W. W. Phelps and John Whitmer; but in the transaction of the business, they bound the Bishop in a heavy mortgage, to pay them the above $2000, in two years from the date thereof, a part of which they had already received, and claim the remainder.

The six counsellors made a few appropriate remarks, none of whom felt to plead for mercy, as it had not been asked on the part of the accused, but all with one consent declared that justice ought to have her demands.

After some remarks by Presidents Marsh and Patten, setting forth the iniquity of those men in claiming the $2000 spoken of, which did not belong to them any more than any other person in the Church, it was decided that William W. Phelps and John Whitmer be no longer members of the Church of Christ of Latter-day Saints, and be given over to the buffetings of Satan, until they learn to blaspheme no more against the authorities of God, nor fleece the flock of Christ.

The Council was then asked, if they concurred with the decision; if so, to manifest it by rising; when they all arose.

The vote was then put to the Congregation, which was carried unanimously.

The negative was called, but no one voted.

Brother Marcellus Cowdery arose and said he wished to have it under-

ing to Thomas B. Marsh, before giving it to him! and in speaking against the authorities of the Church.

A motion was then made by President Patten, that fellowship be withdrawn from Marcellus Cowdery, until he make satisfaction; which was seconded and carried unanimously.

THOMAS B. MARSH, } Presidents.
DAVID W. PATTEN, }
EBENEZER ROBINSON, } Clk. of High Council.

TO BE CONTINUED.

[Selected.]
REALMS OF THE BLEST.

We speak of the realms of the blest,
  Of that country so bright and so fair;
And oft are its glories confessed;
  But what must it be to be there!

We speak of its pathways of gold,
  Of its walls decked with jewels most rare;
Of its wonders and pleasures untold;
  But what must it be to be there!

We speak of its service of love,
  Of the robes which the glorified wear;
Of the church of the first born above;
  But what must it be to be there!

:o:

THE atmosphere is rife with reports of murders, floods, fires, railroad disasters, accidental shooting, ravishings and every species of crime and outrage. The record is simply apalling. Whither is the world tending?—*Independence (Mo.) Gazette.*

:o:

A cyclone in Hungary, Transylvania, and Bukovinia Saturday, swept over several thousand square miles of territory. Hundreds of persons were killed, the crops were destroyed, and enormous damage was done to houses and churches. The districts of Grosswondein, Szegedin, and Mohacs were completely ravaged.

—Verily, the Lord is fulfilling his word.—EDITOR.

DAVIS CITY, IOWA, AUGUST, 1889.

—On the first and second pages of this issue will be found an extract from Elder David Whitmer's Pamphlet to which we wish to call the readers attention, as it briefly gives the items of our faith, and also portrays the main differences between the church of Christ and the Utah and Reorganized churches of Latter Day Saints.

:::

NEW JERUSALEM.—We wish to repeat what we have heretofore said, the gospel of our blessed Lord and Savior, Jesus Christ, is true; and that our heavenly Father will fulfil all he has promised in the bible and book of Mormon; and will add, that ere long a New Jerusalem will be built on this land, by the remnant of the sons of Jacob, the seed of Lehi, assisted by the believing gentiles. Therefore we, gentiles, need not flatter ourselves that we are to take the lead in that glorious work, but only to be helpers, if found worthy to have any part in the matter.

We become Israel by adoption; by being grafted into the vine. Which is greater, the graft, the branch, or the stock that bears it? Let us, gentiles, consider this matter, and not arrogate to ourselves that which does not belong to us.

Read the 11th chapter of Romans, and also the 10th chapter of Nephi, in the latter part of the book of Mormon.

Secret Combinations.

Scientists have made the statement that two distinct races of civilized people have inhabited this country in ages long since past. They have come to this conclusion by the discoveries made in the ruins of the ancient cities, fortifications, canals and highways discovered in many parts of North and South America.

The Book of Mormon gives a brief, but clear and distinct account of these two

THE RETURN.

"Truth, crushed to earth, shall rise again; The eternal years of God are hers."

Vol. 1. No. 8.   DAVIS CITY, IOWA, AUGUST, 1889.   Whole No. 8.

The Return.

PUBLISHED MONTHLY AT $1,00 A YEAR,

Entered at the Post Office at Davis City, Iowa, as second class matter.

EXTRACT,
From David Whitmer's Address.

DEAR READER;

Part first of this pamphlet is a brief address to those who have not read the Book of Mormon, and who are not conversant with the denominations that believe in that book.

Part second is an address to all believers in the Book of Mormon.

There are three distinct denominations that believe the Book of Mormon to be the word of God;

First; *The Church of Christ.*

Second; *The Reorganized Church of Jesus Christ of Latter Day Saints.*

Third; *The Church of Jesus Christ of Latter Day Saints.*

The last named is the church in Salt Lake City; they believe in the doctrine of polygamy, while the two first named churches do not believe in that doctrine. I am an elder in "the Church of Christ." We believe in the doctrine of Christ as it is taught in the New Testament and the Book of Mormon, the same gospel being taught in both these books. The Bible being the sacred record of the Jews who inhabited the eastern continent; the Book of Mormon being the sacred record of the Nephites (descendents of Joseph, the son of Jacob,) who inhabited the western continent, or this land of America. The Indians are the remnant of that people, who drifted into unbelief and darkness about 350 years after Christ appeared to them and established his church among them, after finishing his mission at Jerusalem. We believe in faith in Christ, repentance and baptism for the remission of sins, and the gift of the Holy Ghost. We believe in the laying on of hands as it was practiced in the days of the Apostles. We believe in the resurrection of the dead and eternal judgment. We also believe in the Words of Christ when he said, "*These signs shall follow them that believe.*" Our belief concerning the order of offices in the church, etc., will be found in Part Second of this pamphlet. THE CHURCH OF CHRIST holds to the original doctrine and order that was first established upon the teachings of Christ in the written word, in 1829, when the Lord set his hand the second time to establish the true gospel upon the earth and recover his people, which is in fulfillment of the prophecies in the Bible. We denounce the doctrine of polygamy and spiritual wifeism. It is a great evil, shocking to the moral sense, and the more so because practiced in the name of Religion. It is of man and not of God, and is especially forbidden in the Book of Mormon itself in these words. "*Behold, David and Solomon truly had many wives and concubines, which thing was abominable before me, saith the Lord.* * * * * For there shall not any man among you have save it be one wife: and concubines he shall have none: For I the Lord God, delighteth in the chastity of woman.*" (Book of Mormon, page 116, chap. 2, par. 6.) We do not indorse the teaching of any of the so-called Mormons or Latter Day Saints, which are in conflict with the gospel of our Lord and Saviour Jesus Christ, as

the Father is not in him.". (1 John ii: 15.) "Ye cannot serve God and mammon."(Mate. vi:24.) He who makes up his mind to serve God with an eye single to his glory, the light that is in him will not be darkness to the truth as it is in Christ; such a person will overcome the stumbling-blocks by the Holy Spirit enlightening his mind, and he will see and understand the truth. God works by stumbling blocks. He ordained that Christ should come as a stumbling-block to the Jews, so that all who did not have an eye single to his glory might stumble and not understand. "And He (Christ) shall be for a sanctuary; but for a stone of stumbling and for a rock of offense to booth the houses of Israel, for a sin and for a snare to the inhabitance of Jerusalem. And many among them shall stumble, and fall, and be broken, and be snared, and be taken." (Isaiah viii: 14—15.) (See also 1 Peter ii:7-8, 1 Cor. i:23, Rom. ix; 32-33.) The Jews did not expect the Christ to come in the way he did, because the prophecies about his coming were obscure; so they rejected him.

The Gentiles cannot expect the words of Christ—the Book of Mormon—to come in the way it has, because the prophecies about its coming forth are obscure; so they have rejected it; but the stone which the builders have rejected, the same will become the head of the corner.

The Book of Mormon is the word of God. The prophecies in the scriptures concerning the way in which Christ would come to the Jews, are obscure, but they are just as God wanted them. Likewise are the prophecies in the Bible concerning the coming forth of the word of Christ in these last days, which is "the dispensation of the fullness of time." The prophecies which foretell the coming forth of the Book of Mormon are fully as plain to the Gentiles, as the prophecies were to the Jews concerning Christ's coming.

The people cannot understand why the Lord would bring forth his word from "a book (plates) that is sealed" and was buried in the ground by his ancient prophets on this land: and why He should have the words of the book delivered "to one that is learned," telling him to read it etc.; (see Isa. xxix) but the learned and wise of the world could not read it; God gave to an unlearned boy, Joseph Smith, the gift to translate it by means of a STONE. See the following passages concerning the "Urim and Thummim," being the same means and one by which the Ancients received the word of the Lord. (1 Sam. xxviii:6. Neh. vii: 65. Ezra ii: 63 Num. xxvii: 21. Deut. xxxiii:8. Exodus xxviii:30. Leviticus viii:8.) But this is a great stumbling-block to the people now. They cannot understand why God would work in this manner to bring forth his word; and why he would choose such a man as Joseph Smith to translate it; and they think the canon of scripture is full: and that angels do not minister unto men in these days. But oh kind reader, if you desire to know the truth, be not hasty to condemn and judge, but I pray you to investigate. The scriptures teach that God works in a way least expected by man.

"Neither are your ways my ways, saith the Lord." (Isa. LV : 8). How unsearchable are His judgments, and His ways past finding out." (Rom. xi: 33). Read Isa. xxix whole chapter, which is a prophecy concerning the way in which the Book of Mormon was to come forth. "Out of the ground;" "Out of the dust;" From. "the words of a Book (plates) that is sealed;" The men of the world who are wise and prudent in the eyes of the world, shall be confounded; they will not understand the Lord's way of working. "For the wisdom of their wise men shall perish, and the understanding of their prudent men shall be hid." But the meek and lowly in heart

ill not understand the Lord's way of working. "For the wisdom of their wise men shall perish, and the understanding of their prudent men shall be hid." But the meek and lowly of heart will understand it. "The meek also shall increase their joy in the Lord, and the poor among men shall rejoice in the Holy One of Israel." And those who are spiritually blind and deaf shall "hear the words of the book," and "see out of obscurity, and out of darkness." They also that erred in spirit shall come to understanding, and they that murmured shall learn doctrine;" The above quotations are from the 9th chapter of Isaiah.) John, in his vision on the Isle of Patmos, of "things which must be hereafter," saw "Another angel fly in the midst of heaven, having the everlasting gospel, to preach unto them that dwell on THE EARTH." (Rev. xiv : 6.) In Isaiah xi : 11, 12, it is prophesied as follows: "and it shall come to pass in that day (dispensation) that the Lord shall set his hand again the second time to recover the remnant of his people * * * and he shall set up an ensign for the nations, and assemble the outcasts of Israel, and gather together the dispersed of Judah (the Jews) from the four corners of the earth." The coming forth of the Book of Mormon is only a preparatory work for the great and "marvlous work" of God which is yet to come in gathering scattered Israel, which is spoken of so often through the prophets. The Book of Mormon contains many prophecies which are now and have been during my life, under course of fulfillment. It says that more records are yet to come forth from the "book that is sealed," which book is the sacred scripture or records of the people who inhabited his land of America.

———:o:———

Blessed are the peacemakers; for they shall be called the children of God.—JESUS.

ITEMS OF PERSONAL HISTORY OF THE EDITOR.

No. 5.

INCLUDING SOME ITEMS OF CHURCH HISTORY NOT GENERALLY KNOWN.

(CONTINUED FROM PAGE 121.)

In our last article we gave the proceedings of the High Council in Kirtland, O. that were had on the 29th of May, 1837, and also of the High Council of the church in Far West, Mo., on the 10th of March, 1838; at both of those places David Whitmer and Oliver Cowdery took part. They moved from Ohio to Missouri in the summer or fall of 1837.

On the 7th of Nov. 1837, at a general assembly of the church at Far West, David Whitmer was chosen President of the church in Missouri, (a place he had formerly filled, before he went to Kirtland to be present at the dedication of the temple,) and John Whitmer and W. W. Phelps were chosen to be his counsellors; these three to constitute the three Presidents of the church in Zion, as it was called, and Oliver Cowdery was chosen clerk.

Notwithstanding these men were appointed to these positions yet the disaffection continued, until "at a meeting of the High Council, the Bishop and his council, February 10th, 1838, it was moved, seconded and carried, that Oliver Cowdery, W. W. Phelps and John Whitmer stand no longer as chairman and clerk to sign licenses." And on the 10th of March, further action was had in the cases of Presidents Phelps and John Whitmer, as given on the 120th page of the August No. of THE RETURN.

On the 14th of March, 1838, Joseph Smith, jr., arrived at Far West, with his family, and on the 4th of April Sidney Rigdon also arrived with his family.

Joseph Smith, jr., was held in very high esteem by the masses of the people, members of the church, and looked upon as being invested with powers and qualifications far above all other men, being, as they thought, a great prophet of God, like unto Moses, and that like Elisha, he could tell their actions, and almost their thoughts, when absent from them. They rejoiced to think they were permitted to live to see the day when prophets and apostles were restored to the earth again, therefore there was great rejoicing when he arrived among them, as will be seen by the following extract from a letter writen by him after his arrival, copied from page 130, 16th vol. Millennial Star.

"Far West, March 29th, 1838.
To the Presidency of the church of Jesus Christ of Latter Day Saints in Kirtland.

Dear and well beloved Brethren—Through the grace and mercy of our God, after a long and tedious journey of two months and one day, I and my family arrived safe in the city of Far West, having been met at Huntsville, one hundred and twenty miles from the place, by my brethren with teams and money, to forward us on our journey. When within eight miles of the city of Far West, we were met by an escort of brethren from the city, viz: Thomas B. Marsh, John Corrill, Elias Higbee, and several others of the faithful of the west, who received us with open arms and warm hearts, and welcomed us to the bosom of their society. On our arrival in the city we were greeted on every hand by the Saints, who bid us welcome to the land of their inheritance."

We now quote from the history of Joseph Smith, jr., as found on page 131 of the 16th vol. Millennial Star.

"Far West, April 6th, 1838.
Agreeable to a resolution passed by the High Council of Zion, March 3rd, 1838, the saints in Missouri assembled in this place, to celebrate the anniversary of the church of Jesus Christ of Latter-day Saints, and to transact church business, Joseph Smith, junior, and Sidney Rigdon presiding.

The meeting was opened by singing, and prayer by David W. Patten, after which President Joseph Smith, junior, read the order of the day. * * *

The meeting then proceeded to business. George Morey was appointed Sexton, and Dimick Huntington assistant; John Corrill and Elias Higbee, Historians; George W. Robinson, General Church Recorder, and Clerk to the First Presidency; Ebenezer Robinson, Church Clerk and Recorder for Far West, and Clerk of the High Council; Thomas B. Marsh, President pro tempore of the Church in Zion, and David W. Patten and Brigham Young, his assistant Presidents.

After one hour's adjournment, meeting again opened by David W. Patten. The bread and wine were administered, and ninety-five infants were blessed.

JOSEPH SMITH, junior, President.
E. ROBINSON, Clerk."

We have preserved, and have before us at the present writing, the original minutes of the above meeting as taken down at the time.

It will be seen, that at this meeting Thomas B. Marsh, David W. Patten and Brigham Young were appointed Presidents over the church in Missouri, although David Whitmer still retained his membership in the church, and no charge had been prefered against him except at Kirtland, when the High council broke up in confusion. He had been spoken against in the meeting at Far West, on the 5th of February, by Elder George M. Hinkle, in these words: "<u>David Whitmer's wrong in persisting in the use of tea, coffee and tobacco</u>," as will be seen by reference to the proceedings of that meeting as published on page 118 of the August number of THE RETURN. On that occasion the three Presidents (David and John Whitmer and Phelps,) were voted against, which proceeding evidently, was illegal. Of its legality however, we may speak more fully hereafter.

John Whitmer had been appointed by revelation to write and keep a regular history, and record of the church, as will be seen by the following:

"*Revelation to Joseph Smith, jr., and John Whitmer, given March*, 1831.

1. Behold it is expedient in me

that my servant John should write and keep a regular history, and assist you, my servant Joseph, in transcribinng all things which shall be given you, until he is called to further duties. Again, verily I say unto you, that he can also lift up his voice in meetings, whenever it shall be expedient.

2. And again, I say unto you, that it shall be appointed unto him to keep the church record and history continually, for Oliver Cowdery I have appointed to another office. Wherefore it shall be given him, inasmuch as he is faithful, by the Comforter, to write these things. Even so. Amen."

In conformity with the above command and appointment, he had kept the church history and record, but now it was desirable to have possession of them but he refused to give them up whereupon the following remarkable letter was sent to him, which we copy from the history of Joseph Smith, jr., as found on page 133 of the "Mil. Star," in which the writers seemed to consider their judgment superior to that expressed in the foregoing revelation.

Mr. J. Whitmer: Sir: We were desirous of honoring you by giving publicity to your notes on the history of the church of Latter Day Saints after making such corrections as we thought would be necessary, knowing your incompetency as a historian, that writings coming from your pen, could not be put to press without our correcting them, or else the church must suffer reproach. Indeed, sir, we never supposed you capable of writing a history, but were willing to let it come out under your name, notwithstanding it would really not be yours but ours. We are still willing to honor you, if you can be made to know your own interest, and give up your notes, so that they can be corrected and made fit for the press; but if not, we have all the materials for another, which we shall commence this week to write.

Your obedient servants,

JOSEPH SMITH, jr.
SIDNEY RIGDON,

{ Presid'ts of the whole ch'rch of Lat'r-d'y S'nts

Attest, E. ROBINSON, Clerk.

No attention was paid to the foregoing letter by John Whitmer, as, perhaps, he thought he would not be justified in thus surrendering the work which had been assigned him by revelation. The record was subsequently obtained however, and brought to our house, where we copied the entire record into another book, assisted a part of the time, by Dr. Levi Richards.

On the 11th of April charges were prefered against Oliver Cowdery, and his trial came off on the 12th; and on the 13th charges were prefered against David Whitmer and Lyman (E.) Johnson, and their trial was had the same day, as will be seen by the following quotation from page 133, 16th vol. "Mil. Star."

"April 13th, the following charges were prefered against David Whitmer, before the High Council at Far West, in Council assembled:

1st. For not observing the word of wisdom.

2nd. For unchristian-like conduct in neglecting to attend meetings, in uniting with and possessing the same spirit as the dissenters.

3rd. In writing letters to the dissenters in Kirtland, unfavorable to the cause, and to the character of Joseph Smith, junior.

4th. In neglecting the duties of his calling, and seperating himself from the church while he had a name among us.

5th. For signing himself President of the church of Christ, after he had been cut off from the Presidency, in an insulting letter to the High Council.

After reading the above charges, together with a letter sent to the President of said Council (a copy of which may be found in Far West Record, book A.) the Council considered the charges sustained, and consequently considered him (David Whitmer) no longer a member of the church of Jesus Christ of Latter-day Saints.

The same day three charges were prefered against Lyman E. Johnson which were read, together with a letter from him, in answer to the one recorded in Far West Record, Book A. The charges were sustained and he was cut off from the church."

The above is the *only* trial ever had in David Whitmer's case. The character of the charges speak for themselves. If a failure to keep the word of wisdom was a test of fellowship at the present day, how many members in all churches of the Latter Day Saints, can be found, who use neither *tea, coffee* or *tobacco?* But notice, the Council do not say they either expell or cut David Whitmer off, but, "the Council considered the charges sustained, and consequently *considered* him (David Whitmer) no longer a member of the church of Jesus Christ of Latter Day Saints." There is no account that we can find, of the church ever lifting their hands against him, which is required to be done by the law.

That these trials and proceedings were illegal, and without spiritual force or virtue, is evident from the manner they were conducted.

In the first place, there is no record of their being labored with as the law of Christ demands, which says:

"Moreover, if thy brother shall trespass against thee, go and tell him his fault between thee and him alone: if he shall hear thee, thou hast gained thy brother.

But if he will not hear *thee*, *then* take with thee one or two more, that in the mouth of two or three witnesses every word may be established.

And if he shall neglect to hear them, tell *it* unto the church; but if he neglect to hear the church, let him be unto thee as an heathen man and a publican.—Mat. 18:15, 16, 17.

That the above is the law for the church, we quote from the book of Doctrine and Covenants.

"Thou shalt take the things which thou hast received, which have been given unto thee in my scriptures for a law, to be my law, to govern my church; and he that doth according to these things, shall be saved, and he that doeth them not shall be damned, if he continues."—D. & C. 42:16.

The only mention made of any attempt to labor with these men, was made in the meeting on the 5th of February, more than two months before their trial.

The practice of appointing a committee to go and visit several men as a body, does not comply with the commandment of our Savior, as we understand it. Neither can a trial be considered *legal* where the court are prejudiced, and have expressed an opinion, as had the Presidents and Counsellors done in the case of these men. See the statements made by them in the meeting of February 5, as found on the 118th page of the Aug. number of THE RETURN. Therefore any action taken against David Whitmer, or others, dictated by such an influence and spirit, could not, in the least, affect their spiritual standing before the Lord.

Thus we are fully convinced, from a careful examination of the records, and our personal knowledge of the proceedings, that David Whitmer *never was legally* expelled from the church.

Had these prosecutions of David Whitmer and others satisfied the authorities and members of the church, we would not be called upon to record other scenes enacted, and outrages inflicted upon them, which would disgrace a barbarous people, to say nothing of would be saints; but we leave the unpleasant recital until we reach it in the regular course of events.

In the meantime, that our readers may have as correct an idea of the situation of affairs in the church as possible, we make further quotations from the history of Joseph Smith, jr., giving some of the revelations which he received those days, as found on page 147, 16th vol. "Mil. Star," wherein he says:

"I received the following—*Revelation, given at Far West, April 17, 1838.*

Verily thus saith the Lord, it is wisdom in my servant David W. Patten, that he settle up all his business as soon as he possibly can, and make a disposition of his merchandise, that he may perform a mission unto me next spring, in company with others, even Twelve, including himself, to testify of my name, and bear glad tidings unto all the world; for verily thus saith the Lord, that inasmuch as there are those among you who deny my name, others shall be planted in their stead, and receive their Bishoprick. Amen."

Also I received the following—

Revelation, given to Brigham Young at Far West, April 17, 1838.

Verily thus saith the Lord, let my servant Brigham Young go unto the place which he has bought, on Mill Creek, and there provide for his family until an effectual door is opened for his family, until I shall command him to go hence, and not to leave his family until they are amply provided for. Amen.

I received the following—

Revelation, given at Far West, April 26, 1838, making known the will of God concerning the building up of this place, and of the Lord's House, &c.

Verily thus saith the Lord unto you, my servant Joseph Smith, junior, and also my servant Sidney Rigdon, and also my servant Hyrum Smith, and your Counsellors who are and shall be appointed hereafter; and also unto you my servant Edward Partridge, and his Counsellors; and also unto my faithful servants, who are of the High Council of my Church in Zion (for thus it shall be called), and unto all the Elders and people of my Church of Jesus Christ of Latter-Day Saints scattered abroad in the world; for thus shall my Church be called in the last days, even the Church of Jesus Christ of Latter-Day Saints. Verily I say unto you, all, arise and shine forth, that thy light may be a standard for the nations, and that the gathering together upon the land of Zion, and upon her Stakes, may be for a defence, and for a refuge from the storm, and from wrath when it shall be poured out without mixture upon the whole earth."

Let the city Far West, be a holy and consecrated land unto me, and it shall be called most holy, for the ground upon which thou standest is holy; therefore I command you to build an house unto me, for the gathering together of my Saints, that they may worship me; and let there be a beginning of this work, and a foundation and a preparatory work, this following summer; and let the beginning be made on the 4th day of July next, and from that time forth let my people labor diligently to build a house unto my name, and in one year from this day let them recommence laying the foundation of my house; thus let them from that time forth labor diligently until it shall be finished, from the corner stone thereof unto the top thereof, until there shall not any thing remain that is not finished.

Verily I say unto you, let not my servant Joseph, neither my servant Sidney, neither my servant Hyrum, get in debt any more for the building of an house unto my name; but let an house be built unto my name according to the pattern which I will shew unto them. And if my people build it not according to the pattern which I shall show unto their Presidency, I will not accept it at their hands; but if my people do build it according to the pattern which I shall shew unto their Presidency, even my servant Joseph and his Counsellors, then I will accept it at the hands of my people. And again, verily I say unto you, it is my will that the city of Far West should be built up speedily by the gathering of my Saints, and also that other places should be appointed for Stakes in the regions round about, as they shall be manifest unto my servant Joseph, from time to time; for behold, I will be with him, and I will sanctify him before the people, for unto him have I given the keys of this kingdom and ministry. Even so. Amen."

The next day, after receiving the above temple revelation, Joseph Smith, jr., commenced writing the church history, and continued to write from time to time, besides attending to other duties, as will be seen by the following extracts from his history.—"Mil. Star," pages 148-51.

"April 27th. This day I chiefly spent in writing a history of this church from the earliest period of its existence, up to this date. * *

Monday 30th. The First Presidency were engaged in writing the church history, and in recitation of grammar lessons, which recitations at this period, were usually attended each morning before writing.

May 1st, 2nd, 3rd, and 4th, 1838. The First Presidency were engaged in writing church history, with administering to the sick on the 3rd, and receiving a letter from John E. Page on the 4th. * *

Sunday May 6th. I preached to the saints, setting forth the evils that existed, and would exist, by reason of hasty judgment, or descisions upon any subject given by any people, or in judging before they had heard both sides of the question. I also cautioned the saints againts men who should come amongst them whining and growling about their money, because they had kept the saints, and borne some of the burden with others, and thus thinking that others, who are still poorer, and have borne greater burdens than themselves, ought to make up their loss, &c. I cautioned the saints to beware of such, for they were throwing out foul insinuations here and there, to level as it were a dart, at the best interests of the Church, and if possible to destroy the character of its Presidency. I also gave some instructions in the mysteries of the kingdom of God; such as the history of the planets, &c., &c.; of Abraham's writings upon the planetary systems, &c. * * * * *

Saturday, May 12, 1838, President Rigdon and myself attended the High Council, for the purpose of presenting for their consideration some business relating to our pecuniary concerns. *

We stated to the Council our situation, as to maintaining our families and the relation we now stand in to the Church, spending as we have for eight years, our time, talents, and property, in the service of the Church; and being reduced as it were to beggary, and being still retained in the business and service of the Church, it appears necessary that something should be done for the support of our families by the Church, or else we must do it by our own labors; and if the Church say to us, "help yourselves," we will thank them, and immediately do so; but if the Church say, "serve us," some provision must be made for our sustenance.

The Council investigated the matter, and instructed the Bishop to make over to Presidents Joseph Smith, junior, and Sidney Rigdon, each, an eighty-acre lot of land from the property of the Church, situated adjacent to the city corporation: also appointed three of their number, viz, George W. Harris, Elias Higbee and Simon Carter, a committee to confer with said Presidency, and satisfy them for their services the present year; not for preaching, or for receiving the word of God by revelation, neither for instructing the Saints in righteousness, but for services rendered in the printing establishment,. in translating the ancient records, &c., &c. Said committee agreed that Presidents Smith and Rigdon should receive —$ as a just remuneration for their services this year. * * * *

The above named committee reported to the High Council, at a subsequent meeting, but the sum agreed upon is left blank in the history, as printed. The amount they asked for was ELEVEN HUNDRED DOLLARS each per annum.

The question was warmly discussed by the members of the Council until near sundown. George M. Hinkle bitterly opposed it, as the church had always been opposed to a salaried ministry. A majority of the Council however, favored the measure, so that when the vote

ion of disapprobation
emphatic, that at the
the High Council the
them a salary, was

it, and acted as clerk of
th meetings, therefore
affirm.

r the High Council re-
ary to Joseph Smith jr.
, the TITHING revelation
as given, in which the
ntioned. But more on
fter. We now give fur-
rom the history of Jo-
which he says:

. I left Far West, in
idney Rigdon, T. B.
atten, Bishop Part-
e, S. Carter, Alanson
iny others, for the
ing the North Coun-
off a Stake of Zion;
s, and laying claims
e gathering of the
he benefit of the poor,
ie Church of God.
the mouth of Honey
a tributary of Grand
we camped for the
  * * *
. This morning, we
, and formed a line
ng Grand River at
ney Creek and Nel-
rand River is a large,
and rapid stream,
h waters of spring,
tedly admit of steam
, and other water
ie mouth of Honey
lendid harbor and

our course up the
the timber, about
when we arrived at
Wight's who loves
'ower Hill (a name I
uence of the remains

Rigdon, and clerk, George W. Robinson, for the purpose of selecting
and laying claim to a city plat near
said ferry in Davis county, township
60, range 27 and 28, and sections 25,
36, 31 and 30, which the brethren
called Spring Hill, but by the mouth
of the Lord it was named ADAM-
ONDI-AHAM, because, said He, it is
the place where Adam shall come to
visit his people, or the Ancient of
days shall sit, as spoken of by Daniel
the Prophet."—Mil. Star, page 152
16th vol.

TO BE CONTINUED.

THE RETURN.

PUBLISHED MONTHLY AT $1.00 A YEAR.

E. ROBINSON, EDITOR AND PROPRIETOR.

DAVIS CITY, IOWA, SEPT. 1889.

EDITORIAL.

The extracts we are publishing from the history of Joseph Smith, jr., show conclusively, there has been a great departure from the plain and pure doctrine of Christ. A careful perusal of them must, in our judgment, thoroughly convince every candid, thinking mind, that the course pursued by the leading men of the church, in those days, was not in accordance with the peaceful and heavenly teachings of the Lord Jesus, and his disciples, as set forth in both the New Testament and Book of Mormon.

Jesus says, "Ye cannot serve God and Mammon." Paul says, "to be carnally minded is death, but to be spiritually minded is life and peace." According to this history the carnal strongly predominated over the spiritual; but, unfortunately, we have not reached the worst features of their conduct. But some may say, "Why tell these things?" Our reply is, we feel forced to do it; that if we should hold our peace "the very stones" as it were, "would cry out."

THE RETURN.

"Truth, crushed to earth, shall rise again; The eternal years of God are hers."

Vol. 1. No. 9.   DAVIS CITY, IOWA, SEPTEMBER, 1889.   Whole No. 9.

The Return.

PUBLISHED MONTHLY AT $1.00 A YEAR.

Entered at the Post Office at Davis City, Iowa, as second class matter.

**EXTRACT,
From David Whitmer's Address.**

Continued from the 115th page.

I know that reproach has been brought upon the Book of Mormon. Because some of those who believe it have drifted into wickedness, the world has rejected the book and turned it aside as a thing of naught; but if such persons will stop and think, they will see that they refuse to read this book, which claims to be a message from God, simply because some have transgressed who believe in the book! Such persons are not very earnestly seeking for truth. Those who have read the history of the apostolic church know, that before John wrote the Revelation, many of those who believed in Chirst went into all manner of wickedness and heresies, practicing those things in the name of Christ, and thereby brought reproach upon the name "Christian." Apostolic church history tells us that the Nicolaitanes (Rev. ii: 15,) who departed from the faith by following Nicolas, one of the first seven deacons (Acts. vi; 5,) were also called "Christians;" also that many factions which sprang out of the Christian church, also called themselves "Christians." The Nicolaitanes claimed that Nicolas had received a revelation from God to practice the doctrine of "free love," which is worse than polygamy. (Irenaeus, Epiphanius, Hippolytus.) Reproach was thus brought upon the name "Christian," just as it has been brought upon the words of Christ—the Book of Mormon. History tells us it was a disgrace in the eyes of the world to be called a "Christian," even during the days of the apostles. In Acts xxviii:22 we find that the true church was evil spoken of. "For as concerning this sect, we know that everywhere it is spoken against." Paul speaks of the reproach of Christ in Heb. xi:26 and xiii:13. Christ speaks of the reproach his disciples will have to bear for his name, telling them many times that his disciples would always be persecuted. Peter prophesied (2 Peter ii: 1–2), that damnable heresies will be brought into the church; "and many shall follow their pernicious ways, by reason of whom THE WAY OF TRUTH shall be evil spoken of."

So has it been in these last days. On account of the heresy of polygamy and other heresies, "the way of truth" is evil spoken of; and those who believe in *all* the scriptures of our Lord Jesus Christ, are called by the world "Mormons," and are looked upon by more or less shame by the majority of people; but we are willing to bear the reproach for Him who died for us, for *we know* that the Book of Morom is His word, and by His word we can inherit eternal life if we are faithful in keeping His commandments. God's wisdom is not man's wisdom, and His ways are not man's ways. He work's in a way least expected by man. He does his work in a way that all men may stumble and not understand, unless their whole heart and desire is upon God, and not upon the things of this world. "Love not the world, nor the things that are in the world. If any man love the world, the love of

Vol. 1. No. 10.   DAVIS CITY, IOWA, OCTOBER, 1889.   Whole No. 10.

The Return.

PUBLISHED MONTHLY AT $1.00 A YEAR.

Entered at the Post Office at Davis City, Iowa, as second class matter.

ITEMS OF PERSONAL HISTORY OF THE EDITOR.

No. 6.

INCLUDING SOME ITEMS OF CHURCH HISTORY NOT GENERALLY KNOWN.

(CONTINUED FROM PAGE 137.)

It is with a sorrowful heart that we recount the scenes enacted by the church in Far West, Mo. in June and July, 1838. After having gone through with the form of a trial by the High Council, in which the cases of David and John Whitmer, Oliver Cowdery, W. W. Phelps and L. E. Johnson were disposed of, and Joseph Smith and Sidney Rigdon had written that unfeeling letter to John Whitmer, unbecoming gentlemen, much less professed saints, and after having that remarkable revelation stating that Far West was holy ground, (as published in the Aug. and Sept. numbers of THE RETURN,) a society was organized by the church members, at first called, "The Daughter of Zion," afterwards, "Danites," (or from which came the secret order called "Danites,") to be governed by the following purported Bill of Rights and Articles of organization:

BILL OF RIGHTS OF THE DAUGHTER OF ZION, AND ARTICLES OF ORGANIZATION.

"WHEREAS, in all bodies laws are necessary for the permanent safety and well being of society, we, the members of the society of the Daughter of Zion, do agree to regulate ourselves under such laws as in righteousness shall be deemed necessary for the preservation of our holy religion and of our most sacred rights, and the rights of our wives and children. But to be explicit on the subject, it is especially our object to support and defend the rights confered on us by our venerable sires, who purchased them with the pledges of their lives and fortunes and sacred honors. And now to prove ourselves worthy of the liberty confered on us by them in the providence of God, we do agree to be governed by such laws as shall perpetuate these high privileges of which we know ourselves to be the rightful possessors, and of which privileges wicked and designing men have tried to deprive us by all manner of evil, and that purely in consequence of the tenacity we have manifested in the discharge of our duty towards our God, who had given us these rights and privileges, and a right in common with others, to dwell on this land. But we not having the privileges of others allowed unto us, have determined like unto our Fathers, to resist Tyrany, whether it be in Kings or in people. It is all alike unto us, our rights we must have and our rights we shall have in the name of Israel's God.

ARTICLE 1st.

All power belongs originally and legitimately to the people, and they have a right to dispose of it as they shall deem fit. But as it is inconvenient and impossible to convince the people in all cases, the Legislative powers have been given by them from time to time, into the

ARTICLE 2nd.

The Executive power shall be vested in the President of the whole church and his counsellors.

ARTICLE 3rd.

The Legislative powers shall reside in the President and his counsellors, together with the Generals and Colonels of the society. By them all laws shall be made regulating the society.

ARTICLE 4th.

All offices shall be during life and good behavior, or to be regulated by the law of God.

ARTICLE 5th.

The society reserves the power of electing all its officers with the exception of the Aids and Clerks which the officers may need in the various stations. The nomination to go from the Presidency to his second, and from the second to the third in rank, and so down through all the various grades, branch or department retains the power of electing its own particular officers.

ARTICLE 6th.

Punishments shall be administered to the guilty in accordance to the offence, and no member shall be punished without law, or by any others than those appointed by law for that purpose. The Legislature shall have power to make laws regulating punishments as in their judgement shall be wisdom and righteousness.

ARTICLE 7th.

There shall [be] a Secretary whose business it shall be to keep all the Legislative records of the society, and also to keep a Register of the names of the members of the society, also the rank of the officers. He shall also communicate the laws to the Generals, as directed by laws made for the regulation of such business by the Legislature.

their superiors in rank, according to laws made for that purpose.

Having thus established a military organization within the church, and being exceedingly zealous, were ready to carry out any measure directed, and being determined to rid the community of the presence of the dissenters, therefore, a manifesto was issued, contrary to both the laws of God and the laws of the land, ordering peaceable citizens from their homes, and driving them out of the county, compelling them to flee for their lives.

The following is the first part of the manifesto, or order, notifying the parties to leave the county within three days, or suffer the consequences:

"Far West, June, 1838.

To Oliver Cowdery, David Whitmer, John Whitmer, William W. Phelps and Lyman E. Johnson Greeting: Whereas, the citizens of Caldwell county have borne with the abuses received from you at different times and on different occasions until it is no longer to be endured, neither will they endure it any longer, having exhausted all the patience they have. We have borne long and suffered incredibly, but we will bear nor suffer any longer, and the decree has gone forth from our hearts and shall not return unto us void. Neither think, gentlemen, in so doing we are trifling with either you or ourselves for we are not.

There are no threats from you, no fear of losing our lives by you, or any thing you can say or do will restrain us, for out of the county you shall go and no power shall save you, and you shall have three days after you receive this our communication to you, including twenty-four hours in each day for you to depart with your families peaceably, which you may do undisturbed by any person. But in that time, if you do not depart, we will use the means in our power to cause you to depart, for go you shall.

We will have no more promises to reform as you have already made, and in every instance violated your promise and regarded not the covenant which you had made, but put both it and us at defiance.

We have solemnly warned you, and that in the most determined manner, that if you did not cease that course of wanton abuse of the citizens of this county, that vengeance would overtake you sooner or later, and that when it did come it would be as *furious as the mountain torrent* and as *terrible as the beating tempest*. But you have affected to despise our warnings and to pass them off with a sneer a grin or a threat, and still pursued your former course.

Vengeance sleeps not neither doth it slumber; and unless you heed us this time, and attend to our request, it will overtake you at an hour when you do not expect it and at a day when you do not look for it, and for you there shall be no escape; for there is but one decree for you which is, *depart, depart,* or else a more *fatal calamity shall befall you."*

The italics are ours.

The above manifesto was signed by 83 determined men. Among the names we recognize some of the members of the High Council, and others holding high positions in the church, including that of Hyrum Smith, one of the first Presidency.

The parties heeded the warning, and left in haste late one afternoon in June, a detailed account of which we give as follows: taken from the 9th page of the "*Ensign of Liberty,*" published by W. E. McLellin in March 1847.

"All things seemed to admonish them they only could have safety in flight, consequently near sunset, David, Oliver, John and Lyman, bid farewell to their youthful wives, and their little children, their homes and firesides, and with heavy hearts, and solemn step they left that people who had been enlightened and bro't together, to a great extent, by their labors and "testimony." but alas! who had now fallen, and become their bitterest enemies, and high-handed persecutors. After these men, the "witnesses of truth," had taken an affectionate leave of their innocent families, resigning them into the hands of the Father of lights, they left "the city of their homes" and began to wend their way across those extensive prairies lying south of Far West.

But the darkness of night soon coming on, and being comparative strangers to the way, they directly lost their path. Pensive, mournful and solemn, see them wander they know not where. * * Ah! see that man who sat day after day, week after week, and month after month, and wrote the pages of the Book of Mormon, from the mouth of Joseph Smith, jr., as he translated by the inspiration of Heaven, the words of the holy prophets, who lived and wrote upon this beloved American continent. Yes, see him and his partners in tribulation, wander as the prophets of old; because they had borne a faithful testimony against wickedness in high places. * *

But onward see those men wander until the light of a new day broke in upon that part of the earth, and meeting a stranger he points them to the road that will lead them to an old and tried friend's, who lived about twenty-five miles from Far West. With joy mixed with sorrow, he received them. * * Here they found a home from the "pitiless storm," and remained and refreshed themselves for some days, until their friends had succeeded in bringing to them their families."

Thus they escaped with their lives having wandered all night without food, or shelter, having been driven from their homes by professing SAINTS.

The church, having entered into an independent organization, and taken the law into their own hands, and having driven out these men, (three of whom were witnesses to the Book of Mormon,) and having been commanded by revelation to commence building the temple on the 4th of July, and intending to make a formal *Declaration of Independence*, as did our fore-fathers, extensive preparations were made to have a grand celebration on that day.

A tall liberty pole was raised on which floated the "stars and stripes." A stand was erected for the officers and orator of the day, large enough also to seat several distinguished visitors. An excavation had been made the year previous, for the temple, on the public square, and four large stones had been prepared for corner stones, which were to be laid on that day. Of this celebration Joseph Smith, jr., in his history, speaks as follows, on page 181, 16th vol. Mil. Star.

"July 4th, was spent in celebrating the declaration of Independence of the United States of America, and also in the saints making a declaration of Independence from all mobs and persecutions which have been inflicted upon them, time after time, until they could bear it no longer; * * also in laying the corner stones of the house of the Lord, agreeable to the commandment of the Lord unto us, given April 26, 1838.

Joseph Smith, junior, was President of the day; Hyrum Smith, vice President; Sidney Rigdon, Orator; Reynolds Cahoon, Chief Marshall; and George W. Robinson, Clerk.

The order of the day was splendid. The procession commenced forming at ten o'clock, A. M, in the following order; 1st, the Infantry; 2nd, the Patriarchs of the church; the President, vice President, and Orator; the twelve Presidents of the Stake, and High Council; Bishop and Council; Architects, Ladies and Gentlemen, and the Cavalry in rear."

After the corner stones were laid President Rigdon delivered the oration, from which we make the following extract:

"It is not because we cannot, if we were so disposed, enjoy both the honors and flatteries of the world, but we have voluntarily offered them in sacrifice, and the riches of the world also, for a more durable substance. Our God has promised us a reward of eternal inheritance, and we have believed his promise, and though we wade through great tribulation, we are in nothing discouraged, for we know he that has promised is faithful. The promise is sure, and the reward is certain. It is because of this, that we have taken the spoiling of our goods. Our cheeks have been given to the smiters, and our heads to those who have plucked off the hair. We have not only when smitten on one cheek turned the other, but we have done it again and again, until we are wearied of being smitten, and tired of being trampled upon. We have proved the world with kindness, we have suffered their abuse without cause, with patience, and have endured without resentment, until this day, and still their persecutions and violence does not cease. But from this day and this hour, we will suffer it no more.

We take God and all the holy angels to witness this day, that we warn all men in the name of Jesus Christ, to come on us no more forever, for from this hour, we will bear it no more, our rights shall no more be trampled on with impunity. The man or the set of men, who attempt it, does it at the expense of their lives. And that mob that comes on us to disturb us, it shall be between us and them a war of extermination, for we will follow them, till the last drop of their blood is spilled, or else they will have to exterminate us: for we will carry the seat of war to their own houses, and their own families, and one party or the other shall be utterly destroyed. Remember it then all MEN.

We will never be the agressors, we will infringe on the rights of no peo-

into our streets, to threaten us with mobs, for if he does, he shall atone for it before he leaves the place, neither shall he be at liberty to vilify and slander any of us, for suffer it we will not in this place.

We therefore take all men to record this day, that we proclaim our liberty on this day, as did our fathers. And we pledge this day to one another, our fortunes, our lives, and our sacred honors, to be delivered from the persecutions which we have had to endure, for the last nine years, or nearly that. Neither will we indulge any man, or set of men, in instituting vexatious law suits against us to cheat us out of our just rights, if they attempt it we say wo be unto them.

We this day then proclaim ourselvs free, with a purpose and a determination, that never can be broken, "no never! no never!! NO NEVER!!!""

At the conclusion of the oration the vast multitude shouted, Hosanna! Hosanna!! Hosanna!!! three times, in confirmation of the declaration of Independence made by the speaker. But to show the displeasure of our Heavenly Father, as we verily believe, a few days after, a thunder storm arose, and passing over the place, a shaft of lightning struck the liberty pole and rived it into more than a thousand atoms. This struck dismay into the hearts of some, but we were told at the time, that Joseph Smith, jr., walked over the splinters and prophesied that as he "walked over these splinters, so we will trample our enemies under our feet." This gave encouragement to the fearful and timid.

Is it possible, we ask, that the acts of such a people, under such influences, and dictated by such a spirit, could affect the spiritual standing of any but themselves? We answer, No.

We think we have clearly shown from the records, that the action taken by the tained his priesthood in full force and virtue, which he held equal with Joseph Smith, jr., according to the book of Doctrine and Covenants, for it says expressly: "Wherefore you [David Whitmer, Oliver Cowdery and Martin Harris] have received the same POWER, and the same FAITH, and the same GIFT like unto him" [Joseph Smith, jr.]—D. C. 15:3.

We now dismiss that part of our subject and turn to another.

It will be remembered that on page 187 of the September number of THE RETURN, we gave an account of the High Council at Far West, in June, recinding the vote which had previously passed, granting a salary to Presidents Joseph Smith, jr., and Sidney Rigdon, which left them without a salary. Therefore, four days after their declaration of Independence, Joseph Smith, jr., inquired of the Lord "how much thou requirest of the properties of thy people for a tithing?" notwithstanding it was already stated in a revelation in the book of Doctrine and Covenants what the Lord required of his people for a tithing, and he received the following

TITHING REVELATION:

"*Revelation given at Far West, Mo. July 8, 1838.*

In answer to the question, O Lord show unto thy servants how much thou requirest of the properties of thy people for a tithing?

1. Verily thus saith the Lord, I require all their surplus property to be put into the hands of the bishop of my church of Zion, for the building of mine house, and for the laying the foundation of Zion, and for the priesthood, and for the debts of the presidency of my church; and this shall be the beginning of the tithing of my people; and, after that, those who have thus been tithed shall pay one tenth of all their interest annually; and this shall be a standing law unto them forever,

tithed of their surplus properties, and shall observe this law, or they shall not be found worthy to abide among you. And I say unto you, if my people observe not this law, to keep it holy, and by this law sanctify the land of Zion unto me, that my statutes and my judgments may be kept thereon, that it may be most holy, behold, verily I say unto you, it shall not be a land of Zion unto you; and this shall be an ensample unto all the stakes of Zion. Even so. Amen.—D. C. 106.

There is no mention made of the poor in this revelation, and being personally acquainted with the circumstances under which it was given, we never could feel that the Lord ever gave it for the good of his people, neither can we believe it after seeing its practical workings for fifty years. We verily believe, if the Lord had anything to do with it, it was upon the principle set forth in the 14th chapter of Ezekiel; they evidently had "set up an idol in their hearts," and the Lord answered them "according to their idols."

<u>We feel sure that had the High Council at Far West, carried out the resolution, and paid Joseph Smith, jr. and Sidney Rigdon, the salary they asked for, of eleven hundred dollars each per year, we never would have seen this tithing revelation.</u> The church had been in existence over eight years, and had seen its purest, happiest days before that was given.

That was not the only revelation given on that day, as we learn by reference to the history of Joseph Smith, jr., for, on pages 183-4 of the Millenial Star, he says:

"Also I received the following—

Revelation given to William Marks, Newel K. Whitney, Oliver Granger and others, Zion, July 8, 1838.

Verily thus saith the Lord unto my servant William Marks, and also them awake, and arise, and come forth and not tarry, for I, the Lord, command it; therefore if they tarry it shall not be well with them. Let them repent of all their sins, and of all their covetous desires, before me, saith the Lord, for what is property unto me, saith the Lord? Let the properties of Kirtland be turned out for debts, saith the Lord. Let them go, saith the Lord, and whatsoever remaineth, let it remain in your hands, saith the Lord; for have I not the fowls of heaven and also the fish of the sea, and the beasts of the mountains? Have I not made the earth? Do I not hold the destinies of all the armies of the nations of the earth? therefore will I not make solitary places to bud and to blossom, and to bring forth in abundance, saith the Lord.

Is there not room enough upon the mountains of Adam-ondi-ahman, and upon the plains of. Olaha Shinehah, or the land where Adam dwelt, that you should covet that which is but the drop, and neglect the more weighty matters? Therefore come up hither unto the land of my people, even Zion.

Let my servant William Marks be faithful over a few things, and he shall be a ruler over many. Let him preside in the midst of my people in the city Far West, and let him be blessed with the blessings of my people.

Let my servant N. K. Whitney, be ashamed of the Nicholatine band, and of all their secret abominations, and of all his littleness of soul before me, saith the Lord, and come up to the land of Adam-ondi-ahman, and be a Bishop unto my people, saith the Lord, not in name but in deed, saith the Lord.

And again, I say unto you, I remember my servant Oliver Granger,

earnestly for the redemption of the First Presidency of my church, saith the Lord, and when he falls he shall rise again, for his sacrifice shall be more sacred unto me than his increase, saith the Lord; therefore let him come up hither speedily, unto the land of Zion, and in the due time he shall be made a merchant unto my name, saith the Lord, for the benefit of my people; therefore let no man despise my servant Oliver Granger, but let the blessings of my people be on him for ever and ever.

And again, verily I say unto you, let all my servants in the land of Kirtland remember the Lord their God, and mine house also, to keep and preserve it holy, and to overthrow the money changers in mine own due time, saith the Lord. Even so. Amen"

"Also I received the following—*Revelation, given at Far West, July 8, 1838.*

"Show unto us thy will, O Lord, concerning the Twelve?"

Answer.

Verily, thus saith the Lord, let a Conference be held immediately, let the Twelve be organized, and let men be appointed to supply the places of those who are fallen. Let my servant Thomas remain for a season in the land of Zion, to publish my word. Let the residue continue to preach from that hour, and if they will do this in all lowliness of heart, in meekness and humility, and longsuffering, I, the Lord, give unto them a promise that I will provide for their families, and an effectual door shall be opened for them, from henceforth; and next spring let them depart to go over the great waters, and there promulgate my gospel, the fulness thereof, and bear record of my name. Let them take leave of also my servant John E. Page, and also my servant Wilford Woodruff, and also my servant Willard Richards, be appointed to fill the places of those who are fallen, and be officially notified of their appointment."

The members of the church soon began to bring in their surplus property, as tithing, when, on the 18th of July the following Revelation was received:

"*Revelation given July 18, 1838, making known the disposition of the properties tithed as named in the Revelation of July 8.*

Verily, thus saith the Lord, the time has now come that it shall be disposed of by a Council composed of the First Presidency of my Church, and of the Bishop and his Council; and by my High Council; and by mine own voice unto them, saith the Lord. Even so. Amen.

On July 26, the following disposition of the property was ordered by the Council.—Mil. Star. page 204, 16th vol.

"Thursday 26th. The First Presidency, High Council, and Bishop's Courts assembled at Far West, to dispose of the public properties of the Church in the hands of the Bishop, many of the brethren having consecrated their surplus property according to the Revelations.

It was agreed that the First Presidency should keep all their properties that they could dispose of to advantage, for their support, and the remainder be put into the hands of the Bishop or Bishops, according to the commandments.

TO BE CONTINUED.

:-o-:

INDIAN SCHOOL.

The Indian school at Carlisle, Pa. has the oldest pupil of any educational institution in the United States. He is more than 60 years of age. Crazy Head is his name, and

prayers and the Lord blesses us oftimes with a goodly portion of the holy spirit. But as we live so we do receive. The nearer we live to God, the greater our blessings, My desires are to continue faithful ever clinging to that rod of iron neither turning to the right hand nor to the left, but ever by the assisting grace of God pressing onward.

On Sabbath, the fifteenth of Sept. my husband and I met with Brother W. P. Brown, and the few there, that have taken upon them the name of Christ. The meeting was at Bro. Brown's house, and he administered the holy sacrament, and each rose as they felt moved by the spirit, and bore their testimony to the goodness of God to us his children, and I can truly say the blessings of the Lord was with us.

Brother Brown has been at quite an expense in fitting up and making a good comfortable room, to hold meetings in. It is over his store room, and he run up a good stairway from the outside. He intended to seat the room with chairs, and there he intends to preach, and show clearly to the minds of all who will come and hear him, the blessed truths of this glorious gospel as taught in the new Testament and Book of Mormon. May the Lord give him strength of body and his holy spirit to guide him into all truth.

Ever praying for the welfare of God's children, and that we may each be worthy of a part in the first Resurrection.

Your sister in Christ.

:-o-:

An Elder in the Reorganized church, under date of October 28 '89, writes:

"E. ROBINSON, DEAR BRO. I wrote to you some time ago to stop "THE RETURN" which was sent to my address, sending you 50 cents to pay September, as I d complete file.

I am much interes sonal history, hope y it, am also changing siderable in regard Saintism. Send me Whitmer's address, close stamp. If you THE RETURN circul Saints in this countr me back numbers, a they are put in the who are likely to re: you will find many little paper.

Yours for

:o:

Sound A
[Lord Color

Never, under an read a bad book; ar serious hour in re rate book. No w state the mischief of bad book will ofte his whole life long. membered when mu gotten; it intrudes i solemn moments, a the best feelings Reading trashy, so is a grievous waste the first place, the many more first-rate can ever master; an place, you cannot r book without giving tunity of reading a Books, remember, ar affect character; and neglect any other m cast upon you.

:o:

Who is free? Th ters himself. Who who can control his

The devil speaks a passion.

THE RETURN.

PUBLISHED MONTHLY AT $1.00 A YEAR.

E. ROBINSON, EDITOR AND PROPRIETOR.

DAVIS CITY, IOWA, NOV. 1880.

EDITORIAL.

—When we commenced publishing our personal history, we did not anticipate occupying the space we are doing, but when we come to examine the records, and the material at our command, we find so many things that we think will be of interest to our readers, that we seem to be making but slow progress.

Notwithstanding our apparent slow progress, we have omitted several incidents that we believe would be interesting to many readers, but thought best to pass them by for the present, lest we become tedious.

Judging from the tenor of letters we are receiving, not only from members of our church, and elders and members of the Reorganized church, but also from gentlemen holding high official positions in other states, we find our effort is being appreciated; we therefore purpose continuing it, hoping it may be a record worth preserving, and be instrumental in doing good, as that is our earnest desire.

—:o:—

—We rejoice greatly to learn from Elder Solomon Thomas' letter, that bro. Homer C. Hoyt has united with the church of Christ. We became acquainted with brother Hoyt when he was a young man, living in his fathers' family near Boonville, Oneida county, N. York, when on a mission to that state, in the summer of 1836. He was a sober, exemplary young man, of goodly parentage. They united with the church of Latter Day Saints in that place. It is good to be associated with old and tried friends. May the Lord bless him and his household, together with all Israel, is our earnest desire and prayer.

—o—

—We feel gratified and very thankful for the reconciliation which has taken place between brethren W. P. Brown and George F. Robinson. The misunderstanding that had existed between them has been a source of grief to us. We always feel sorry to see our brethren at variance one with another. Our experience has taught us that all men are mortal, and that we need not look for perfection in any, that we are all subject to like pasion as other men, and to err is human, but we must forgive each other, as we hope for forgivness, for our heavenly Father has established a fixed law, that is immutable, as revealed by his Son, Jesus Christ, when he said:

"For if ye forgive men their trespasses, your heavenly Father will also forgive you.

But if ye forgive not men their trespasses, neither will your Father forgive your trespasses."—Mat. 6: 14-15.

ITEMS OF PERSONAL HISTORY OF THE EDITOR.

No. 7.

INCLUDING SOME ITEMS OF CHURCH HISTORY NOT GENERALLY KNOWN.

(CONTINUED FROM PAGE 151.)

We make further quotations from the history of Joseph Smith, jr., from the fact that we were personally acquainted with, and present during many of the scenes spoken of, therefore, the relation of them here answers a threefold purpose.

First. They relate incidents in our personal experience, a knowledge of which no man can defraud us.

Second. They give our readers a better idea of the true condition of things in the church in those days, than they could have without a relation of those scenes.

Third. They will enable the reader to more readily judge of the spirit which actuated the First Presidency in the part they took in these transactions, they themselves being witnesses.

At the council held on the 26th of July, 1838, as given on page 151, in the Oct. No. of THE RETURN, the following resolutions were passed:

ahman, equally by the Bishop of each place.

2nd. That all the travelling expenses of the First presidency shall be defrayed.

3rd. That the Bishop be authorized to pay orders coming from the East, inasmuch as they will consecrate liberally, but this is to be done under the inspection of the First Presidency.

4th. That the First Presidency shall have the prerogative to say to the Bishop, whose orders shall or may be paid by him in this place, or in his jurisdiction." * *

Thus the First Presidency were to have their travelling expenses paid, in addition to the 80 acres of land adjoining the city plat, given to each, and the surplus tithing given them; also they reserved the right and prerogative to dictate to the Bishop who, of their eastern creditors, he should pay, "inasmuch as they, [the eastern people,] *consecrate* freely" to the church funds. Consecration is not tithing. We further quote from the history of Joseph Smith, jr., as found on page 204, 16th vol. Millennial Star.

"Saturday 28th. I left Far West for Adam-ondi-ahman, in company with President Rigdon, to transact some important business, and to settle some Canadian brethren in that place, as they are emigrating rapidly to this land from all parts of the country.

Elder Babbit with his company from Canada has arrived, and brother Turley is with him.

Sunday 29th. Elders Kimball and Hyde preached at Far West, having just returned from England.

Monday 30th. The Circuit Court sat in Far West, Judge King presiding.

I returned this evening from Adam-ondi-ahman to Far West, with President Rigdon.

Journal" was printed at Far West, in this month of July. (Two numbers had been printed at Kirtland, Ohio, before the printing office was burned there.) Joseph Smith, jr., editor, Thomas B. Marsh publisher, who employed the writer hereof as printer. We printed four numbers during the summer, when we were compelled to desist on account of the mob, and the press was taken down and the type hastily boxed and buried, in the night, and a haystack put over it.

It will be remembered with what assurance the declaration of Independence, was made on the 4th of July, in which it is declared:

"That mob that comes on us to disturb us, it shall be between us and them a war of extermination, for we will follow them, till the last drop of their blood is spilled, or else they will have to exterminate us; for we will carry the seat of war to their own houses, and their own families, and one party or the other shall be utterly destroyed. Remember it all MEN."—S. Rigdon's oration.

Let it be distinctly understood that President Rigdon was not alone responsible for the sentiment expressed in his oration, as that was a carefully prepared document, previously written, and well understood by the First Presidency, but Elder Rigdon was the mouth piece to deliver it, as he was a natural orator, and his delivery was powerful and effective.

Several Missouri gentlemen of note, from other counties, were present on the speaker's stand at its delivery, with Joseph Smith, jr., President, and Hyrum Smith Vice President of the day, and at the conclusion of the oration, when the President of the day led off with the shout of Hosanna, Hosanna, Hosanna, and joined in the shout by the vast multitude, these Missouri gentlemen began to shout hurrah, but they soon saw that did not time with the other, and they ceased shouting.

A copy of the oration was furnished the editor, and printed in "The Far West," a weekly newspaper printed in Liberty, the county seat of Clay county. It was also printed in pamphlet form, by the writer of this, in the printing office of the Elders' Journal, in the city of Far West, a copy of which we have preserved.

This oration, and the stand taken by the church in endorsing it, and its publication, undoubtedly exerted a powerful influence in arousing the people of the whole upper Missouri country.

Little did they think when driving David and John Whitmer, Oliver Cowdery and Lyman E. Johnson out of Caldwell county, that the words of Jesus, where he said, "the same measure that you mete shall be measured to you again," would be so soon fulfilled upon their own heads, and brought about, in a great measure, through their unwise and wicked words and actions. Let the cause be what it may, it soon came "as *fierce* as the mountain torrent, and as *terrible* as the beating tempest."

We mourn when we think of these transactions, they were so different from the teachings of our blessed Lord and Master. But our heart-felt regrets will not undo the past, but a relation of these experiences may deter others from being drawn into such a snare.

In less than thirty-five days after that boastful and daring declaration was made what would be done if a mob should come upon us again, a mob commenced their wicked and outrageous treatment upon some of our brethren at the election at Gallatin, in Davies county, as will be seen by the following quotation from the history of Joseph Smith, jr., as found on page 229, of the 16th vol. Mil. Star.

"Tuesday morning, August 7th, 1838. A report came to Far West, by way of those not belonging to the Church, that at the election at Gallatin, yesterday, two or three of our brethren were killed by the Missourians, and left upon the ground, and not suffered to be interred; that the brethren were prevented from voting, and a majority of the inhabitants of Davies County were determined to drive the Saints from the county.

On hearing this report I started for Gallatin, to assist the brethren, accompanied by President Rigdon, brother Hyrum Smith, and fifteen or twenty others, who were armed for their own protection; and the command was given to George W. Robinson.

On our way we were joined by the brethren from different parts of the country, some of whom were attacked by the mob, but we all reached Colonel Wight's that night in safety, where we found some of the brethren who had been mobbed at Gallatin, with others, waiting for our council. Here we received the cheering intelligence that none of the brethren were killed, although several were badly wouned.

From the best information, about one hundred and fifty Missourians warred against from six to twelve of our brethren, who fought like lions. Several Missourians had their skulls cracked. Blessed be the memory of those few brethren who contended so strenuously for their constitutional rights and religious freedom, against such an overwhelming force of desperadoes.

Wednesday 8th. After spending the night in counsel at Colonel Wight's, I rode out with some of the brethren to view the situation of affairs in that region, and, among others, called on Adam Black, Justice of the Peace, and Judge elect for Davies County, who had some time previous sold his farm to brother Vinson Knight, and received part pay according to agreement, and afterwards united himself with a band of mobbers to drive the Saints from, and prevent their settling in Davies county. On interrogation, he confessed what he had done, and in consequence of this violation of his oath as magistrate, we asked him to give us some satisfaction so that we might know whether he was our friend or enemy, whether he would administer the the law in justice; and politely requested him to sign an agreement of peace; but being jealous, he would not sign it, but said he would write one himself to our satisfaction, and sign it, which he did, as follows—

'I, Adam Black, a Justice of the Peace of Davies county, do hereby Sertify to the people coled Mormin, that he is bound to *suport* the Constitution of this State, and of the United State, and he is not attached to any mob, nor will attach himself to any such people, and so long as they will not molest me, I will not molest them. This the 8th day of August, 1838.

ADAM BLACK. J. P.

Hoping he would abide his own decision, and support the law, we left him in peace, and returned to Colonel Wight's at Adam-ondi-ahman.

In the evening some of the citizens from Mill Port called on us, and we agreed to meet some of the principal men of the county in Council, at Adam-ondi-ahman the next day at twelve o'clock.

The Committee assembled at Adam-ondi-ahman at twelve, according to previous appointment, viz., on the part of citizens, Joseph Morin, Senator elect; John Williams, Representative elect; James B. Turner, Clerk of the Circuit Court, and others: on the part of the Saints, Lyman Wight, Vinson Knight, John Smith, Reynolds Cahoon, and others. At this meeting both parties entered into a covenant of peace, to preserve each other's rights, and stand in their defence; that if men should do wrong, neither party should uphold them or endeavour to screen them from justice, but deliver up all offenders to be dealt with according to law and justice. The assembly dispersed on these friendly terms, myself and friends returning to Far West, where we arrived about midnight and found all things quiet."

We left our work in t and went with the party ty, thinking it to be ou to aid our brethren in and was present at Ada he signed that paper gi party went with a deter him signed such a paper to be an exceedingly un

The election took plac seph Smith, jr., and pa vies county on the 7th, on the 8th, and on the 1 nent citizens of Davies P. Peniston, Wm. Bow Kinney and John Nethe Austin A. King, of Ra of the 5th judicial circu that "a body of armed ber of one hundred ar committed violence aga by surrounding his ho him in a violent manne him to great indignities under threats of instan paper writing of a very acter, and by threatenin to all the old setlers an vies county." *

The result was, a con county visited Far We and soon after a commi ton county, and the w souri country was aro seen by the following history of Joseph Smit 16th vol. Mil. Star.

"Saturday, Septe

There is great exci ent among the Misso if possible en occas They are continually provoking us to an one sign of threatenin but we do not fear Lord God the Eterne God, and Jesus the Saviour, and in the our strength and con

We have been di time, and that witl smitten again and without provocation proved the world wi

and our liberties to be taken from us; we have not avenged ourselves of those wrongs; we have appealed to magistrates, to sheriffs, to judges, to Government and to the President of the United States, all in vain: yet we have yielded peaceably to all these things. We have not complained at the Great God, we murmured not, but peaceably left all, and retired into the back country, in the broad and wild praire, in the barren and desolate plains, and there commenced anew; we made the desolate places to bud and blossom as the rose; and now the fiend-like race are disposed to give us no rest. Their father the Devil, is hourly calling upon them to be up and doing, and they, like willing and obedient children, need not the second admonition; but in the name of Jesus Christ the Son of the living God, we will endure it no longer, if the great God will arm us with courage, with strength and with power, to resist them in their persecutions. We will not act on the offensive, but always on the defensive; our rights and our liberties shall not be taken from us, and we peaceably submit to it, as we have done heretofore, but we will avenge ourselves of our enemies, inasmuch as they will not let us alone.

Sunday 2nd. The whole upper Mo. is in a u ro w a ico ifusio t.

This evening I sent for General Atchison, of Liberty, Clay county, who is the Major General of this division, to come and counsel with us, and to see if he could not put a stop to this collection of people, and to put a stop to hostilities in Davies County. I also sent a letter to Judge King containing a petition for him to assist in putting down and scatter-ing the mob, which are collecting at Davies.

last. I was at home day.

This evening Gener rived in Far West.

Tuesday 4th. Th in Council with Gen He says he will do all to disperse the mob, ployed him and Doni ner) as our Lawyers a in Law. They are first lawyers in Upper

President Rigdon a: menced this day the under the instruction Atchison and Do think, by diligent can be admitted to th months."

This last movement of idents to become lawyer ted at the bar. was new not noticed it until the amining the history.

It is marvelous to se had strayed from the co by the Lord, for them t revelation given to Jose July, 1830, he had been ral labors thou *shalt no* for this *is not thy callin*

Notwithstanding this tion, how persistantly t poral things, having trie city lot speculation, sea hidden treasure in Sal Joseph Smith received *all Salem* should be give its *gold* and *silver,"* and of which had so signa that they thought it be Kirtland, Ohio, in haste in his history, that they in the night time, on t 1838, riding on horse b first night. See page 1 Star.

It does seem that all should have taught the

ness of the above declaration, but they seemed to be ready to try a new turn of the wheel of fate, and soon proved the truthfulness of the saying, "man proposes, but God disposes," for, instead of being admitted to the bar, they were soon overcome by their enemies and incarcerated in prison, as will be seen in our next number.

(TO BE COTINUED.)

---o---

ONE WIFE OR MANY.

Some person has sent us a pamphlet with the above title, for which they will please accept our thanks.

The pamphlet was written by Joseph Smith, with an addenda written by W. W. Blair, Presidents of the Reorganized church of Latter Day Saints, and is for sale at the Herald office at Lamoni, Iowa at 25 cents per dozen.

President Smith shows very clearly, to our understanding, that monogamy, and *not polygamy*, is the Lord's order in establishing the marriage relation between male and female. But where he attempts to make the reader believe that his father, Joseph Smith, and his uncle, Hyrum Smith, were innocent of having any thing to do with helping establish polygamy in Nauvoo, he greatly errs.

His uncle, Hyrum Smith, taught polygamy to *our certain knowledge*, for he taught it to the writer in 1843, to which we made oath on the 29th of Dec. 1873. Our companion, who was then living, joined us in the affidavit, as she was present when he taught it.

There is a good brother living in Lamoni, a member of the Reorganized church, whose word will be taken as readily and believed as firmly as that of any other man in that church, who was living in Nauvoo, Illinois, in the years 1843 and 1844, whom we have heard state on different occasions, that his "father and mother went to Hyrum Smith for their patriarchal blessing, (as he was the patriarch for the church of Latter Day Saints,) and when there Hyrum Smith taught them the doctrine of polygamy, and that when they returned home his mother walked the house and *wrung her hands and wept*, day and night, for several days."

On page 739 of the Saints' Herald for Dec. 1, 1873, Joseph S[mith], refering to his [un]cle Hyrum:

"Neither Joseph [nor] their compeers, ever [built an]amy; nor did they [have] the necessary concor[d]

He concluded the [article with these] words:

We have not cha[nged our senti]ment, in respect to t[hese assump]tions one shade, nor [do we intend] to.—So, "if this be [treason make] the most of it."

After reading that st[atement I wrote] and sent him the follow[ing letter:]

Pleasanton, Iowa, D[ate...]

Bro. Joseph; I re[gret very much] the position taken i[n the Herald] of the 1st inst., o[n the subject of] polygamy, wherein [you say nei]ther Joseph nor Hy[rum nor their] compeers, ever built [it up.]

Now, if teaching [a doctrine and] recommending othe[rs to believe] and practice it, is no[t building it up,] then I do not unders[tand the En]glish language. Th[is is what] Hyrum did. He ca[lled on me] in Nauvoo, Ill., in t[he month of Nov]ember and Decem[ber 1843, and] taught the doctrine [of spiritual] wife, more than o[nce, and] gave me special i[nstructions how] I could manage the [matter, so as] to have it known to [but few. I] seemed displeased w[ith it, and] declined entering in[to the practice.]

Your father never [taught me the] doctrine, but I hav[e understood] from what your Un[cle Hyrum and] others told me, to [believe that he] did teach it.

This is an unple[asant subject to] write upon, but I d[o think you] ought to know the f[acts and allow] for an error, or fals[e statement will] not stand the test in [time to come.]

If you will recoll[ect, I told you] on one occasion whe[n I was] with you in your bug[gy alone,] when we were talkin[g on this sub]ject, "That your fat[her taught] me that doctrine,

Hyrum did." You asked none of the particulars, and I gave none; so I presume you had forgotten the remark.

Hoping that all things may work together for good to them who love the Lord, and are the called according to his purpose.

I am Respectfully and Truly your Brother in the great work of the last days.

E. ROBINSON.

In addition to these testimonies, the writers of the above named pamphlet have seen copies of affidavits made by several parties who testify that Joseph Smith, jr., taught the doctrine, and the affidavits of other reliable witnesses who testify that the revelation on polygamy was read before the High Council in Nauvoo, in August, 1843, by Hyrum Smith; yet, with all this testimony before them they still persist in the innocence of Joseph and Hyrum Smith in the matter, in proof of which reference is made to a letter of Hyrum Smith's, published in the Times and Seasons of March 15, 1844. We append that letter entire, and let the reader judge of its character. The italics are ours. Where Hyrum had italics we put small caps. We quote from the Times and Seasons.

We certainly feel sorry for, and pity the men who will persist in maintaining a false position against such a cloud of witnesses, knowing that nothing but truth will stand in the Judgement; then the "refuge of lies" will be swept away; but they have deliberately chosen their position, and therefore must abide the consequences.

Now comes John K. Sheen's pamphlet, entitled "Polygamy, or The Veil Lifted," in which, among other things, he gives lengthy extracts from a document entitled, "The Elders' Pocket Companion," which he claims was written by "William Smith, one of the Twelve," (a brother of Joseph and Hyrum Smith,) in 1844, the next year after the polygamous revelation was given, which refers, as he claims, to several sections of that revelation; which document, he says came into his father's possession early in 1850, two years before Brigham Young presented the revelation to the church in Utah.

Thus the evidence accumulates. This pamphlet can be obtained, as we understand, by sending 10 cents to John K. Sheen, York, Nebraska.

HYRUM SMITH'S LETTER.

Nauvoo, March, 15, 1844.

To the brethren of the Church of Jesus Christ of Latterday Saints, living on China Creek, in Hancock County, Greeting:—Whereas brother Richard Hewitt has called on me to-day, to know my views concerning some doctrines that are preached in your place, and states to me that some of your elders say, that a man HAVING A CERTAIN PRIESTHOOD may have as many wives as he pleases, and that doctrine is taught here: I say unto you that that man teaches FALSE DOCTRINE for there is no such doctrine taught here; neither is there any such thing practised here. And any man that is found teaching privately or publicly any such doctrine, is culpable, and will stand a chance to be brought before the High Council, and lose his license and membership also: therefore he had better beware what he is about.

And again I say unto you, an elder has no business to undertake to preach mysteries in any part of the world, for God has commanded us all to preach nothing but the first principles unto the *world*. Neither has any elder any authority to preach any mysterious thing to any branch of the church *unless* he has a *direct* commandment from God to do so. Let the matter of the grand councils of heaven, and the *making of gods*, worlds, and *devils* ENTIRELY ALONE; for *you* are not called to teach any such doctrine—for neither you nor the *people* are capacitated to understand any such principles—less so to teach them. For when God commands men to teach such principles the saints will receive them. Therefore beware what *you* teach! for the *mysteries* of God are not given to *all men*; and unto *those* to whom they are *given* they are placed under restrictions to impart *only such* as God will command them; and the *residue* is to be kept in a *faithful breast*, otherwise he will be brought under condemnation. By *this* God will prove his faithful servants, who will be called and numbered WITH THE CHOSEN.

And as to the celestial glory, all will enter in and possess that kingdom that obey the gospel, and continue in faith in the Lord unto the end of his days. Now therefore, I say unto you, you must cease preaching your miraculous things, and let the *mysteries alone until bye and bye*. Preach faith in the Lord Jesus Christ; repentance and baptism for the remission of sins; the laying on of hands

The Return.

PUBLISHED MONTHLY AT $1.00 A YEAR,

Entered at the Post Office at Davis City, Iowa, as second class matter.

THE CHILDREN of ISRAEL.

END OF THE GENTILE NATIONS.

We watch with intense interest, the movements of the children of Israel, and their gathering home to the land of their fathers. That act alone portends wonderful consequences not only to that people, but also to the nations of the earth. Jesus hath said "Jerusalem shall be trodden down of the gentiles until the times of the gentiles be fulfilled."—Luke 21:24.

Paul also, speaking on this subject says: "For I would not, brethren, that ye should be ignorant of this mystery, lest ye should be wise in your own conceits, that blindness in part is happened to Israel until the fulness of the gentiles be come in."—Romans 11:25. And in another place, when preaching to the Athenians, he says:

"Then Paul stood in the midst of Mars' hill, and said, Ye men of Athens, I perceive that in all things ye are too superstitious.

For as I passed by, and beheld your devotions, I found an altar with this inscription, TO THE UNKNOWN GOD. Whom therefore ye ignorantly worship, him declare I unto you.

God that made the world and all things therein, seeing that he is Lord of heaven and earth, dwelleth not in temples made with hands;

Neither is worshipped with men's hands, as though he needed any thing, seeing he giveth to all life, and breath, and all things.

And hath made of one blood all nations of men for to dwell on all the face of the earth, and hath determined the times before appointed, and the bounds of their habitation."—Acts 17:22-26.

Here Paul declares positively that God "made of one blood all nations of men for to dwell on all the face of the earth, and hath determined the times *before appointed* and the *bounds of their habitation.*" This being true, as we verily believe, then when we read the word of the Lord, as declared by one of his holy prophets, "That he that scattered Israel will gather him and keep him as a shepherd doth his flock;" and when we see that gathering has commenced, and is now taking place; and that the Lord has restored the former and the latter rain to the land of Palestine, after it had been withheld for so many ages; and that the planters have commenced to plant out the vines, in fulfillment of the word of the Lord, where he says: "Thou shalt yet plant vines upon the mountains of Samaria: the planters shall plant, and shall eat them as common things;" which is being literally fulfilled, as we are credibly informed one colony of Jews have planted *two millions of vines* in Palestine.

And when we read of their widening and improving the highways of that land, it reminds us of the commandment of the Lord to Israel, what they should do after their return, viz; "Go through, go through the gates; prepare ye the way of the people; cast up, cast up the highway: gather out the stones; lift up a standard for the people." How literally and beautifully this will be fulfilled when the railroads are completed in the holy land.

In view of all these things which are now transpiring, we rejoice greatly with

with an eye single to the glory of God, "having faith, hope, and charity," or we "cannot assist in this work," as the Lord notified the Elders in the beginning of his work in the last days.—D. C. 6. 7.

Remember we are called upon to help prune the vineyard of the Lord for the last time, and that we must labor in gentleness, in kindness, and forbearance, in much long suffering and patience, knowing that by so doing we ourselves will bring forth good fruit, and assist others in so doing, for the Lord of the vineyard to lay up against the season, for the end draweth near.

ITEMS OF PERSONAL HISTORY OF THE EDITOR.

No. 8.

INCLUDING SOME ITEMS OF CHURCH HISTORY NOT GENERALLY KNOWN.

(CONTINUED FROM PAGE 174.)

During the summer of 1838, a settlement was established by the church at De Witt, on the Missouri river, in the lower part of Carroll county, Mo. Two members of the High Council at Far West, viz: George M. Hinkle and John Murdock had moved there.

In the latter part of September a mob began to gather, and threatened to drive the members of the church from that place. The brethren armed themselves in self defense, and on the 2nd of October the mob commenced firing on them, which they repeated on the 3rd and 4th, when the brethren returned the fire.

On the 5th Joseph Smith, jr., left Far West and arrived in De Witt on the 6th, as we learn by the following quotation from his history; page 342, 16th vol. Millennial Star.

"Saturday Oct. 6th. I arrived at De Witt, and found that the accounts of the situation of that place were and ingress as well as egress. I found my brethren, who were only a handful in comparison to the mob by which they were surrounded, in this situation, and their provisions nearly exhausted, and no prospect of obtaining any more. We thought it necessary to send immediately to the Governor, to inform him of the circumstances, hoping, from the Executive, to raise the protection which we needed; and which was guaranteed to us in common with other citizens. Several gentlemen of standing and respectability, who lived in the immediate vicinity, who were not in any way connected with the Church of Latter-day Saints, who had witnessed the proceedings of our enemies, came forward and made affidavits to the treatment we had received, and concerning our perilous situation; and offered their services to go and present the case to the Governor themselves."

A messenger was dispatched to the Governor, who returned on the 9th, as seen by the following quotation from the history of Joseph Smith, jr,, page 376, 16th vol. Mil. Star.

"The messenger, Mr. Caldwell, who had been dispatched to the Governor for assistance, returned, but instead of receiving any aid or even sympathy from his Excellency, we were told that "the quarrel was between the Mormons and the mob," and that "we might fight it out."

About this time a mob, commanded by Hyrum Standly, took Smith Humphrey's goods out of his house, and said Standly set fire to Humphrey's house and burned it before his eyes, and ordered him to leave the place forthwith, which he did by fleeing from De Witt to Caldwell County. The mob had sent to Jackson County and got a cannon, powder, and balls, and bodies of armed men had gathered in, to aid them, from Ray, Saline, Howard, Livingston, Clinton, Clay, Platte, and other parts of the State, and a man by the name of Jackson from Howard County was appointed their leader.

The Saints were forbid to go out of the town, under the pain of death, and were shot at when they attempted to go out to get food, of which they were destitute. As fast as their cattle, horses, or other property got where the mob could get hold of it, it was taken as spoil. By these outrages the brethren were obliged, most of them, to live in wagons or tents.

Application had been made to the judge of the Circuit Court, for protection, who ordered out two companies of Militia, one commanded by Captain Bogart, a Methodist priest, and mobocrat of the deepest die; the whole under the command of General Parks, another mobber, if his letters speak his feelings, and his actions did not belie him, for he never made the first attempt to disperse the mob, and when asked the reason of his conduct, he always replied that Bogart and his company were mutinous and mobocratic, that he dare not attempt a dispersion of the mob. Two other principal men of the mob were Major Ashly, *Member of the Legislature*, and Cercil (Sashiel) Woods, a *Presbyterian Clergyman*.

General Parks informed us that a greater part of his men under Captain Bogart had mutinied, and that he should be obliged to draw them off from the place, for fear they would join the mob; consequently he could offer us no assistance.

We had no hopes whatever, of successfully resisting the mob, who kept constantly increasing; our provisions were entirely exhausted, and we being wearied out, by continually standing on guard, and watching the movements of our enemies, who, during the time I was there, fired at us a great many times. Some of the brethren died for the common necessaries of life, and perished from starvation; and for once in my life, I had the pain of beholding some of my fellow creatures fall victims to the spirit of persecution, which did then, and has since, prevailed to such an extent in Upper Missouri; men, too, who were virtuous, and against whom no legal process could for one moment be sustained, but who, in consequence of their love to God, attachment to His cause, and their determination to keep the faith were thus brought to an untimely grave."

The following quotation can be found on page 395 10th vol Mil. Star.

"Seeing no prospect of relief, the Governor having turned a deaf ear to our entreaties, the Militia having mutinied, and the greater part of them being ready to join the mob; the brethren came to the conclusion to leave that place, and seek a shelter elsewhere; and gathering up as many wagons as could be got ready, which was about seventy, with a remnant of the property they had been able to save from their matchless foes, left De Witt, and started for Caldwell on the afternoon of Thursday, October 11, 1838. They travelled that day about twelve miles, and encamped in a grove of timber near the road.

No sooner had the brethren left De Witt, than Sashiel Woods called the mob together, and made a speech to them, that they must hasten to assist their friends in Davies County.

"On my arrival in Caldwell, I was informed by General Doniphan, of Clay County, that a company of mobbers, eight hundred strong, were marching toward a settlement of our people in Davies County. He ordered out one of the officers, to raise a force and march immediately to what he called Wight's Town, and defend our people from the attack of the mob, until he should raise the Militia in his and the adjoining Counties to put them down. A small company of Militia, who were on their route to Davies County, and who had pass-

were "damned rotten hearted."

Sunday 14th. I preached to the brethren at Far West, from the saying of the Saviour—"Greater love hath no man than this, that he lay down his life for the brethren." At the close, I called upon all that would stand by me to meet me on the Public Square the next day.

Monday 15th. The brethren assembled on the Public Square, and formed a company of about one hundred, who took up a line of march for Adam-ondi-ahman; and here let it be distinctly understood, that this company were Militia of the County of Caldwell, acting under Lieutenant Colonel Hinkle, agreeable to the order of General Doniphan, and the brethren were very careful in all their movements to act in strict accordance with the constitutional laws of the land.

The special object of this march was to protect Adam-ondi-ahman, and repel the attacks of the mob in Davies County. Having some property in that county, and having a house building there, I went up at the same time. While I was there, a number of houses belonging to our people were burned by the mob, who committed many other depredations, such as driving off horses, sheep, cattle, hogs, &c. A number of those whose houses were burned down, as well as those who lived in scattered and lonely situations, fled into the town for safety, and for shelter from the inclemency of the weather, as a considerable snow storm took place on the 17th and 18th. Women and children, some in the most delicate situations, were thus obliged to leave their homes, and travel several miles in order to effect their escape. My feelings were such as I cannot describe when I saw them flock into the village, almost entirely destitute

eral Parks arrived at Davies County, and was at the house of Colonel Lyman Wight on the 18th, when the intelligence was brought that the mob were burning houses; and also when women and children were fleeing for safety, among whom was Agnes M. Smith, wife of my brother Don Carlos Smith, who was absent on a mission in Tennessee, her house having been plundered and burned by the mob, she having travelled nearly three miles, carrying her two helpless babes, and having had to wade Grand River.

Colonel Wight, who held a commission in the 59th Regiment under his (General Park's) command, asked what was to be done. He told him that he must immediately call out his men and go and put them down. Accordingly a force were immediately raised for the purpose of quelling the mob, and in a short time were on their march, with a determination to drive the mob, or die in the attempt; as they could bear such treatment no longer.

The mob, having learned the orders of General Parks, and likewise being aware of the determination of the oppressed, broke up their encampment and fled."

When President Joseph Smith, jr., preached the sermon, on the 14th, as named in the foregoing quotation, and called for volunteers, there was a ready response. A company was organized on the 15th, and marched to Davies county, under the immediate command of David W. Patten, one of the twelve Apostles, as captain, and Parley P. Pratt, another of the twelve Apostles, as first lieutenant, and the writer hereof in the double capacity as second lieutenant and also, as ensign, for, as we marched into Adam-ondi-Ahman, we served as standard bearer, floating the stars and stripes, in fulfillment, we suppose, of a declaration

ering in Davies county, with avowed determination of driving the Mormons from the county, and we began to feel as determined that the Missourians should be expelled from the county.

We had pledged, on the 4th of July preceeding, that if any mob should come upon us hereafter, it should "be between us and them a war of extermination,** for we will carry the seat of war to their own houses, and their own families, and one party or the other shall be utterly destroyed." S. Rigdon's oration.

The church having thus deliberately made their own declaration and threats, and the mob having commenced their work, it now remained to be seen how those threats would be carried out.

Unfortunately for the church, they now felt to act upon that declaration. A company of 60 were detailed to go to the East fork of Grand River, to bring and guard in some families of the church who had settled there, the writer being one of the number.

We made an early start, and by a forced march, reached the place of destination about 2 oclock P. M. and hurriedly packed the families into wagons and detailed about 10 men to accompany the wagons as guard, the ballance of the company immediately started on our return march, with a determination to attack the camp of the mob that night, if we could find them. They had been encamped near Millport, in Grand River timber, some 6 or 8 miles from Adam-ondi-ahman.

We reached the neighborhood of their encampment about one or two o'clock in the morning, but failed to find them. After exploring in the timber some time, and not finding the camp, marched into Millport, thinking we would undoubtedly find some trace of the mob there, but failed to find them, when we returned to Adam-ondi-ahman, where we arrived just after day light.

once or twice during the night, which accounted for our not finding them.

As stated in the history of Joseph Smith, jr., as herein quoted, the mob soon broke up and left, together with several Missourians, who now seemed to be aroused to the gravity of the situation. Some lingered, but soon after left in a hurry, for "prairie fires" (as they were termed) became frequent, and with them one, or more, of the Missourians' houses went up in flame and smoke, and settled down in a bed of embers and ashes, fired by the hands of some of those who had pledged to "carry the seat of war to their own houses," &c. A swift retribution however, soon followed.

We further quote from the history of Joseph Smith jr., page 406, 16th vol. Mil. Star.

"It was reported in Far West, today, that Orson Hyde had left that place, the night previous, leaving a letter for one of the brethren, which would develope the secret.

Monday 22nd. On the retreat of the mob from Davies, I returned to Caldwell, with a company of the brethren, and arrived at Far West about seven in the evening, where I hoped to enjoy some respite from our enemies, at least for a short time; but upon my arrival there, I was informed that a mob had commenced hostilities on the borders of that county, adjoining to Ray County, and that they had taken some of our brethren prisoners, burned some houses, and had commited depredations on the peaceable inhabitants.

Tuesday 23rd. News came to Far West, this morning, that the brethren had found the cannon, which the mob brought from Independence, buried in the earth, and had secured it by order of General Parks.

Wednesday 24th. Austin A. King and Adam Black renewed their inammatory communications to the Governor as did other citizens of Richmond.

Thomas B. Marsh, formerly President of the Twelve, having apostatized, repaired to Richmond, and made affidavit before Henry Jacobs, Justice of the Peace, to all the vilest calumnies, aspersions, lies, and slanders, towards myself and the Church, that his wicked heart could invent. He had been lifted up in pride, by his exaltations and the Revelatons of Heaven concerning him, until he was ready to be overthrown by the first adverse wind that should cross his track, and now he has fallen, lied and sworn to it, and is ready to take the lives of his best friends. Let all men take warning by him, and learn that he who exalteth himself, God will abase.

Orson Hyde was also at Richmond, and testified to most of Marsh's statements.

The following letter, being a fair specimen of the truth and honesty of a multitude of others which I shall notice, I give it in full—

Carrolton, Mo., Oct. 24, 1838.

Sir—We were informed, last night, by an express from Ray County, that Captain Bogart and all his company, amounting to between fifty and sixty men, were massacred by the Mormons at Buncombe, twelve miles north of Richmond, except three. This statement you may rely on as being true, and last night they expected Richmond to be laid in ashes this morning. We could distinctly hear cannon, and we know the Mormons has had one in their possession. Richmond is about twenty-five miles west of this place, on a straight line. We know not the hour or minute we will be laid in ashes—our country is ruined—for God's sake give us assistance as quick as possible. Yours &c.

SASHIAL WOODS,
JOSEPH DICKSON.

These mobbers must have had very acute ears to hear cannon (a six pounder) thirty seven miles. So much for the lies of a priest of this world. Now for the truth of the case. This day about noon, Captain Bogart, with some thirty or forty men, called on brother Thoret Parsons, where he was living, at the head of the east branch of Log Creek, and warned him to be gone before next day at ten in the morning, declaring also that he would give Far West thunder and lightning before next day noon, if he had good luck in meeting Neil Gillum, who would camp about six miles west of Far West that night, and that he should camp on Crooked Creek, and departed towards Crooked Creek.

Brother Parsons despatched a messenger with this news to Far West, and followed after Bogart to watch his movements. Brothers Joseph Holbrook, and ——Judith, who went out this morning to watch the movements of the enemy, saw eight armed mobbers call at the house of brother Pinkham, where they took three prisoners (Nathan Pinkham, brothers William Seely and Addison Green,) and four horses, arms, &c., and departed, threatening Father Pinkham, if he did not leave the State immediately, they "would have his damned old scalp;" and having learned of Bogart's movements, returned to Far West near midnight, and reported their proceedings, and those of the mob.

On hearing the report, Judge Higbee, the first Judge of the county, ordered Lieutenant Colonel Hinkle, the highest officer in command in Far West, to send out a company to disperse the mob and retake their prisoners. whom, it was reported, they intended to murder that night. The trumpet sounded, and the brethren were assembled on the Public Square about midnight, when the facts were stated, and about seventy-five volunteered to obey the Judge's order, under command of David W. Patten, who immediately commenced their march on horseback, hoping to

company were detached from the main body, while sixty continued their march till they arrived near the ford of Crooked River (or Creek,) where they dismounted, tied their horses, and leaving four or five men to guard them, proceeded towards the ford, not knowing the location of the encampment. It was just at the dawning of light in the east, when they were marching quietly along the road, and near the top of the hill which descends to the river, when the report of a gun was heard, and young O'Banion reeled out of the ranks and fell mortally wounded. Thus the work of death commenced, when Captain Patten ordered a charge and rushed down the hill on a fast trot, and, when within about fifty yards of the camp, formed a line. The mob formed a line under the bank of the river, below their tents. It was yet so dark that little could be seen by looking at the west, while the mob, looking towards the dawning light, could see Patten and his men, when they fired a broadside, and three or four of the brethren fell. Captain Patten ordered the fire returned, which was instantly obeyed, to great disadvantage in the darkness which yet continued. The fire was repeated by the mob, and returnd by Captain Patten's Company, and gave the watchword "God and Liberty," when Captain Patten order a charge, which was instantly obeyed. The parties immediately came in contact, with their swords, and the mob were soon put to flight, crossing the river at the ford and such places as they could get a chance. In the pursuit, one of the mob fled from behind a tree, wheeled, and shot Captian Patten, who instantly fell mortally wounded, having received a large ball in his bowels.

The ground was soon cleared, and in the rear, one in the shoulder, one through the hips, one through both thighs, one in the arms, all by musket shot. One had his arm broken, by a sword. Brother Gideon Carter was shot in the head, and left dead on the ground, so defaced that the brethren did not know him. Bogart reported that he had lost one man. The three prisoners were released, and returned with the brethren to Far West. Captain Patten was carried some of the way in a litter, but it caused so much distress he begged to be left, and was carried into brother Winchester's, three miles from the city, where he died that night. O'Banion died soon after, and brother Carter's body was also brought from Crooked River, when it was discovered who he was.

I went with my brother Hyrum and Amasa Lyman, to meet the brethren on their return, near Log Creek, where I saw Captain Patten in a most distressing condition. His wound was incurable.

Brother David W. Patten was a very worthy man, beloved by all good men who knew him. He was one of the Twelve Apostles, and died as he lived, a man of God, and strong in the faith of a glorious resurrection, in a world where mobs will have no power or place. One of his last expressions to his wife was—"Whatever you do else, O! do not deny the faith."

How different his fate from that of the apostate, Thomas B. Marsh, who this day vented all the lying spleen and malice of his heart towards the work of God, in a letter to brother and sister Abbot, to which was annexed an addenda by Orson Hyde."

The battle of Crooked River was the only one fought during these troubles. We may speak of it and also of the massacre at Haun's Mill, hereafter.—ED.

(To be continued.)

The Return.

PUBLISHED MONTHLY AT $1,00 A YEAR,

Entered at the Post Office at Davis City, Iowa, as second class matter.

CHRIST THE WAY.

Our readers will please bear in mind that our heavenly Father sent his beloved Son, Jesus Christ of Nazareth, to show us the way that leads to life everlasting, to eternal rest and peace. He set the example before us how to enter into, and walk in that way, and said: "He that will be my disciple let him take up his cross and follow me." In another place he says: "I am the way, the truth and the life." Again: "I am the door: by me if any man shall enter in, he shall be saved, and shall go in and out and find pasture."

By these scriptures we learn that we must enter the sheepfold in and through Christ Jesus, by a willing obedience to the gospel, as he willingly obeyed his Father, when he went to John the Baptist and demanded baptism to fulfill all righteousness, because it is the straight gate, (baptism,) that the children of men must pass through in order to enter the "narrow way" which leads to eternal life; for after they pass through that gate, they receive the gift of the Holy Ghost, which introduces them to the Father and the Son, whom it is necessary to know, in order to escape the burning, and obtain eternal life: as we clearly learn by the following scriptures:

"And this is life eternal, that they might know thee the only true God, and Jesus Christ whom thou hast sent."—John 17:3.

Paul also testifies as follows:

"And to you who are troubled, rest with us, when the Lord Jesus shall be revealed from heaven, with his mighty angels, In flaming fire, taking vengeance on them that know not God, and that obey not the gospel of our Lord Jesus Christ; Who shall be punished with everlasting destruction from the presence of the Lord, and from the glory of his power;"—2nd Thess.1:7-9.

That knowledge of God and his Christ, comes through the manifestation of the Holy Ghost, as Paul says:

"Wherefore I give you to understand, that no man speaking by the Spirit of God calleth Jesus accursed: and that no man can say that Jesus is the Lord, but by the Holy Ghost."—1 Cor. 12, 3.

This manifestation of the Holy Ghost came upon Jesus *after* he was baptized; and Peter, on the day of Pentecost, when preaching to the people, said:

"Repent, and be baptized every one of you in the name of Jesus Christ, for the remission of sins, and ye shall receive the gift of the Holy Ghost."—Acts 2, 38.

By these and other scriptures, we learn that baptism is essential to qualify us for the reception of the Holy Ghost, by which we can testify that Jesus is the Christ, and become acquainted with our blessed Father who is in heaven, and can truthfully cry, "Abba, Father."

Jesus also taught us the manner of life we should lead after we have entered into the narrow way, in his sermon on the mount. By a careful and faithful observance of the rules and commandments given by Jesus, we receive joy and gladness here, and have a bright hope of a glorious reward hereafter, to which the faithless and unbelieving are strangers.

Now, reader, do not let us, for one moment, flatter ourselves that we can

instead of the "setting sun." But our government is putting up its now strong arm, and saying to this Chinese tide from the west, "Thou must not come." This, to our mind, is contrary to the spirit and genius of our free institutions, and is one indication that we are fast ripening in iniquity. The corner stone on which our national superstructure rests, is the equality of man.

"We hold these truths to be self-evident that all men are created equal: that they are endowed with certain unalienable rights, among which are life, liberty and the pursuit of happiness." Thus declared our fore fathers.

The mighty God of Jacob strengthened their arm when defending that heaven-born truth. Will he sustain their sons in waring against it? We think not.

Another indication that we are nearing the end, is the introduction of the railroad system throughout the world, as it indicates that we are living in the day of the Lord's preparation as Nahum says:

"The shield of his mighty men is made red, the valiant men are in scarlet: the chariots *shall be* with flaming torches in the day of his preparation, and the fir-trees shall be terribly shaken.

The chariots shall rage in the streets, they shall jostle one against another in the broad ways: they shall seem like torches, they shall run like the lightnings."—Nahum 2:3-4.

Another sure indication that the end is near, is the return of the Jews to Jerusalem and the promised land. We have many assurances in the scriptures that this will take place immediately preceeding the second coming of the Son of man, but we defer giving them here, as we only intended to extend a friendly greeting to our patrons and friends. May the Lord bless you all.—*Ed.*

-----:o:-----

A friend in California writes:

"BRO. E. ROBINSON: Inclosed you will find P. O. order for $1, for which you will please send me THE RETURN another year. I am well pleased with it, and am only sorry it can't come oftner. My desire, and earnest prayers are that I may be worthy a membership of the cause it advocates, at the first opportunity."

ITEMS OF PERSONAL HISTORY OF THE EDITOR.

No. 9.

INCLUDING SOME ITEMS OF CHURCH HISTORY NOT GENERALLY KNOWN.

(CONTINUED FROM PAGE 191.)

In our last we gave an account of a company of brethren volunteering at Far West, at the call of Joseph Smith, jr. and marching to Davies county, with David W. Patten as captain, who was one of the twelve apostles of the church. We esteemed him very highly, as a good man, and loved him as such. He was brave to a fault. So much so, that he was styled and called, "*Captain Fearnought.*" He seemed reckless of his life, as though it was scarce worth preserving. He had said to us, before there was any indication of a mob, or difficulty with the people of Missouri, "If I dare to do it, I could wish myself dead." We did not feel at liberty to ask him any reason for such a wish, but presume it was on account of those things transpiring in the church, as we did not know of his having any domestic or financial troubles.

An account of the battle at Crooked River, and of his death, we gave in the last No. of THE RETURN, on page 191, as quoted from the history of Joseph Smith jr. He was buried with the honors of war, and at his grave a solemn covenant was made to avenge his death.

The attack upon Bogart, and the mob under his command at Crooked River, added wonderfully to the excitement already existing in Upper Missouri, and created wide spread alarm, on account of the exaggerated statements made with regard to it.

The report went abroad, and circulated like wild fire, "that Bogart, and all his company, amounting to between fifty and sixty men, were massacred by the Mormons, except three," whereas only one of his men was killed.

The brethren lost three killed and several wounded, as heretofore stated. They took one prisoner, who was releas-

He went in the direction told, but did not escape being shot, as some one shot and wounded him, not fatally however, as he recoved, and appeared as a witness afterwards against the brethren, when on trial in Richmond.

The writer of these papers did not accompany this expedition, therefore was not present to witness any of its scenes, as we declined to go when called upon the night before, consequently were at home, thirteen miles away from the scene of the engagement, when it took place.

After the Governor sent word to the brethren by their messenger, as stated in our last, that "if they had got into a difficulty with the citizens they must fight it out," they felt justified in pursuing the course they did in plundering the store in Gallatin, and burning the houses in Davies county; which action, together with the attack on Bogart's camp, completely aroused the whole upper country.

Rumors came to Far West of mobs gathering in large numbers, and committing terrible depredations against the brethren, the most brutal of which was

THE MASSACRE AT HAUN'S MILL,

a brief account of which we extract from the history of Joseph Smith, jr.. found on page 587, 16th vol. Mil. Star, as follows:

"About the time of the battle with Captain Bogart, a number of our people who were living near Haun's Mill, on Shoal Creek, about twenty miles below Far West, together with a number of emigrants who had been stopped there in consequence of the excitement, made an agreement with the mob which was about there, that neither party should molest the other, but dwell in peace. Shortly after this agreement was made, a mob party of from two to three hundred, many of whom are supposed to be from Chariton County, some from Davies, and also those who had without any ceremony, notwithstanding they begged for quarter, shot them down as they would tigers or panthers. Some few made their escape by fleeing. Eighteen were killed, and a number more were severely wounded.

This tragedy was conducted in the most brutal and savage manner. An old man, after the massacre was partially over, threw himself into their hands and begged for quarter, when he was instantly shot down; that not killing him, they took an old corn cutter and literally mangled him to pieces. A lad of ten years of age, after being shot down, also begged to be spared, when one of them placed the muzzle of his gun to his head and blew out his brains. The slaughter of these not satisfying the mob, they then proceeded to rob and plunder. The scene that presented itself after the massacre, to the widows and orphans of the killed, is beyond description. It was truly a time of weeping, of mourning, and of lamentation."

This was a cold blooded butchery, and shows very clearly the terrible state of feeling existing in the country at the time. The perpetrators of this terrible crime were never called to an account by the authorities of Missouri. Some of them publicly boasted of the part they took in this barbarous transaction.

Eighteen of the victims were buried in one well. Thrown in promiscuously, without shroud or coffin.

A writer in the Missouri "Globe Democrat," over the signature of "Burr Joice," has given a detailed account of this terrible affair, which was published in the "Saints' Herald," of Oct. 22, 1887.

While these were transpiring in Davies and Caldwell counties, messengers were being sent to the Governor with exciting and highly exagerated statements which induced him to order out a large number of troops, and to issue, Nero like, his

free republican government, such as ours. The innocent should never be punished with the guilty, more than is incidental in the just execution of the law.

We here insert some of the communications sent to the Governor, and his order calling out troops, and also his exterminating order, copies of which were obtained some time afterwards, but at the time, the brethren had no intimation of what was passing with the Governor.

The following letters and Governor's orders are copied from the history of Joseph Smith jr., as found on pages 444, and 446, 16th vol. Mil. Star.

"The following letter will show the state of public feeling in the country,

Lexington, 6 o'clock, A. M.
Oct. 25, 1838.

To Messrs. Amos Rees and Wiley C. Williams.

Gentlemen—This letter is sent on after you on express, by Mr. Bryant of Ray County, since you left this morning. Mr. C. R. Morehead came here on express for men to assist in repelling a threatened attack upon Richmond to night. He brought news that the Mormon armed force had attacked Captain Bogart this morning at day-light, and had cut off his whole company of fifty men. Since Mr. Morehead left Richmond, one of the company (Bogart's) has come in and reported that there were ten of his comrades killed, and the remainder were taken prisoners, after many of them had been severely wounded; he stated further that Richmond would be sacked and burned by the Mormon banditti to-night. Nothing can exceed the consternation which this news gave rise to. The women and children are flying from Richmond in every direction. A number of them have repaired to Lexington, amongst whom is Mrs. Rees. We will have sent from this county since one o'clock this evening, about night. You will see the necessity of hurrying on to the City of Jefferson, and also of imparting correct information to the public as you go along. My impression is, that you had better send one of your number to Howard, Cooper, and Boone Counties, in order that volunteers may be getting ready and flocking to the scene of trouble as fast as possible. They must make haste and put a stop to the devastation which is menaced by these infuriated fanatics, and they must go prepared and with the full determination to exterminate or expell them from the State *en masse*. Nothing but this can give tranquillity to the public mind, and re-establish the supremacy of the laws. There must be no further delaying with this question any where. The Mormons must leave the State, or we will, one and all, and to this complexion it must come at last. We have great reliance upon your ability, discretion and fitness for the task you have undertaken, and we have only time to say, God speed you.

Yours truly,
E. M. RYLAND.

"The brethren had *not thought* of going to Richmond—it was a lie of whole cloth.

GOVERNOR BOGG'S ORDER FOR TROOPS.

Friday, Head Quarters of the Militia,
City of Jefferson, Oct. 26, 1838.
General John B. Clark, 1st Division, Missouri Militia.

Sir—Application has been made to the Commander-in-Chief, by the citizens of Davies County, in this State, for protection, and to be restored to their homes and property, with intelligence that the Mormons, with an armed force, have expelled the inhabitants of that county from their homes, have pillaged and burnt their dwellings, driven off their stock, and were destroying their crops; that they (the Mormons) have burnt to ashes the towns of Gallatin and Mill Port in said county; the former being the county seat of said county, and including the Clerk's Office and all the public records of the county, and that there is not now a civil officer within said county. The Commander-in-Chief therefore orders, that there be raised, from the 1st, 4th, 5th, 6th, and 12th Divisions of the Militia of this State, four hundred men each, to be mounted and armed as Infantry or Riflemen, each man to furnish himself with at least fifty rounds of ammunition, and at least fifteen days' provisions. The troops from the 1st, 5th, 6th, and 12th, will rendezvous at Fayette, in Howard County, on Saturday, the 3rd day of next month (November,) at which point they will receive further instructions as to their line of march. You will therefore cause to be raised the quota of men required of your division (four hundred men,) without delay, either by volunteer or drafts, and rendezvous at Fayette, in Howard County, on Saturday, the 3rd of next month (November,) and there join the troops from the 5th, 6th, and 12th Divisions. The troops from the 4th Division will join you at Richmond, in Ray County. You will cause the troops raised in your Division, to be formed into companies, according to law, and placed under officers already in commission. If volunteer companies are raised they shall elect their officers. The preference should always be given to volunteer companies already organized and commissioned. You will also detail the necessary field and staff officers. For the convenience of transporting the camp equipage, provisions and hospital stores for the troops under your command, you are authorized to employ two or three baggage wagons.

By order of Commander-in-Chief,
B. M. LISLE, Adj.-General.

Governor Boggs' Exterminating Order was issued from—

Head Quarters Militia, City of Jefferson, Oct. 27 1838.

SIR—Since the order of the morning to you, directing you to cause four hundred mounted men to be raised within your division, I have received by Amos Rees, Esq., and Wiley E. Williams, Esq., one of my aids, information of the most appalling character, which changes the whole face of things, and places the Mormons in the attitude of open and avowed defiance of the laws, and of having made open war upon the people of this State. Your orders are therefore, to hasten your operations and endeavour to reach Richmond, in Ray County, with all possible speed. The Mormons must be treated as enemies, and *must be exterminated* or driven from the State, if necessary, for the public good. Their outrages are beyond all description. If you can increase your force, you are authorized to do so, to any extent you may think necessary. I have just issued orders to Major-General Wallock, of Marion county, to raise five hundred men, and to march them to the northern part of Davies, and there to unite with General Doniphan, of Clay, who has been ordered with five hundred men to proceed to the same point, for the purpose of intercepting the retreat of the Mormons to the north. They have been directed to communicate with you by express; you can also communicate with them if you find it necessary. Instead, therefore, of proceeding, as at first directed, to reinstate the citizens of Davies in their homes, you will proceed immediately to Richmond, and there operate against the Mormons. Brigadier-General Parks, of Ray, has been ordered to have four hundred men of his brigade in readiness to join you at Richmond. The whole force will be placed under your command.

L. W. BOGGS,
Governor and Commander-in-Chief.
To General Clark.

THE RETURN.

Great excitement now prevailed, and mobs were heard of in every direction, who seemed determined on our destruction. They burned the houses in the country, and took off all the cattle they could find. They destroyed corn fields, took many prisoners, and threatened death to all the Mormons.

Head Quarters of the 3rd and
4th Div. Missouri Militia,
Richmond, Oct. 28, 1838.

To the Commander-in-Chief, Missouri Militia.

Sir—From late outrages committed by the Mormons, civil war is inevitable. They have set the laws of the country at defiance, and are in open rebellion. We have about two thousand men under arms to keep them in check. The presence of the Commander-in-Chief is deemed absolutely necessary, and we most respectfully urge that your Excellency be at the seat of war, as soon as possible.

Your most obedient servants,
DAVID R. ATCHISON, M. G. 3rd Div.
SAMUEL D. LUCAS, M. G. 4th Div."

In the afternoon of the 30th of October, 1838, a large body of armed men were seen approaching Far West, whom we supposed were mobbers coming to attack the city, as at that time we did not know of the Governor's order calling out the Militia, consequently felt it our duty to make as successful a resistance as possible.

Our men were collected upon the public square, where President Joseph Smith, jr., delivered an address, in which he endeavoured to inspire the hearts of his hearers with courage, and deeds of valor, in defence of our families, our homes, and our firesides, in which he made this declaration that if the mob persisted in coming upon us. "We will play h—l with their apple cart."

At the conclusion of the address, our men formed into companies under their respective officers, and marched out of town, on to the open prairie on the south of town, as the army was coming in from the south, and formed in line of battle, in single column, stretched out as far as we could, by stationing the men several feet apart, so that, to an observer at a distance, we made a very formidable appearance.

Goose creek, a small stream running from the northwest to the southeast, passed nearly one mile south of town. The army that was coming, crossed over this stream and formed in line of battle, and marched towards the city. Their army being in the valley, and ours on the high prairie, with the brow of the descending ground and hazle brush intervening, could not see each other, but we could distinctly hear their officers give the word of command.

Their commanding officer, as he came out of the hazle brush, was in full view of our little army of about 800 men, but spread out as we were, appeared to him a host; he immediately ordered a "halt," and soon ordered his army to "right about face," and marched them back to Goose creek, where they went into camp for the night.

Our men returned into the city, and went immediately at work throwing up a barricade on that side of the city, composed of fence rails, house logs, building material, wagons, or any and every thing moveable we could get.

We stationed a guard around the city, and the writer hereof officiated as sergeant of the guard for that night, until four o'clock the next morning. And to show the impression made upon that army by our little band of men spread out to such an extent upon the prairie, we learned afterwards, they estimated our force at 2000 strong, while they had only 1500. With this impression upon their minds, they evidently expected an attack from our men during the night. Four different times during the night, while attending to our guard duties, we heard them give the alarm, and their officers called the men "to arms," which we could distinctly hear in the stillness of the night. We were told they were called "to arms" once after we laid down at four o'clock, making five times during the night.

The sound that came from the camp, after the call "to arms," resembled more the buzzing of a large swarm of bees when the hive is disturbed, than anything else we can compare it to.

They evidently were very much excited, and we have no doubt, had we made an attack their army could easily have been routed, but we had no such thought; our whole effort was directed in making preparation for self defence.

The next morning their army marched up towards the city, and we repaired to our breast work, expecting an attack. They however, after a short time, withdrew to their camp, and we returned into the city, but to be ready at a moment's notice for any emergency.

Of the imprisonment of Joseph Smith, jr., and others, and of our surrender, we will speak hereafter.

(*To be continued.*)

CORRESPONDENCE.

Forsyth, Taney Co. Mo. Nov. 24, '89.

Bro. E. Robinson: I have been preaching for the last two years about once a month, but the people here were prejudiced that when I began they would hardly listen to me, but their prejudice gradually gave way, so now it is no trouble to get a hearing. I had to contend with the preachers of the different denominations several times, but that had a good effect; the people soon saw wherein they were trying to pervert scriptures of divine truth.

I did not debate with them, but I let them preach first that they might set forth their faith, then I would set forth our faith in Christ and his gospel, by the new testament, as I had to be very careful not to say very much about the Book of Mormon though I know it must be taught; but we must first get the people to believe in their own Book, then if we can get them to believe the gospel of Christ, and in the promises of Christ to those who obey the gospel, and also the prophets in the bible, so they can see that God does reveal his mind and will to those that obey the gospel of Christ, then they are better prepared to receive the evidence in favor of the Book of Mormon, and the work of the Latter days.

Now I want to say to all who may read this letter, as sure as God rules in heaven and on earth, the Book of Mormon is of Divine origin. God has revealed it to me in such a plain manner, and with such power that I know beyond a doubt in my own mind. Now whether any one can believe me or not, I have heard a voice several times speaking to me. I was privileged to read in the Book of Mormon, while in a vision, the name of the Church of Christ, and a voice said unto me, *and that Book shall lead you to the Church of Christ.*

Brethren and sisters, I know that God knows the secret thoughts and the intentions of our heart, and we must all give an account of all we say, that is not truth, at the great day of God Almighty. As sure as there is a God in heaven, what I have written is truth, and the time is close at hand when God is going to manifest his power in great destructions upon the unbelieving of the gentile nations, in order to bring about his purposes in behalf of the house of Israel; and if the righteous scarcely be saved, where shall the ungodly and unbelievers appear? Now as we are in the Church of Christ, let us work the works of Christ in love and union, with an eye single to the honor and glory of God.

I did not think of writing in this way when I began to write, but God knows what purpose he had in impressing me to write what I have; to God belongs all honor and glory. May God, through Christ, bless the church with great power and great blessings. Amen.

W. C. KINYON.

—:x:—

BRAZIL AND HER BLOODLESS REVOLUTION.

It is difficult to believe that the Empire of Brazil has really become the Republic of Brazil. A "nation shall be born in a day" said the old Hebrew seer, but here we have the fifth nation of the globe, in territorial extent, effecting in a

shed to earth, shall rise again; The eternal years of God are hers."

DAVIS CITY, IOWA, JANUARY, 1890. Whole No. 13.

Return.

NTHLY AT $1,00 A YEAR,

Post Office at Davis City, second class matter.

RTICLE.

offices in the church of
d some of the duties
the same.

JOHN C. WHITMER.

and Saviour, Jesus twelve apostles at Jer- sa twelve apostles Jesus y to the lost sheep of Israel. After Jesus icified and arose from nd this language, when nto the eleven apostles, ot had fallen, so his nt,) in Mathew 28th ning at the 18th verse: came and spake unto ll power is given unto and earth. Go ye d teach all nations, m in the name of the of the Son, and of ost; teaching them to ug whatsoever I have ou; and, lo, I am with you unto the end of the m." See also Mark beginning at the 14th rward he appeared un- s they sat at meat, and hem, go ye into all the ach the gospel to every that believeth and is be saved; but he that hall be damned.. And ll follow them that be- Luke 24: 49, "And be- hold, I send the promise of my Father upon you; but tarry ye in the city of Jerusalem, until ye be endowed with power from on high." Also Acts of the apostles 1: 4-5, "And, being assembled together with them, commanded them that they should not depart from Jerusalem, but wait for the promise of the Father, which, saith he, ye have heard of me. For John truly baptized with water; but ye shall be baptized with the Holy Ghost not many days hence." Same chapter, 8th verse: "But ye shall receive power, after that the Holy Ghost is come upon you: and ye shall be witnesses unto me both in Jerusalem, and in all Judea, and in Samaria, and in the uttermost part of the earth.

I will now refer to the call of Matthias and his ordination, Acts 1: 21-22, "Therefore of these men which have companied with us all the time, that the Lord Jesus went in and out among us, beginning from the baptism of John, unto the same day that he was taken up from us, must one be ordained to be a witness of his resurrection, 26th verse, and they gave forth their lots; and the lot fell on Matthias; and he was numbered with the eleven apostles."

The 2nd chapter of the Acts of the apostles shows us when they received the promise of the Father, the comforter, the Holy Ghost, which was to guide them into all truth. Acts 2: 24. "And suddenly there came a sound from heaven as of a rushing mighty wind, and it filled all the house where they were sitting, and there appeared unto them cloven tongues like as of fire, and it sat upon each of them, and they were all filled with the Holy Ghost, and be-

The Return.

PUBLISHED MONTHLY AT $1,00 A YEAR.

Entered at the Post Office at Davis City, Iowa, as second class matter.

ITEMS OF PERSONAL HISTORY OF THE EDITOR.

No. 10.

INCLUDING SOME ITEMS OF CHURCH HISTORY NOT GENERALLY KNOWN.

(CONTINUED FROM PAGE 207.)

On the 31st of October, 1838, Col. Geo. M. Hinkle, W. W. Phelps, and, we believe, Capt. Arthur Morrison, went out of the city, with a white flag, and had an interview with Gen. Samuel D. Lucas, who was then in command of the army. Gen. Lucas informed them that his army was the state militia ordered out by the Governor, and he demanded the presence of Joseph Smith, jr., Sidney Rigdon, Lyman Wight, Parley P. Pratt, and Geo. W. Robinson, as hostages, (as he states in his report to the Governor,) with the declaration that if they did not come by "one hour by sun in the evening, he would make an attack upon the town."

Col. Hinkle and companions returned to the city, and reported the result of their interview to Pres't. Joseph Smith, jr., and the other brethren named above, who, after a serious, deliberate consultation, concluded to go to the army, but instead of being treated as hostages were taken into custody, and treated as prisoners of war.

Parley P. Pratt, speaking of this transaction, says:

"Col. Hinkle waited on Messrs. J. Smith, S. Rigdon, Hyrum Smith, L. Wight, G. W. Robinson, and myself, with a polite request from Gen. Lucas, that we would surrender ourselves as prisoners and repair to his camp, and remain over night, with assurance that as soon as peaceable arrangements could be entered into next morning, we should be released. With this request we readily complied, as soon as we were assured by the pledge of the honor of the principal officers, that our lives should be safe; we accordingly walked near a mile voluntarily, towards the camp of the enemy; who, when they saw us coming came out to meet us by the thousands, with Gen. Lucas at their head. When the haughty General rode up to us, and scarcely passing a compliment, gave orders to his troops to surround us, which they did very abruptly, and we were marched into camp surrounded by thousands of savage looking beings, many of whom were painted like Indian warriors. These all set up a constant yell, like so many blood hounds let loose on their prey, as if they had achieved one of the most miraculous victories which ever dignified the annals of the world. In camp we were placed under a strong guard, and before morning, A. Lyman and several others were added to our number.—*P. P. Pratt's history of the persecutions.*

That night, about sixty of those who had been engaged in the Crooked River battle, made arrangements, and fled on horse back, north to the Indian country of Iowa, thus escaping the vengeance of the authorities of Missouri, which was about to be poured out upon all those who participated in that affair. They were advised to leave, being looked upon

fence of their brethren, and their friends wished them to escape the wrath of their persecutors.

The next morning, Thursday, Nov. 1, the brethren in the city were told that it was deemed advisable to lay down our arms and surrender to the army, which, instead of being a mob, were the militia of the state, ordered out by the Governor, and acting under legally commissioned officers. And also, that it was the wish of President Joseph Smith, jr., that we should do so.

Accordingly, about 10 o'clock, A. M. we marched out on to the open prairie south of town, where the army was stationed, forming three sides of a hollow square, leaving the north side open, through which our little army marched, and formed a hollow square inside of the square of the army. They had their artillery stationed on the south side of the square, with their guns pointing to the north in such a manner that in case anything should occur, making it necessary to use them, they could rake us fore and aft, without endangering their own men.

Our men were stationed in our hollow square with our faces inward, and at the word of command laid down our guns, and taking off our powder horns or flasks, laid them down also; seeing this Maj. Seymour Bronson passed around the square, and speaking low to the men, told us to take up our powder and bullet acoutrements, as we were not required to give them up, whereupon we took them up, which caused a stir among the soldiers.

When the writer laid his gun upon the ground, and as it lay there, a spirit of much greater strength came upon us than we had enjoyed while carrying it, and we asked our heavenly Father to witness the scene, and to give us grace and strength to keep his commandments the remainder of our days, when a spirit of resignation and calmness filled our soul, and we rejoiced in the Lord.

Our guns were gathered up and taken possession of by the soldiers, which is the last we ever saw of them.

A strong guard were placed around us and we were detained at the place of surrender until near night, while the main body of the army, now numbering 2500 men, went into the town. They placed a guard entirely around the city, so that persons inside could not go out, or those outside come in without a permit. Some time before sunset, we were marched back into the city and disbanded, after being charged by their commanding officer, that whenever we heard the drum beat on the public square, we must immediately repair to that place and await further orders.

President Joseph Smith, jr., and those brethren taken prisoners with him, were taken to Jackson county, Mo.

On Friday the 2nd, or on Saturday the 3rd, (we do not distinctly remember which day, but we remember the circumstance perfectly well,) the drum beat, and we repaired to the public square, according to previous orders, where the soldiers were formed in a hollow square with a table standing inside, with a deed of trust and writing material thereon, and officers sitting by it, who required each one of us to sign the deed. In this act they informed us that we signed away *all* our property, both *personal* and *real*, to pay the expenses of the war.

Thus, within the short space of four months from the time the church made that threatning boast that if a mob should come upon us again, "we would carry the war to their own houses, and one party or the other should be utterly destroyed," we found ourselves prisoners of war, our property confiscated, our leaders in close confinement, and the entire church required to leave the state or be exterminated.

<u>We admonish all christian people to let this be a solemn warning to never suffer themselves to make a threatening boast of what they would do under certain circumstances, as we are not our own keepers, and we feel certain the Lord will not help us fight any such battles.</u> But to return to our narrative.

On Sunday night, the 4th, our spiritual monitor notified us that, individually, we had not experienced the worst. So strong was this impression that when the drum beat on the public square on

Monday afternoon, the writer declined to go, hoping that possibly we might escape the coming sorrow. But our remaining at home did not avail us, for soon a soldier came and asked if Ebenezer Robinson lived here? We assured him that was our name, when he said: "Gen. Clark wants to see you on the public square." Putting on our cap, started with him, he going behind us with the muzzle of his gun close to our back. We soon met an officer on horseback, to whom our guard said, "I have got him," to this the officer replied, "make him run, d—n him." At this we started out on a brisk trot.

On the public square the soldiers were formed in a hollow square as before, and Gen. Clark and other officers therein. Our guard, taking us inside the hollow square, addressed Gen. Clark, and said: "Here is Mr. Robinson." The General commanded us to step five paces forward. This brought us in line with several brethren who had preceded us. Looking along the line we noticed bishop E. Partridge, Isaac Morley, and several others considered some of the best brethren in the church. This encouraged us, feeling assured they would prove good companions in tribulation. Several other brethren were brought and placed in our company, until they obtained near fifty. They marched us to a hotel, before the door of which two columns of soldiers were stationed, extending out about forty feet from the door, facing each other, with their guns poised so their muzzles were about breast high, between which we marched into the hotel.

After we had been taken to the hotel Gen. Clark made the following speech to the brethren on the public square:

"Gentlemen, you whose names are not attached to this list of names, will now have the privilege of going to your fields and providing corn, wood, &c., for your families. Those who are now taken will go from this to prison, be tried, and receive the due demerit of their crimes. But you (except such as charges may hereafter be preferred against) are now at liberty, as soon as the troops are removed that now guard the place, which I shall cause to be done immediately. It now devolves upon you to fulfill the treaty that you have entered into, the leading items of which I shall now lay before you—

The first requires that your leading men be given up to be tried according to law; this you have already complied with.

The second is, that you deliver up your arms; this has been attend to.

The third stipulation is, that you sign over your properties to defray the expenses of the war; this you have also done.

Another article yet remains for you to comply with, and that is, that you leave the State forthwith; and whatever may be your feelings concerning this, or whatever your innocence, it is nothing to me; General Lucas, who is equal in authority with me, has made this treaty with you—I approve of it—I should have done the same, had I been here—I am therefore determined to see it fulfilled. The character of this State has suffered almost beyond redemption, from the character, conduct, and influence that you have exerted, and we deem it an act of justice to restore her character to its former standing among the States, by every proper means.

The orders of the Governor to me were, that you should be exterminated, and not allowed to remain in the State, and had your leaders not been given up, and the terms of the treaty complied with, before this, you and your families would have been destroyed and your houses in ashes.

There is a discretionary power vested in my hands, which I shall exercise in your favor for a season; for *this* lenity you are indebted to *my* clemency. I do not say that you shall go now, but you must not think of staying here another season, or of putting in crops, for the moment you do this the citizens will be upon you. If I am called here again, in case of a non-compliance of a treaty made, do not think that I shall act any more as I have done—you need not expect any mercy, but extermination, for I am determined the Governor's order shall be executed. As for your leaders, do not once think—do not imagine for a moment—do not let it enter your mind, that they will be delivered, or that you will see their faces again, for their *fate is fixed*—THEIR DIE IS CAST—THEIR DOOM IS SEALED.

I am sorry, gentlemen, to see so great a number of apparently intelligent men found in the situation that you are; and oh? that I could invoke that *Great Spirit*, THE UNKNOWN GOD, to rest upon you, and make you sufficiently intelligent to break that chain of superstition, and liberate you from those fetters of fanaticism, with which you are bound—that you no longer worship a man.

I would advise you to scatter abroad, and never again organize yourselves with Bishops, Presidents, &c., lest you excite the jealousies of the people, and subject yourselves to the same calamities that have now come upon you.

You have always been the aggressors— you have brought upon yourselves these difficulties by being disaffected and not being subject to rule—and my advise is, that you become as other citizens, lest by a recurrence of these events you bring upon yourselves irretrievable ruin.

After making the above speech on the public square, Gen. Clark came into the hotel and said to us, that we were charged with "treason, murder, burglary, arson, robbery and larceny, and that tomorrow you will be taken to Richmond, to be tried for the above crimes." They then took us to a vacant store room that was to serve for our quarters during the night. They then permitted us to go to our homes under guard, to bid our families farewell, and to procure blankets for our bedding, and also have our families furnish our supper and breakfast, as no provision had been made for us by the officers of the army.

The soldier who accompanied the writer to his home, was a very humane man, as he would not enter to witness the parting scene. We soon returned to the store room where they detained us until near noon the next day, our families bringing us our supper and breakfast, but we made no further provision for food, expecting to be supplied from the Quarter-Master's stores of the army, but in this we were disappointed.

Tuesday Nov. 6, we started for Richmond, under a strong guard mounted; we, the prisoners, walked about thirteen miles, when they camped for the night. Having had no dinner, we felt the want of food. The officers of the army having made no preparation for us, our only resort was to get ears of corn, which had been provided for the horses, and roast them in the fire, and eat, which the writer and others did, and we confess it proved a sweet and delicious repast.

(TO BE CONTINUED.)

DAVID WHITMER'S BLESSING.

We received a few days since, in a letter from Elder W. C. Kinyon, a copy of a "blessing of David Whitmer," in the hand writing of J. L. Traughber, jr., of Forsyth, Mo., as herein given, together with Mr. Traughber's statement with regard to it.

BLESSING OF DAVID WHITMER, DELIVERED BY JOSEPH SMITH, JR., IN *Kirtland, Ohio, 1836. Oliver Cowdery being scribe.*

Blessed of the Lord is brother David, for he is truly a faithful friend to mankind; and he should be beloved by all because of the integrity of his heart. All his words are steadfast as the pillars of heaven, because truth is his only meditation, and he delights in it, and shall rejoice in it forever. The Lord God of Abraham, of Isaac and Jacob shall be on his right hand and his left, and shall go before his face, and shall be his rearward, and his enemies shall become an easy prey unto him; for, behold, he it is whom the Lord hath appointed to be the captain of his host, under the guidance and direction of him who is appointed to say unto the strength of the Lord's house, Go forth, and build up the waste places. A mighty shaft shall he be in the quiver of the Almighty in bringing about the redemption of Zion, and in avenging the wrongs of the innocent. He shall yet stand upon the land of Zion, from which he has been driven, and shall find an inheritance therein, and shall be a ruler in Zion until he is well stricken in years, and shall enjoy an abundance of the precious things of the lasting mountains, and shall have part with his brethren in all the good things of the earth, and shall never want a friend. He shall bring down his adversaries under his feet, and shall walk upon their ashes when their names are blotted out. His name shall be a blessing among all nations, and his testimony shall shine as fair as the sun, and as a diamond, shall it remain untarnished. There shall not be spot upon his character while he liveth, neither his seed after him to the last posterity. He shall not be forsaken, nor his seed be found begging bread. Amen.

On the other side of the sheet containing the above blessing is the following statement:

A FEW ITEMS CONCERNING THE BLESSING OF DAVID WHITMER.

I would state that I have twice seen and read the original of which a copy is found on the other side of this sheet. The first time was Thursday, May 30th, 1878, when David at his house in Richmond, Mo., showed me the manuscript of the Book of Mormon, a printed copy of the Book of Commandments of 1833, and the first edition of Doctrine and Covenants, (1835.) The next time I saw the blessing was Sept. 2nd, 1879. As nearly as I can now remember, David related the circumstances of the delivery of the blessing about as follows:

He was out attending to some business for the church, buying provisions I think, and while he was away, some persons had Joseph to inquire for them. After they had received something, Oliver Cowdery asked, "Is there not something for brother David?" With tears running down his cheeks, Joseph answered, "Yes, there is," and proceeded to dictate the blessing found on the other side, which was written by Oliver Cowdery, and by him presented to David when he returned home to Kirtland.

The language of the blessing attests the truth of this statement, as it speaks of David but is not addressed to him as though he were present.

I have no doubt the blessing was delivered and written just as it stands; but till time proves the issue, we have no means of telling how far it is true or false as it relates to the work of David Whitmer.—Sept. 19, 1886. J. L. TRAUGHBER, Jr.

The above blessing is being literally fulfilled, where it says: "His name shall be a blessing among *all nations*, and his *testimony* shall shine as fair as the sun, and as a diamond shall remain untarnished." One gentleman in California has already received over thirty copies of Elder Whitmer's pamphlets, some of which he purposed sending to crowned heads in Europe, as he informed us in one of his letters. Thus his testimony is going forth to the nations, and will continue to go, until our heavenly Father has accomplished all his purposes in it.

The Lord sent him to Richmond and *commanded* him to *remain* there, which he did for fifty years, (lacking only a few months,) where he established a character for truth and veracity far above reproach, which he could not have done if he had been moving about from place to place. When his heavenly Father moved upon him by his Holy Spirit to speak, he spoke, and his words are now going to the nations. It would have been useless for him to have spoken sooner. "God's ways are not as man's ways."—EDITOR.

No. 11.

INCLUDING SOME ITEMS OF CHURCH
HISTORY NOT GENERALLY KNOWN.

(CONTINUED FROM PAGE 212.)

At Richmond we were taken into the court house, which was a new unfinished brick building, with no inside work done except a floor laid across one end, some 16 or 20 feet wide. There were two large fire places built in the wall where the floor was laid. A railing was built across the room at the edge of the floor, and we were quartered inside the railing as our prison, with a strong guard inside and outside the building.

Two 3 pail iron kettles for boiling our meat, and two or more iron bake kettles, or dutch ovens, for baking our corn bread in, were furnished us, together with sacks of corn meal and meat in the bulk. We did our own cooking. This arrangement suited us very well, and we enjoyed ourselves as well as men could under similar circumstances. We spread our blankets upon the floor at night for our beds, and before retiring we sang an hymn and had prayers, and practiced the same each morning before breakfast.

The soldiers inside the building usually gave good attention during these devotions. Some of them were heard to tell other soldiers to come and hear these Mormons sing, for, said they: "They have composed some of the d—dst prettyest songs about Diahman you ever heard in your life."

Some of the guard however, at times, were very rude in speech and actions. One was heard to cry out to another: "Shoot your Mormon, I have shot mine." From this we concluded he helped compose the mob that committed that brutal, unhuman massacre at Haun's mill.

Robinson, were brought from Independence to Richmond, and placed in another building, and chained together in a cruel and barbarous manner.

Tuesday, Nov. 13, A space on the south end of the floor in the court house was appropriated for the use of the court, which convened on that day, with Austin A. King on the bench, and Thomas C. Burch, state's attorney, when the prisoners named above, together with those confined in the court house, were arraigned for trial, viz:

Caleb Baldwin, Alanson Ripley, Washington Voorhees, Sidney Tanner, John Buchanan, Jacob Gates, Chandler Holbrook, George W. Harris, Jesse D. Hunter, Andrew Whitlock, Martin C. Alred, William Alred, George D. Grant, Darwin Chase, Elijah Newman, Alvin G. Tippets, Zedekiah Owens, Isaac Morley, Thomas Beck, Moses Clawson, John T. Tanner, Daniel Shearer, Daniel S. Thomas, Alexander McRea, Elisha Edwards, John S. Higbee, Ebenezer Page, Benjamin Covey, Ebenezer Robinson, Luman Gibbs, James M. Henderson, David Pettigrew, Edward Partridge, Francis Higbee, David Frampton, George Kimball, Joseph W. Younger, Henry Zabriski, Allen J. Stout, Sheffield Daniels, Silas Maynard, Anthony Head, Benjamin Jones, Daniel Carn, John T. Earl, and Norman Shearer.

All the above named prisoners were severally charged with high treason against the state, murder, burglary, arson, robbery and larceny.

The charge of murder was made on account of the man that was killed in the Bogart battle, wherein one Missourian and three of our men were killed. Fortunately, most of our brethren who had participated in that battle had left the state, consequently only a few of our fellow prisoners had anything to do with that unfortunate affair.

After the trial had pregressed a few days, we understood the judge to say that "nothing but hanging would answer the law," thinking perhaps, from the testimony, that we were all guilty of treason. On another occasion we understood him to say, speaking of the prisoners, that, "if they would deny the book of Mormon they might go clear."
These things were talked over among the prisoners, but not one of our number would accept of freedom upon such unholy terms, notwithstanding it might possibly save them from the gallows. In view of these things, when we were seriously contemplating the worst, judge of our happy surprise when, on Saturday, the 24th, the judge issued the following order:

"Defendants against whom nothing has been proven, viz: Amasa Lyman, John Buchanan, Andrew Whitlock, Alvah L. Tippets, Jedediah Owens, Isaac Morley, John T. Tanner, Daniel S. Thomas, Elisha Edwards, Benjamin Covey, David Frampton, Henry Zobriski, Allen J. Stout, Sheffield Daniels, Silas Maynard, Anthony Head, John T. Earl, Ebenezer Brown, James Newberry, Sylvester Hulet, Chandler Holbrook, Martin Alred, William Alred. The above defendants have been discharged by me, there being no evidence against them.

AUSTIN A. KING, Judge, &c.
November 24, 1838."

As will be seen, the writer's name does not appear in the list of those discharged. The reason undoubtedly is because our name had been mentioned by W. W. Phelps, one of the witnesses for the state as having seen us with a burnt gun barrel. The circumstance was this, during the burning in Davies county, the writer accompanied a party of our men who visited a farm house belonging to a Missourian, which was deserted by its owner. Some of the party set fire to the house and barn and the party left the place. After getting some half a mile away, we heard the report of a gun in the burning barn.

The next day a few of us rode out to the place, and in the a found a gun barrel, took back to camp and cumstance of finding it those in camp, and this present. Thus this, gun barrel became und cipal cause of our being a prisoner.

The above was the o present at any house b the troubles.

It seemed to be the a ecuting attorney to in of the prisoners as poss gart battle, so much s man Gibbs, one of the honest hearted soul, th ate himself, stepped up open court, and said: " all, I staid back and horses." The writer p his coat, and urged hi but it was too late, destiny.

The court continued days after the discharg above, when some oth ed, and the remainder r

The trial was a one fair. as our witnesse badly, and intimidated it was considered usele make an extended defe

Joseph Smith, jr., i found on page 565 16 Star, says:

"Wednesday, 28. member of the State General Clark. tha battle [mob] at Ha thirty-one "Mormon and seven of his par

The remaining p released, or admited Lyman Wight, Cale rum Smith, Alexan ney Rigdon, and m sent to Liberty, Cla to stand our trial murder—the treas whipped the mob County, and takin from them; and the

THE RETURN.

man killed in the Bogart battle; also Parley P. Pratt, Morris Phelps Luman Gibbs, Darwin Chase, and Norman Shearer, who were put into Richmond jail to stand their trial for the same crimes.

During the investigation, we were mostly confined in chains, and received much abuse.

The matter of driving away witnesses or casting them into prison, or chasing them out of the country, was carried to such a length, that our lawyers, General Doniphan and Amos Rees, told us not to bring our witnesses there at all; for if we did, there would not be one of them left for final trial; for no sooner would Bogart and his men know who they were, than they would put them out of the country.

As to making any impression on King, if a cohort of angels were to come down, and declared we were clear. Doniphan said it would all be the same; for he (King) had determined from the beginning to cast us into prison.

We never got the privilege of introducing our witnesses at all; if we had, we could have disproved all they swore."

Joseph Smith, jr., Hyrum Smith, Sidney Rigdon, Lyman Wight, Caleb Baldwin, and Alexander M'Rea were taken to the Liberty, Clay county jail, and the remainder of the prisoners, eighteen in number, were removed from the court house to the Richmond jail, and put up stairs into the debtors' room, all of whom were subsequently released on bail except Parley P. Pratt, Luman Gibbs, Morris Phelps, Darwin Chase and Norman Shearer.

The first or second night they put us down into the dungeon, which was strongly built without light or ventilation. We spread our blankets down in a circle, which completely filled the place except a small space in the center occupied by an iron kettle.

The only entrance to this dark place, that we discovered, was through a trap door from the room above, and a light ladder put down when necessary for persons to enter or leave it, and then the ladder taken up and the trap door fastened, making it a dungeon in very deed.

In the morning they opened the trap door, and putting down the ladder we gladly made our way into the light of day, thanking the Lord for the privilege of seeing the beautiful sunlight, and breathing the sweet, pure air of heaven. This was the only experience we ever had in a dungeon.

The remainder of the time the writer remained in prison we were permitted to sleep in the debtors' room. The jail was a two story hewed log building, the upper story unfinished. The space between the logs was not plastered, and only indifferently chinked, consequently a cold uncomfortable place, but being so many of us, we made it as cheerful and comfortable as possible.

We were taken there on the 28th of November. Winter set in early that season. A considerable snow had fallen, and the weather became severely cold by the first of December. An amusing scene occurred one cold night. Brother Luman Gibbs, of whom we have heretofore spoken, lodged in the same bed with the writer, and after retiring for the night, he put his feet out of the bed and said: "Stay there and freeze. It serves you right; bring me here all the way from Vermont to be in prison for murder and never thought of killing any body in all my life." The act was so unexpected and so ludicrous, it convulsed his fellow prisoners with laughter, except Parley P. Pratt, he seemed to get out of humor, and gave him a good scolding. We may have occasion to speak of Bro. Gibbs hereafter.

After a few days confinement in jail we were released upon a light bail; James M. Henderson, one of our fellow prisoners, signed our bail bond, and we returned to our home in Far West, feeling thankful to our heavenly Father for our freedom.

On the 13th of December, met with the High Council, as will be seen by the following quotation from the history of Joseph Smith, jr., as found on page 602,

Mil. Star. And also again, as seen on page 333, same paper.

"Thursday, Dec. 13th, 1838.

Agreeable to appointment, the standing High Council met, when it was found that several were absent, who (some of them) have had to flee for their lives; therefore it being necessary that those vacancies be filled, the meeting was called for that purpose, and also to express each other's feelings respecting the word of the Lord; President Brigham Young presiding.

The Council was opened by prayer by Elder Kimball. After prayer, President Young made a few remarks, saying he thought it all important to have the Council re-organized, and prepared to do business. He advised the Counsellors to be wise and judicious in all their movements, and not hasty in their transactions. As for his faith it was the same as ever; and he fellowshipped all such as loved the Gospel of our Lord and Saviour Jesus Christ, in act as well as word. * *

Jared Carter responded to President Brigham Young's feelings, and wished still to walk with the brethren.

Thomas Grover said he was firm in the faith, and he believed the time would come when Joseph would stand before kings, and speak marvellous words.

David Dort expressed his feelings in a similar manner.

Levi Jackman says his faith is the same as ever, and he has confidence in brother Joseph as ever.

Solomon Hancock says he is a firm believer in the Book of Mormon and Doctrine and Covenants, and that brother Joseph is not a fallen Prophet, but will yet be exalted and become very high.

John Badger says his confidence in the work is the same as ever, and his faith, if possible, is stronger than ever. He believes that it was necessary that these scourges should come.

George W. Harris says that, as it respects the scourges which have come upon us, the hand of God was in it, &c.

Samuel Bent says that his faith is as ever, and that he feels to praise God in prisons and in dungeons, and in all circumstances.

After some consultation it was thought expedient to nominate High Priests to fill the vacancies.

The Council was organized as follows—Simeon Carter, No. 1; Jared Carter, 2; Thomas Grover, 3; David Dort, 4; Levi Jackman, 5; Solomon Hancock, 6; John Badger, 7; John Murdock, 8; John E. Page, 9; George W. Harris, 10; John Taylor, 11; Samuel Bent, 12.

Voted that John Murdock fill the vacancy of John P. Green, No. 4, and David Dort the place of Elias Higbee, No. 11, and John Badger the place of George Morey, No. 7, and Lyman Sherman the place of Newell Knight, until he returns.

Council adjourned until Friday evening, six o'clock. Closed in prayer by President Young.

E. ROBINSON, Clerk.

The High Council of Zion met in Far West, Wednesday, December 19th, 1838.

The Council was organized as follows—Ebenezer Robinson No. 1, Jared Carter No. 2, Thomas Grover 3, Reynolds Cahoon 4, Theodore Turley 5, Solomon Hancock 6, John Badger 7, John Murdock 8, Harlow Redfield 9, George W. Harris 10, David Dort 11, Samuel Bent 12. The Council was opened by prayer by President Brigham Young who presided.

Harlow Redfield gave a statement of his feelings. He said his faith was as good as it ever was, notwithstanding he did not feel to fellowship all the proceedings of the brethren in Davis County; he thought they did not act as wisely as they might have done, &c.

Voted by the Council that John E. Page and John Taylor be ordained to the Apostleship, to fill vacancies in the Quorum of the Twelve; when they came forward and received their ordination under the hands of Brigham Young and Heber C. Kimball.

Voted that we send a petition to the General Goverment, and send it by mail.

Voted that Edward Partridge and John Taylor be a committee to draft the above mentioned petition: also it is their privilege to choose another person to assist them.

Council adjourned until next Wednesday at one o'clock, at same place.

E. ROBINSON, Clerk.

(To be continued.)

CORRESPONDENCE.

Temple, Bell Co., Texas,
Feb. 15th, 1890.

BROTHER E. ROBINSON.—I was baptized on Jan. 29th, by Bro. Elias Land. It is the earnest desire of my heart, as well as my sincere prayer, that this blessed gospel may be preached in all churches.

It is my desire to advocate nothing but what is pure in the sight of the living God, and if this doctrine taught by Brother Elias Land, is not the very same that was taught by our blessed Lord and Savior, Jesus Christ, then there is certainly none in existence. It is indeed strange to me, that men will close their eyes, and stop their ears, and be led, as I term it, right straight into hell, and yet I myself was once blind; but now I see, and it is the earnest desire of my heart, to persuade others to see their danger, and turn ere it is too late.

I was a member of the Baptist church, now I can very plainly see they have not the true religion, they too would say so if they will only lay all prejudice aside, and investigate our doctrine, and not only them but all other denominations. I read THE RETURN nearly every night, also the Book of Mormon, and the Bible, and I thank God that through his goodness and mercy they have given me that light on the gospel, that I did not know ever existed before.

May God bless you forever Amen. Your humble servant, and searcher after Truth, and a believer in Jesus Christ. Respectfully Yours.

T. J. POLK.

Danbury, Iowa, Feb. 21st 1890.
ELDER E. ROBINSON,
—EDITOR OF RETURN.

I have been reading your little paper, ever since first published, and am pleased with the sentiment contained in it. I gave them away about as fast as I read them.

I received three of Elder D. Whitmer's pamphlets. I tried hard to keep one of those, but I felt anxious that others should read them, and thus gave them away, also I can truly say I never read a book that did me so much good as David Whitmer's pamphlet. When I began reading it, I never wanted to stop, it seemed to rejoice me so much; there is so much meaning contained in his words. After reading it I took it with me wherever I went, and showed it to the people, and talked to them and left it with them. I do think it is a great work; and one that will do a great deal of good.

I like THE RETURN also, although I have heard the History of the Church rehearsed often, it makes one think the writer has been there, there is but one church in Danbury, our little village, the M. E. church.

Yours in hope of a glorious resurrection. ELIZABETH R. BOWSER.

A friend in the west writes:

DEAR BRO. I would suggest that the first volume of THE RETURN be bound, cheaply, with a soft back, as durable as possible, to lend out to such as are interested in the latter day work, I will want at least one or two copies.

The word of God is often sweeter than my necessary food. Truly the book of Mormon is now like an unsealed treasure, in which I often look and find pearls of great worth.

It is written to the churches of Asia that in some points they came short of being complete, may we not profit by them of old, and overcome the world, or the flesh, and the evil one, who, in these perilous times, will counterfeit the pure gospel of the Son of God. Many will not understand the depths of Satan in this regard; discernings of the spirit is one of the gifts of the spirit.

"To him that overcomes will I make a pillar in the temple of my God, and he shall go no more out; and I will write upon him the name of my God." St. Paul says: The Holy Ghost witnesseth that bonds and suffering awaited him, but he adds: "none of these things move me." he endured to the end, so must we overcome even as our great Captain overcame.

Having been called lately to pass through what seemed hard to endure, yet the trial was a means of bringing me nearer to God.

Please send me one or two copies of David Whitmer's address. I am without; I find it difficult to keep an address in the house.

J. B.

ALONE WITH GOD.

In every instance the man who prevails in prayer is the man who is alone as he prays to God. Abraham leaves Sarah behind when he pleads with Him for Sodom, and if he fails, it is because he ceases to ask before God ceases to grant. Moses is by himself beside the bush in the wilderness. Joshua is alone when Christ comes to him as an armed man. Gideon and Jephtah are by themselves when commissioned to save Israel. Once does Elijah and Elisha raise a child from the dead, and in each case not even the mothers came in while the prophets, alone with God, asks and receives. So of Ezekiel, so of Daniel.

Although others are present, Saul journeying to Damascus is alone with Christ after that he breaks upon him. Cornelius is praying by himself when the angel flashes upon his solitude; nor is any one with Peter upon the house-top when he is preparing to go to the Gentiles for the first time. One John is alone in the wilderness; another John is by himself in Patmos when nearest God. It is when alone under his fig-tree in prayer that Jesus sees Nathaniel. All religious biography, our own closest communion and success with God, show what Christ means when, as if it were the only way to pray, He says: "And thou, when thou prayest, enter into thy closet and pray to thy Father which is in secret, and thy Father which seeth in secret shall reward thee openly."—*Rev. Wm. Baker.*

PALESTINE.

The greatest amount of rain tabled in any year during the period of observation is eighty-five inches, which fell in the year 1850-51. In 1889 there fell thirty-five inches. It is calculated that the average annual fall of rain throughout the United States is about forty-five inches. In California it averages only about twenty inches. Thus we see that we have about one fourth more rain in Palestine than in the Atlantic region of the United States.

We believe God is beginning to turn the captivity of the land which has lain so many centuries in desolation. The increase in the annual rainfall, the reclaiming of barren tracts of land, the continual improvement in the roads, all warrant this conclusion. These facts speak loudly to those who have ears to hear of the times in which we live.—*Hebrew Christian for Jan. 1890.*

—WE TAKE the following extract from a series of articles written on the "Jewish legends of hell," and printed in the *Jewish Messenger*, which may be interesting to some of our readers.

In these legends the idea is presented of degrees of punishment in the lower regins, on the same principle that Paul assures us there are degrees of glory in heaven. Paul says: "There is one glory of the sun, and another glory of the moon,

The Return.

PUBLISHED MONTHLY AT $1.00 A YEAR.

Entered at the Post Office at Lamis City, Iowa, as second class matter.

COMMUNICATIONS.

THE BOOK OF MORMON.

THE FULLNESS OF THE GOSPEL.

All that is necessary for our Salvation and government, is recorded in the New Covenant Scriptures:

This heading is what I honestly believe, and I shall endeavor to substantiate the same by the words of divine truth. Some have thought, as the B. of M., was only an abridgement of the Nephite Record, that it did not contain all the gospel. Now kind reader, are you willing to let the Book answer for itself?

Christ, when he was talking to the Nephites concerning his words which they should write, which should come forth by way of gentile, to the remnant of their seed, (the Lamanites,) calls it the fulness of his gospel, and also tells them what will happen to the gentiles if they reject the fulness of his gospel. Book of Nephi, chap. 6, par. 4. Also read the 3rd chap. and 43rd par. of first Nephi, where the angel said unto Nephi. "and the words of the Lamb shall be made known in the records of thy seed (the B. of M.) as well as in the record of the twelve Apostles of the Lamb, (the Bible.) Now I believe the Angel knew what he was talking about. In another place it says that those things were to come forth to us as the fulness of t[he] kind reader how d[o] swer? will you wrest Now, if this be tru look any farther in pel and the great p[l]

Now let us hea[r] Revelator. John s[aw] another Angel fly heaven having the [everlasting gospel] to preach unto th[ose that dwell on] the earth, and to e[very nation,] kindred and tongu[e.] Those who believe [the Book of] Mormon, generally the coming forth o[f the Book of Mormon] vision was literally if the book of Mor[mon that John] saw, he says it wa[s the everlasting] gospel. Now if J[ohn said that] the angel have the ness of the gospel, have said: I saw a[ngel flying in] the midst of heave[n having] an abridgement of [the] gospel. I believe he was saying. .

Now I wish to ca[ll your attention] to some revelations day, (doubtless th as recorded in the D[octrine & Cove]nants, See. 19. p (Lamoni Edition.) necessary for you t[o read all] of this section to g[et an understand]ing of what I shall the remainder of th[is section will con]tain all those par[ticulars] which my holy Pr[iesthood and] also my Disciples prayers should con[cerning my] people; and I said should be granted ing to their faith yea, this was their pel (all my gospel)

The Return.

PUBLISHED MONTHLY AT $1.00 A YEAR.

Entered at the Post Office at Davis City Iowa, as second class matter.

ITEMS OF PERSONAL HISTORY OF THE EDITOR.

No. 12.

INCLUDING SOME ITEMS OF CHURCH HISTORY NOT GENERALLY KNOWN.

(CONTINUED FROM PAGE 238.)

As will be seen by the extracts published in our former article, that immediately on our return to Far West, from Richmond, we were called to take part in the affairs of the church.

On the 13th of December we officiated as clerk of the High Council. Again, on the 19th, officiated not only as clerk, but also as a member of the High Council, or which occasion Elders John Taylor and John E. Page were appointed and ordained Apostles to fill vacancies in the quorum of the twelve.

Early in January, 1839, at a local election the writer was elected Justice of the Peace, and duly commisioned as such, and attended to the duties of that office during our stay in that state.

In consequence of the Governor's order, expelling the church from the state preparations were being made to carry out said order within the time specified and as there were a large number of poor families requiring help to get away, a committee was appointed to see that all were cared for in the removal, as will be seen by the following quotation from the history of Joseph Smith, jr., as found on pages 711 and 712 19th vol. Millennial Star.

Saturday, J

A meeting of a resp of the citizens of Ca members of the C Christ of Latter-day at Far West, accordi notice, to devise and sideration such meas thought necessary in complying with the Executive to remove of Missouri immedi known by General C zens of said county, November last.

The meeting was by Don C. Smith, John Smith was una o the chair, and F pointed Secretary.

The object of th then stated by the briefly adverted to tl and called for an ex iment on the best co sued in the present e

Several gentlemer neeting on the subje il from the State, a impossibility of com orders of the Govern in consequence of th erty of many, which them by being drive place, deprived of th 'l rights and privile if this, and the Uni were of the opinion he citizens of I might to be made, so ondition, and clain ance towards furnis he removal of th ountv out of the St ight and our due in

On motion, Res

...mittee of seven be appointed to make a draft of a preamble and resolutions in accordance with the foregoing sentiments, to be presented to a future meeting for their consideration.

The following were then appointed, viz.—John Taylor, Alanson Ripley, Brigham Young, Theodore Turley, Heber C. Kimball, John Smith, and Don C. Smith.

Resolved: That the committee be farther instructed to ascertain the number of families who are actually destitute of means for their removal, and report at the next meeting.

Resolved: That it is the opinion of this meeting that an exertion should be made to ascertain how much can be obtained from individuals of the society, and that it is the duty of those who have, to assist those who have not, that thereby we may, as far as possible, within and of ourselves, comply with the demands of the Executive.

Adjourned to meet again on Tuesday, the 28th instant, at twelve o'clock. M.

JOHN SMITH, Chairman,
E. SMITH, Secretary.

Tuesday, 28th. The brethren met according to adjournment. John Smith was again called to the chair, and Elias Smith appointed Secretary. The committee appointed to draw up a preamble and resolutions to be presented to the meeting for consideration, presented by their chairman, John Taylor, a memorial of the transactions of the people of Missouri towards us since our first settlement in this State; in which was contained some of our persecutions by the authority of the State, and our deprivation of the rights of citizenship guaranteed to us by the Constitution, which was yet in an unfinished state, owing to causes which were stated by the committee; and they further apologized for not drawing it up in the form of resolutions, agreeable to vote of the former meeting.

The report was accepted as far as completed, and by a vote of the meeting, the same committee were directed to finish it, and prepare it for, and send it to, the Press for publication, and were instructed to dwell minutely on the subject relating to our arms, and the fiend-like conduct of the officers of the militia in sequestering all the best of them after their surrender, on condition of being returned to us again, or suffering them to be exchanged for others not worth half their value, in violation of their bond, and of the honour of the commander of the forces sent out against us by the State.

On motion of President Brigham Young, it was Resolved, that we this day enter into a covenant to stand by and assist each other to the utmost of our abilities in removing from this State, and that we will never desert the poor who are worthy, till they shall be out of the reach of the exterminating order of General Clark, acting for and in the name of the State.

After an expression of sentiments by several who addressed the meeting on the propriety of taking efficient means to remove the poor from the State, it was resolved, that a committee of seven be appointed to superintend the business of our removal, and to provide for those who have not the means of moving till the work shall be completed.

The following were then appointed, viz.—William Huntington, Charles Bird, Alanson Ripley, Theodore Turley, Daniel Shearer, Shadrach Roundy, and Jonathan H. Hale.

Resolved: That the Secretary draft an instrument expressive of the sense of the covenant entered into this day, by those present, and that those who were willing to subscribe to the covenant should do it, that their names might be known, which would enable the committee more judiciously to carry their business into effect.

The instrument was accordingly

THE RETURN.

drawn; and by vote of the meeting. the Secretary attached the names of those who were willing to subscribe to it.

Adjourned to meet again on Friday, the 1st of February next, at twelve o'clock. M.

JOHN SMITH, Chairman."

We find 214 names to the covenant, which was carried out to the letter.

It will be seen by the foregoing quotation, that it is no small matter for a whole church, or community, numbering, as it was estimated, some ten or twelve thousand, to be compelled to move out of a state in the dead of winter, as was required to be done. Of the heartless cruelty in issuing such an order by the Governor, we leave every one to judge.

Knowing there was no alternative but to leave, the writer began to make arrangements as well as he could to that end. In the latter part of January, in company with three other brethren, we walked from Far West, Mo. to Quincy, Illinois, through the snow, where we arrived on the first day of February, having one dollar left, after paying our ferriage across the Mississippi river.

Some families of brethren had preceded us, among whom was Elder John P. Green and family, with whom we stopped a day or two.

Not knowing what to do, as Quincy was being overrun with laborers, and hearing there were some parties about forty miles north, in Hancock county, favorable to our people, we concluded to go there; and after leaving Bro. Green's to go north, the thought occurred to us that it would not be wise to leave the place without first visiting the printing offices there. Accordingly, we stepped into the "*Quincy Whig*" printing office, conducted by Messrs. Bartlett and Sullivan.

For some reason, we felt a little delicate about introducing our business, therefore asked them if they had any papers from western Missouri. They replied: "Ye*", and gave us one to look at One of them soon asked if we belonged to that people who were compelled to leave Missouri. We re[plied in the affirm]ative, and told them we [were seeking] a situation in a printi[ng office, as that] was our occupation. [They said they did] not need any help, but [had some] job work and blank pri[nting if we would] give us a few days' w[ork at ...] per day, and we coul[d have our] in board, (as they kept [boarders,] them being married,) [and we would] share of the provisio[ns at one] dollar and fifty cents p[er week.]

We gladly accepted [the offer] and considered it a gr[eat favor,] to thank our heavenly [father, and] put it into their hea[rts to be kind] to us.

We soon had means t[o hire] a team and had ou[r families moved] to Quincy, where we [rented a] room at $5 per mont[h and worked] with Messrs. Bartlett a[nd Sullivan] in the month of May, [without] employment.

The citizens of Quinc[y received our peo]ple with open arms, [held public] meetings, and appoint[ed committees to] solicit money and cloth[ing and other nec]essaries for those who w[ere destitute;] also adopted resolutio[ns requesting] the citizens to give em[ployment to all] willing to labor, and t[o refrain from] say anything calcula[ted to injure the] feelings of the strange[rs thrown in their] midst, which caution [was very thought]ful and timely.

During the winter [months all] the prisoners at Liberty [were released] except Joseph and H[yrum, and in] April they were taken [to Gallatin] where bills of indite[ment were found] against them. They [obtained a change of] venue to another coun[ty, and the sheriff] detailed a guard to a[ccompany them on] their removal. The [prisoners and] guard were allowed t[o get drunk, and] when the prisoners n[oticed this they got] horses and quietly rod[e away to Illi]nois. A few weeks lat[er they saw] the Sheriff at Quinc[y, named] Smith, jr., a friendly [man, and offered to] pay for the h[orses.]

The prisoners in F[ar West had all] been liberated except

Morris Phelps, Luman Gibbs and King Follett. These took a change of venue, and were removed to Boone county, where they remained until the 4th of July, when Elders Pratt and Phelps made their escape.

Believing it will be interesting to many of our readers, we give Elder Pratt's account of their escape copied from his history of the persecutions as found in the history of Joseph Smith jr., on page 342 of the 17th vol. Mil. Star, as follows:

Sister Phelps, Orson Pratt, and sister Phelps' brother came from Illinois on horseback and visited with us for several days. On the fourth of July we felt desirous as usual to celebrate the anniversary of American Liberty; we accordingly manufactured a white flag, consisting of the half of a shirt, on which was inscribed the word "Liberty," in large letters, and also a large American eagle was put on in red; we then obtained a pole from our jailor, and on the morning of the fourth, this flag was suspended from the front window of our prison, overhanging the public square, and floating triumphantly in the air to the full view of the citizens who assembled by hundreds to celebrate the National Jubilee.

With this the citizens seemed highly pleased, and sent a portion of the public dinner to us and our friends who partook with us in prison with merry hearts, as we intended to gain our liberties or be in paradise before the close of that eventful day.

While we were thus employed in prison, the town was alive with troops parading, guns firing, music sounding, and shouts of joy resounding on every side. In the mean-time we wrote the following toast, which was read at their public dinner, with many and long cheers—

"The patriotic and hospitable citizens of Boone County: opposed to tyranny and oppression, and firm to the original principles of republican liberty; may they, in common with every part of our wide spreading country, long enjo[y] which flow from t[he] American Independe[nce]

Our dinner being brethren took leave for Illinois, (leaving still visit with her had preceded a mi road then took into finally placed their thicket within one t[he] the prison, and ther[e] anxious suspense un[til] the meantime we p[ut] and hats and waite[d] sun.

With prayer and deliverance from th[e] ous bondage, and fo[r] the society of our f[ami]lies, we then sung lines—

Lord cause their foo[d]
And let them fain[t]
Our souls would q[uit]
And fly to Illinois
To join with the em[igrants]
Who are with fre[e]
That only bliss for [us]
With them a whil[e]
Give joy for grief—
Take all our foes
But let us find our [way]
In this eventful d[ay]

Thus ended the c[elebration of] National liberty; b[ut] our own was the gr[eat] now before us. I [as] the sun was setting; rived—the footste[ps] were heard on the s[tairs] flew to his feet, an[d the] door. The great d[oor] and our supper har[d] small hole in the in[ner] still remained lock[ed] the key was turned in the pot of coffee the key turned th[e] jerked open, and three of us were [out] down the stairs, t[he] and out into the Phelps cleared him[self]

ing after us, some on horseback, and some on foot, prepared with dogs, guns, and whatever came to hand. But the flag of Liberty, with its eagle, still floated on high in the distance; and under its banner, our nerves seemed to strengthen at every step.

We gained the horses, mounted, and dashed into the wilderness, each his own way. After a few jumps of my horse, I was hailed by an armed man at pistol shot distance, crying, "Damn you, stop, or I'll shoot you!" I rushed onward deeper in the forest, while the cry was repeated in close pursuit, crying "Damn you, stop, or I'll shoot you," at every step, till at length it died away in the distance. I plunged a mile into the forest—came to a halt—tied my horse in a thicket—went a distance, and climbed a tree, to await the approaching darkness.

Being so little used to exercise, 1 fainted through over exertion, and remained so faint for near an hour that I could not get down from the tree; but calling on the Lord, He strengthened me, and I came down from the tree. But my horse had got loose and gone. I then made my way on foot for several days and nights, principally without food, and scarcely suffering myself to be seen.

After five days of dreadful suffering, with fatigue and hunger, I crossed the Mississippi, and found myself once more in a land of freedom. Mr. Phelps made his escape also; but King Follett was retaken and carried back.

Luman Gibbs sent for his wife who came and lived with him in the jail. He was a basket maker, and we were told the jailor let him go into the forest and cut and prepare the material, when he would return to the jail and make his

at Quincy on the 22nd. On the 24th President Joseph Smith, jr., Bishop Vincent Knights and Alanson Ripley were appointed a committee to select a location for the church, by a council of the official members of the church convened at Quincy, at which council a resolution passed advising the brethren "to move north to Commerce as soon as they possibly can."

On the 25th the committee left Quincy on their mission. After examining different localities in Lee County, Iowa, and Commerce, Hancock County, Illinois, they decided upon the latter place.

On the 1st day of May the committee purchased of Hugh White, a farm of 135 acres for five thousand dollars, and also of Isaac Galland, a farm adjoining the White farm, for nine thousand dollars.

Joseph Smith, jr., moved to Commerce on the 10th of May, and settled on the White farm, and Sidney Rigdon and Geo. W. Robinson settled, about the same time, on the Galland farm, and other brethren commenced moving in. These farms were soon laid out into city lots.

The following is a description of the place by Joseph Smith, jr., copied from page 276 17th vol. Mil. Star.

"Tuesday, June 11th, 1839.

About this time Theodore Turley raised the first house built by the Saints in this place; it was built of logs, about twenty-five or thirty rods north north-east of my dwelling, on the north-east corner of lot 4, block 147 of the White purchase. When I made the purchase of White and Galland, there were one stone house, three frame houses, and two block houses, which constituted the whole of Commerce. Between Commerce and Mr. Davidson Hibbard's, there was one stone and three log houses, including the one that I live in, and these were all the houses in this vicinity, and the place was literally a

but believing that it might become a healthy place by the blessing of heaven to the Saints, and no more eligible place presenting itself, I considered it wisdom to make an attempt to build up a city.

(*To be continued.*)

CORRESPONDENCE.

Magnolia, Iowa, March 17, 1890.

To THE READERS OF THE RETURN.

As I have previously stated in a letter published in RETURN, July, 1889, that I had been dissatisfied for some time, with the Reorganized Church of Latter Day Saints, I have thought perhaps, I had better give a few of the many reasons that caused me to become dissatisfied.

In my younger days, I did not read much in the Bible, book of Mormon, or Doc. and Covenants; consequently I drifted along with the tide, thinking all was well with Zion. In after years I began to take notice of things, and it seemed to me there was a great lack of the Spirit and power; quite frequently I heard it spoken of by the elders, and the cause was most always laid to the saints not living humble and faithful enough.

I did not believe this was the whole cause, for it did seem to me that many of the saints that I was personally acquainted with, were trying to live their religion according to the best of their ability.

I also noticed that secret combinations were in the church, and once I heard Joseph F. McDowell say in one of his sermons, that he defied any one to find anything against beneficiary societies, such as Masonry, Oddfellows, Knights of Pythias, in any of these three books, pointing communications. Wherefore the Lord commandeth you, when ye shall see these things come among you, that ye shall awake to a sense of your awful situation, * * for it is built up by the devil, who is the father of all lies.". Found in Book of Mormon, Ether; chap. 3, par. 12-13.

When I see no effort made by church authorities to rid the church of secret combinations, and a few lights in the church, calling secret combinations, beneficiary societies, it seems more safe for the wellfare of my soul to "Leave the poor old stranded wreck, and pull for the shore."

By comparing book of Doctrine and Covenants, with the Book of Mormon, it seems there are additions in the book of Doctrine and Covenants not found in the gospel of Christ. In section 77, the revelation says, "the time has come that the people must organize, to advance the cause which they had espoused, and if they were not equal in earthly things, they could not be equal in obtaining heavenly things."

"Wherefore a commandment I give unto you, to prepare and organize yourselves by a band or everlasting covenant that cannot be broken. And he who breaketh it shall loose his office and standing in the church, and shall be delivered over to the buffetings of satan until the day of redemption." By this revelation it seems that the gospel of Christ could not save those that break this band or covenant, and they were turned over to satan, to do with them as he pleased.

Book of Mormon, Nephi, chap 5, par. 9. Christ says, "And again I say unto you, ye must repent, and be baptized in my name, and become as a little child, or ye can in no wise inherit the kingdom of God. Verily, verily I say unto you, that this is my doctrine, and whoso buildeth upon this, buildeth upon my rock; and the gates of hell shall not prevail against them. And whoso shall declare more or less than this, and establish it for my doctrine, the same cometh of evil, and is not built upon my rock, but he buildeth upon a sandy foundation, and the gates of hell standeth open to receive such, when the floods come, and the winds beat upon them."

Doctrine and Covenants, section 64, par. 6, says: "Behold it is said in my laws or forbidden, to get in debt to thine enemies; but behold, it is not said at any time, that the Lord should not take when he please, and pay as seemeth him good, wherefore, as ye are agents, and ye are on the Lord's errand; and whatever ye do according to the will of the Lord, is the Lord's business, and he hath set you to provide for his saints in these last days."

By this revelation it seems the elders are to provide for the saints; but when we turn to section 106 we find, that the saints are tithed to provide for the "priesthood, and the debts of the presidency of the church."

Doctrine and Covenants, section 77, par. 3. "Michael has the keys of salvation under the counsel and direction of the holy one. And it seems by reading section 110, par. 21, that Michael and Adam are one and the same. If this revelation in section 77 is divinely inspired, then Brigham Young was right, when he said that, "Adam is our Father and our God, and the only God with whom we have to do."

The question now comes to our mind why were so many people blind in regard to these doctrines, "privily" brought in to the church. Turn to section 19. "Wherefore, meaning the church, thou shalt give heed unto all his words, and commandments, which he shall give unto you, as he receiveth them, walking in all holiness before me;, for his words ye shall receive as if from mine own mouth." After such a revelation as this, there was no need of taking, "heed lest ye be deceived," or turning to the "Law and the testimony."

Let no one think by reading this letter, that I have drifted away from Mormonism. I believe that pure Mormonism is the gospel of Christ. The gospel was preached at Jerusalem, and also to the Nephites without the aid of the book of Doctrine and Covenants.

I will close hoping that a great desire to investigate, may rest upon the honest in heart.

Yours for truth;
Mrs. CHARLOTTE LOCKLING.

———:x:———

ELDER ROBINSON:

Dear Sir: I have been reading THE RETURN, and I must say I thank you very much for the pleasure derived and knowledge gained therefrom.

I have been a member of the Reorganized Church a good many years. I have been blessed many times in answer to prayer. We take the *Herald* and *Hope*, and have for seventeen years. When I joined the church I had only heard the gospel three times preached. I had heard no preaching for more than a year before I was baptized. I had asked the Lord to guide me into all truth and give me a knowledge of his will, and when I was baptized I felt the assurance that I had taken upon me that which bound me to the service of God. I have sought earnestly to obey the Law the Savior gave us that we love one another. I find that the more we try to serve God, and the closer we watch ourselves, lest we fail to serve him properly, the more love we have for all; and will not be so liable to find fault with others.

THE RETURN.

"Truth, crushed to earth, shall rise again; The eternal years of God are hers."

Vol. 2. No. 5.   DAVIS CITY, IOWA, MAY, 1890.   Whole No. 17

The Return.

PUBLISHED MONTHLY AT $1.00 A YEAR.

Entered at the Post Office at Davis City. Iowa, as second class matter.

ITEMS OF PERSONAL HISTORY OF THE EDITOR.

INCLUDING SOME ITEMS OF CHURCH HISTORY NOT GENERALLY KNOWN.

No. 13.

Continued from page 246.

In the month of May, 1839, the writer moved from Quincy to Commerce, Illinois, to which place our people were rapidly gathering. The only chance for a house was the body of a log house situated on the high ground in the woods near the river, about one mile north of Commerce. For the want of lumber, were under the necessity of going into the forest and spliting out oak clapboards, or *shakes*, three feet long, for the roof, floor and doors, which furnished a temporary shelter.

At a council of the First Presidency and other authorities of the church, early in June, it was decided to let Don Carlos Smith, and the writer, (as we were practical printers,) have the printing press and type which had been saved from the mob in Missouri, by having been buried in the ground and a haystack placed over it, and that we should publish a paper for the church, or a church paper, at our own expense and responsibility, and recieve all the profits arising therefrom. The council named said paper *Times and Seasons*. Accordingly we undertook the task, and after purchasing fifty dollars worth of type on credit, from Dr. Isaac Galland, and cleaning the Missouri soil from the press and type that had been saved, and hiring from one of the brethren, fifty dollars in money, which we sent for paper, we issued the prospectus for the *Times and Seasons*, and sent it to brethren residing in different states.

[Heretofore, in "Items of personal history," when speaking of myself, have used the pronoun *we*, as is customary with Editors, but having formed a Co-partnership with Don Carlos Smith, it seems necessary that a change be made in the manner of expression, therefore hereafter, when speaking of our company affairs, will use the term, *we*, but when speaking of myself, individually, will use the pronoun I and my. The reader must not consider it egotism at the frequent appearance of these terms, as it cannot well be avoided.]

The only room that could be obtained for the printing office, was a basement room in a building formerly used as a warehouse, but now occupied as a dwelling, situated on the bank of the Mississippi river. The room used for the printing office had no floor, and the ground was kept damp by the water constantly trickling down from the bank side. Here we set the type for the first number of the paper, which we got ready for the press in July, and had struck off only some two hundred copies, when both Carlos and the writer were taken down with the *chills and fever*, and what added to our affliction, both our families were taken down with the same disease. My wife was taken sick the very next day after I was, which sickness continued ten months. This was a year of suffering for the citizens of the place, as it was estimated at one time, there was not one well person to nearly ten that were sick. Five adults died out of one family in one week.

Before our sickness we had wet down paper sufficient for two thousand copies of the *Times and Seasons*, which paper mildewed and spoiled. Afterwards another batch of paper was wet down by Francis Higbee, who thought he could print the papers, but he failed and that paper was lost.

Subscriptions for the paper soon commenced coming in, in answer to the prospectus, and the two hundred copies sent out, which enabled us to provide for our families; and also to have a small, cheap frame building put up, one and a half stories high, the lower room to be used for the printing office, and our friends moved myself and wife into the upper room, or chamber, in the latter part of August. We were moved upon our bed, and a portion of the time in those days, neither of us was able to speak a loud word. This was a happy change for us, as it gave a clean sweet room to dwell in, and the benefit of near neighbors, it being in town.

In the month of November we secured the services of a young printer from Ohio, Lyman Gaylord, and resumed the publication of the paper. In the winter of 1839-40, brother Carlos and myself had each of us a log house built on a lot donated to us by the church, situated on a block next to the one on which the printing office was located, and moved into the same in early spring. The deed to our lot was signed by Joseph Smith jr. and Emma Smith.

The persecutions in Missouri, and expelling the church from the State, instead of having a tendency to destroy Mormonism, had the very opposite effect. An increased interest was manifest in the work, and calls were made for the Book of Mormon, but there were none on hand to supply the demand.

There had been two editions printed of that book: the first by E. B. Grandin, in Palmyra, N. Y., in 1830. The second edition was printed in the church printing office in Kirtland, Ohio, in the winter of 1836-7. The writer helped set the type for the second edition.

In the spring of 1840 consultation was held upon the subject of getting another edition of the Book of Mormon printed, to supply the demand, when, in view of our extreme poverty, consequent upon our so recently having been driven from our homes, the idea was abandoned, for want of the necessary funds to accomplish such a work.

My health had so far recovered that I was able to walk from my house to the printing office, when, early in May, 1840 as I was walking to the office, I received a manifestation from the Lord, such an one as I never received before or since. It seemed that a ball of fire came down from above and striking the top of my head passed down into my heart, and told me, in plain distinct language, what course to pursue and I could get the book of Mormon stereotyped and printed. I went into the printing office, and in a few moments brother Joseph Smith, jr., he who translated the book of Mormon by the gift and power of God, as I verily know, stepped into the office, when I said to him, "Brother Joseph, if you will furnish $200, and give us the privilege of printing two thousand copies of the book of Mormon, Carlos and I will get $200 more and we will get it stereotyped and give you the plates." He dropped his face into his hand for a minute or so, when he said, "I will do it." He asked how soon we would want the money. I replied, in two weeks.

Brother Carlos and I made an effort immediately to obtain our $200. We found a brother in the church who would let us have $120, until the next April at thirty-five per cent interest, the interest to be incorporated in the note, and all to draw six per cent interest, if not paid when due. We consented to the terms, and got the money. A few days after, the same brother brought us $25 more, on the same terms, making $145. I took the money and put it away. In a few days brother Joseph Smith came to the printing office and said, "Brother Robinson, if you and Carlos get the Book of Mormon stereotyped you will have to furnish the money, as I cannot get the $200." I replied, that if he would give us the privi-

We were considerably in debt to different persons, and our creditors were repeatedly pressing us for money, so that after a little time we began to draw a few dollars from the $145. We knew that it would not do to be paying thirty-five per cent interest for money to pay ordinary debts with, so Carlos said to me, one day in June, "Brother Robinson you take that money and go to Cincinnati and buy some type and paper, which we must have." I said "Yes, I will go, but I will not come home until the Book of Mormon is stereotyped," for it was as fire shut up in my bones, both day and night, that if I could only get to Cincinnati the work could be accomplished. He replied that "that was out of the question, as it could not be done with our limited means." Brother Hyrum Smith also said it could not be done, but brother Joseph Smith did not say it could not be done, when I told him, but he said, "God bless you."

Brother Joseph and I immediately went to work and compared a copy of the Kirtland edition with the first edition, by reading them entirely through, and I took one of the Kirtland edition as a copy for the stereotype edition.

On the 18th of June, 1840, I took passage on board the steam packet, "Brazil," which made regular trips from Cincinnati, Ohio, to Galena, Illinois, stopping at Nauvoo, as she passed each way. At St. Louis, while the steamer was waiting for passengers and freight, I foolishly stepped into a mock auction store, when the auctioneer had up a fancy box filled with *valuable articles*,(?) among which was a *gold watch*, or what the autioneer claimed to be took $.23 from my already limited purse. I left that auction room, if not a better, I trust, a wiser man. Since writing the above sentence, the thought has occurred to me that perhaps it was a good thing that it occurred, as it had a tendency to try my faith just that much more, and the sequel proved to me that the Lord is abundantly able and willing to provide means for the accomplishment of his purposes, when we follow his directions.

After arriving at Cincinnati I purchased a quantity of paper and put on board the "Brazil" to take to Nauvoo on her return trip. After paying for the paper and paying my passage, I had $105.06¼ left. Now came the trial of my faith. I had not yet taken my trunk from the steamer. The adversary of all righteousness said to me, "Get more paper and some type and go home; it is folly to think of getting the Book of Mormon stereotyped, for you can not do it." I replied that "I came for that purpose, and did not propose to return until it was done," but I assure you he made the big drops of sweat roll from my face, but I did not give up to him for one instant, or swerve from my purpose, although I was there a stranger in a strange city, not knowing a single person there, except those who came with me on the steamer.

I took the Book of Mormon in my pocket and made inquiry for a stereotype foundry. I was informed there was one on Pearl street. I found the place, and as I stepped into the office a feeling of horror came over me and it seemed as though I was in prison. A gentlemanly appearing man was there, and I asked him what they

...arged for stereotyping a book, giving him the size as near as I could without naming or showing him the book. He told me what they charged for one thousand ems, a term which I understood. I then asked him if there was another stereotype foundry in the city. He said, "Yes, one in Bank Alley, off Third street, owned by Gleason and Shepherd." I felt in an instant that that was the place for me to apply to, and bidding the gentleman "Good day," left, breathing freer when I stepped into the street. I soon found the other foundry, and as I entered the office, I saw three gentlemen standing by the desk, in conversation. I asked if Messrs. Gleason and Shepherd were in. A gentleman stepped forward and said, "My name is Gleason." I said, "I have come to get the Book of Mormon stereotyped." Mr. Shepherd stepped forward and said, "When that book is stereotyped I am the man to stereotype it." I then handed him the book and told him what size type I wanted it done in. He took the book and went to a case of type the size I had named, and set up one line and counted the ems in the line. then counted the number of lines in the page and multiplied the two numbers together, and then counted the number of pages in the book, and multiplied the number of pages by the number of ems in a page, when he said the stereotyping would amount to *five hundred and fifty dollars*. I told him that I had one hundred dollars to pay in hand, and would pay two hundred and fifty dollars more in three months, or while he was doing the work, and the remaining two hundred dollars within three months after the work was done. He said he would do that, and sat down and immediately wrote out a contract accordingly, which we both signed, which contract I have to this day. I then told him I wished to see a book binder and contract for the binding of two thousand copies of the book. He said I will go with you to a good book binder around on Main street, and taking me by the arm, we went directly to the book binder, who said he would bind two thousand copies in good leather for two hundred and fifty dollars, which was twelve and a half cents apiece. I told him I would give him eighty dollars while he would be doing the work, and the remainder within six weeks after the work was done. He agreed to that, and wrote out a contract to that effect, which we both signed. I told Mr. Shepherd I wanted to engage paper enough for the two thousand books, when we went from the bindery to the paper warehouse where I had just purchased the paper I sent to Nauvoo; but the paper dealer, the proprietor, was not in, so we left word for him to come to Mr. Shepherd's the next morning, which he did, when I engaged the paper from him amounting to nearly two hundred and fifty dollars to be paid for in payments similar to the stereotyping and binding, but we did not write the contract. After we had concluded our bargain the paper dealer said, "Mr. Robinson, you are a stranger here, and it is customary to have city reference in such cases when we deal with strangers." Mr. Shepherd stepped forward and said, "I am Mr. Robinson's backer, sir." "All right," said the paper dealer, "you can have the paper, Mr. Robinson." This was the only place where any reference, or backing was required.

Mr. Shepherd purchased a font of new type the day we made the contract, and put three compositors (type setters) immediately at work on the book, and I was to remain and assist in reading the proof, so as to be sure it was done according to copy. I was to have twenty-five cents an hour for what time I would be engaged at that, or any other service

isher of his stereotype plates, and paid him the five dollars I had left, after paying Mr. Shepherd the one hundred on his contract, leaving me only 6¼ cents (an old fashioned Spanish six-pence) on hand. The five dollars was soon boarded out, and there I was, a stranger in a strange city, with contracts on hand amounting to over one thousand dollars on which only one hundred had been paid, and board bill due and nothing to pay with. I confess that for a time, viewed from a worldly standpoint, it looked quite gloomy, but I never for a moment lost faith in the final success, or literal fulfillment of the previous promise of the Lord made to me in Nauvoo. In the mean time I had written to Bro. Don Carlos Smith telling him what I had done, and also to several brethren in the eastern states requesting them to get subscribers for the book, offering them one hundred and twenty books for every one hundred dollars sent us in advance, in time to meet our engagements. It was several weeks before I received a responce.

The first money I received brother Don Carlos Smith sent me a twenty dollar bill on the state bank of Indiana, a specie paying bank, the bills of which were at a premium of 13 per cent, so that I realised $22.60 for the $20. This relieved me of present financial embarrasment. Not long after this, my brother, Joseph L. Robinson, who resided in Boonville, Oneida county, New York, whom I had baptized into the church, when on a mission to that state in the summer and fall of 1836, sent me a draft on the Leather Manufacturer's Bank of New York City, for $96. This was also at a premium of 13 per cent. Bro. John A. Forgeus, of Chester county, Pennsylvania, who loan, which I afterwards paid him in Nauvoo. Several other brethren sent me money in advance for books, so that I paid Mr. Shepherd all his money before it became due, and gave the book-binder eighty dollars on his contract before he had done any work on it, and when I was ready for the paper to print them on, the paper dealer with whom I had contracted for the paper on time, did not have it on hand of the size and quality I wanted, when I went to another paper dealer who had the article I wanted, and paid him all cash in hand for the paper, and had the books printed on a power press, for which I paid the cash in hand as the work was done.

I had the printing progressing before the stereotyping was finished, so that by the time the last twenty-four pages of stereotype plates were finished, the printer had the book all printed, except the last form, of twenty-four pages, and the printed sheets were in the hands of the book-binder being folded, so that soon after this last form was printed, the book-binder had several hundred copies bound, ready for me to deliver to those who had advanced their money for the books. This was strictly in accordance with the instruction I received in the first manifestation made to me in Nauvoo.

Thus the work was accomplished, and all paid for before the time specified in the contracts, and I had nearly one thousand copies left. The work was finished in October.

I then purchased from Mr. Shepherd and other parties several fonts of type, and material for a stereotype foundary and book-bindery, and a winter's supply of news and book paper, and took to Nauvoo, a considerable portion of which I paid for down, and got credit for the balance

Mr. Shepherd endorsed one note for me of four hundred dollars, payable in four months, which money I sent him before it became due.

In June, 1841, I went to Cincinnati and settled all up with Mr. Shepherd, and paid him what was due him, (his bills altogether amounting to about $1,000,) when he arose and said, "Mr. Robinson, do you want to know what made me do as I did when you came here last summer, it was no business way, it was not what I saw in you, but what I felt here," putting his hand upon his heart.

This voluntary statement of Mr. Shepherd's afforded me great pleasure, as it was a practical illustration of the ease with which the Lord can move upon the hearts of the children of men to assist in the accomplishment of his work and purposes; and to our Heavenly Father be all the praise and glory, now and ever, Amen.

From the foregoing experience, together with many other evidences which I have received of the truth of the divine origin of the Book of Mormon, I bear record that it is true, and that the promises and prophecies contained therein are being and will be fulfilled to the letter. May the Lord help us to walk according to its holy precepts, that we may be able to stand in the day of his visitation and power, which is coming as a whirlwind upon the nations, and that we may be worthy to enter into his rest, is my earnest desire.

E. ROBINSON.
(TO BE CONTINUED.)

COMMUNICATIONS.

HE THAT GIVETH
TO THE POOR, LENDETH TO THE LORD.

Speaking of the brotherhood Christ came to establish, we find in the scriptures that we are to do unto others as we would have them do unto us, or have care one for the other. If one is honored all rejoice with that one, if any one is afflicted, all sympathise with that one. How should we show our sympathy? By administering unto their wants as far as our circumstances will permit. For an example, we will say one of our brethren is very poor, and cannot make a living for his family; he is willing to do all he can. Now is the time for this brother to be helped, and how is the best way to do it? I will give you my thoughts.

Brother A has a small farm more than he needs to support his family, say of 15 or 20 acres; he lets this poor Brother move on to it, and tells him "all I will charge you for a time, is to keep the place in good repair as it is now, except the natural wear of the land." Brother B loans him a horse to cultivate this little farm. Brother C loans him another horse when he needs more than one to do the work on this farm. Brother D loans him a cow, to give milk for his children. This brother being helped in this way, and no one suffering loss, feels that he is among true brethren.

The way to help those who stand in need, is to put them in the way to help themselves. Those who are sick or disabled must be helped by those who are able to help. Those who are not able, if they say in their hearts, if I had I would give, then they are excusable. Amulek, speaking on this subject, says: "And now behold, my beloved brethren, I say unto you, do not suppose this is all; for after ye have done all these things, if ye turn away the needy, and the naked, and visit not the sick and the afflicted, and impart of your substance if ye have to those who stand in need; I say unto you, if ye do not any of these things, behold, your prayer is vain, and availeth you nothing, and ye are as hypocrites who denieth the faith."—Alma 26:29

The apostle, John, tells us in his first letter to the brethren in the 3rd chapter and 17th verse, "Whoso

signed to have his brethren live a practical life in this Brotherhood, for he said ye are as a city that is set on a hill, whose light cannot be hid; a brotherhood that would live as we have been speaking, their light could not be hid for their joy would be so great that they could not hold their peace.

Some will say, if the brethren would live in this way there would be none very poor. So I say, for the Lord would bless those brethren that discharged their whole duty. Then we would have care one for another, and as all have not the same gift to make money, who is responsible? God has made provisions for his children, and holds all responsible for their stewardship over the gifts that he has given them, either spiritual or temporal.

Suppose here is a brother who is a devout christian in all his ways, yet has not enough of this world's goods to keep his family without improving all his time, and the Lord calls him to go and preach the gospel, and endows him with all the necessary qualifications for the work of the ministry. This brother had only gift enough to make a common living by working all the time, and God calls him into another field to labor. Now the Master looks around and sees a brother that he gave a gift to make money and has made money, yet has no gift to preach, and as God has a work for all to do in this brotherhood, what must this brother do?

Suppose I have two men working for me; they are out on the farm at work, they find a piece of work that needs to be done, and A is able to do the work if he had the *instrument* to do it with. B has the instrument but cannot do the work himself, nor comply with my wishes? I gave them the means and told them they were co-laborers for *me*.

I often think what the apostle James says: "Go to now, ye rich men, weep and howl for your miseries that shall come upon you, your riches are corrupted, and your garments are moth-eaten, your gold and silver is cankered; and the rust of them shall be a witness against you, and shall eat your flesh as it were fire. Ye have heaped treasure together for the last days." Amen.

Your brother in Christ,
P. A. PAGE.

———o———

A GRAVE And A BALL of FIRE.

Along the shore of the Oneida Lake there is an Indian's grave where at times a wierd and supernatural light makes its appearance. It is described as a ball of fire about the size of a large orange, and sways to and fro in the air about thirty feet from the ground, confining its irregular movements within a space about 100 feet square. People have attempted to go near enough to solve the mystery, but it would suddenly disappear before reaching it. A very peculiar story is told by the neighbors around the spot. They claim that many years ago the locality was the part of an Indian reservation. A man by the name of Belknap frequently dreamed that there was a crock in the Indian cemetery containing immense treasures, and that if he went there at the hour when the graveyards yawn he could secure it. These dreams were repeated so often that they had a strong effect, and he went there with pick and shovel according to instructions, but he failed to turn round three times when he found the crock, as the dream direct-

of God that they should be ordained to the ministry, and go forth to prune the vineyard for the last time, or the coming of the Lord, which was nigh—even *fifty-six years* should wind up the scene.

* * *

President Joseph Smith, jun., after making many remarks on the subject of choosing the Twelve, wanted an expression from the brethren, if they would be satisfied to have the Spirit of the Lord dictate in the choice of the Elders to be Apostles; whereupon all the Elders present expressed their anxious desire to have it so.

A hymn was then sung, "Hark, listen to the trumpeters," &c. President Hyrum Smith prayed, and meeting was dismissed for one hour.

Assembled pursuant to adjournment, and commenced with prayer.

President Joseph Smith, jun., said that the first business of the meeting was, for the three witnesses of the Book of Mormon, to pray, each one, and then proceed to choose twelve men from the Church, as Apostles, to go to all nations, kindreds, tongues and people.

The three witnesses, viz., Oliver Cowdery, David Whitmer, and Martin Harris, united in prayer.

These three witnesses were then blessed by the laying on of the hands of the Presidency.

The witnesses then, according to a former commandment, proceeded to make choice of the twelve. Their names are as follows:
1. Lyman E. Johnson. 2. B. Young. 3. Heber C. Kimball, 4. Orson Hyde. 5. David W. Patten, 6. Luke Johnson. 7. Wm. E, McLellin. 8. John F. Boynton, 9. Orson Pratt, 10. William Smith. 11. Thos. B. Marsh, 12. Parley P. Pratt.

Lyman E. Johnson, Brigham Young and Heber C. Kimball came forward; and the three witnesses laid their hands upon each one's head and prayed seperately.

The blessing of Lyman E. Johnson was, in the name of Jesus Christ, that he should bear the tidings of salvation to nations, tongues, and people, until the utmost corners of the earth shall hear the tidings; and that he shall be a witness of the things of God to nations and tongues, and that holy angels shall administer to him occassionally; and that no power of the enemy shall prevent him from going forth and doing the work of the Lord; *and that he shall live until the gathering is accomplished*, according to the holy Prophets; and he shall be like unto Enoch; and his faith shall be like unto his; and he shall be called great among all the living; and Satan shall tremble before him; and he shall see the Saviour come and s'and upon the earth with power and great glory.

The blessing of Brigham Young, was, that he should be strong in body, that he might go forth and gather the elect, preparatory to the great day of the coming of the Lord; and that he might be strong and mighty, declaring the tidings to nations that know not God; that he may add ten talents; that he may come to Zion with many sheaves. He shall go forth from land to land, and from sea to sea; and shall behold heavenly messengers going forth; and his life shall be prolonged; and the holy Priesthood is conferred on him, that he may do wonders in the name of Jesus; that he may cast out devils, heal the sick, raise the dead, open the eyes of the blind, go forth from land to land and from sea to sea; and that heathen nations shall even call him *God himself, if he do not rebuke them.*

----o----

ON A MISSION TO THE LAND OF MY FATHERS.

REV. ISAAC LEVINSHON IN "THE JEWISH HERALD."

Here was the site of the ancient and

MEMORABLE GILGAL,

and it was here that the stones were piled up in memory of Israel's great events and triumphs! And here the tribes of Israel pitched their tents the first night they entered the promised land; and here took place the solemn renewal of God's covenant in the observances of the Passover and Circumcision. Joshua at this place also beheld the captain of the Lord's host with a drawn sword in hand. The Tabernacle rested here until it was removed to Shiloh. Here was the cradle of Israel's national life, here Saul was made King, whose life ended in disaster. It was here that the brave warriors and friends of David assembled to re-establish him on his kingly throne, on his return from exile. Here also was the school of prophets—happy residence of Elijah, Elisha, and others. As we beheld the filthy mud hovels, and saw the faces of the inhabitants, which betrayed them, it made us feel the necessity of being on our guard, as the people are mostly corrupt rogues. As we gazed upon the landscapes all around us, fearless of the thievish inhabitants, we read carefully Joshua iv. 5; 1

as the choice of drinking the water out of their water-pots, I am not sure which we would have done! We certainly refused to drink their kindly offered water, but quickly offered them backshish thinking it would satisfiy them. They took the backshish given, and continued following us, demanding more. We were annoyed, and asked of Ibrahim and our Bedouin guide to rid us of this company of dirty followers, feeling that they were dangerous company. All at once our Bedouin, with a voice as of a wild beast, declared most passionately that unless they returned to their homes, and ceased to follow us, by the head of the prophet he would shoot and kill them, and walk over their carcasses. Evidently they believed in the earnestness of the man, and they blessed and thanked us for previous gifts. Very soon after we saw no more of them. Soon after we found ourselves at the site of ancient Jericho. After inspecting the site we hastened on to the next village, the

MODERN JERICHO

The country round here is the most lovely and fertile that we ever saw. So far as the land itself and its fertility is concerned, it seems as if the primeval curse has not touched this place. The soil is marvelously fertile. Fountains of water pour forth their streams over the picturesque plain. Here we remained for the rest of the afternoon and evening, and slept a night in an inn kept by a Russian. How strange were our feelings; a night spent in Jericho! Our inn was beautifully situated. Splendid orchards were planted around the house. Closely by the house runs a stream of water from the mountains behind. Being very thirsty we gladly drank of the lage and plains was magnificent. Shepherds were leading their flocks, Bedouins were singing their war songs, girls were dancing in a most frantic manner for backshish. With the slightest effort the soil here becomes like a most fruitful garden, and yet how truely the curse still rests upon Jericho. "Cursed be the man before the Lord, that riseth up and buildeth this city Jericho; he shall lay the foundation thereof in his firstborn, and in his youngest son shall he set up the gates of it" (Joshua vi. 26; see also 1 Kings xvi. 34). As the sun was now gradually setting, we undertook a walk around Jericho. How interesting was the view of the Sultan's Spring, doubtless the very

SPRING HEALED BY ELISHA.

Here we read with renewed interest the sacred page, "And the men of the city said unto Elisha, behold, I pray thee, the situation of the city is pleasant, as my Lord seeth; but the water is nought, and the ground barren. And he said, bring me a new cruse, and put salt therein. And they brought it to him. And he went forth unto the spring of the waters, and cast the salt in there, and said, Thus saith the Lord, I have healed these waters; there shall not be from thence any more death or barren land. So the waters were healed unto this day, according to the saying of Elisha which he spake" (2 Kings ii. 19-22). Near the spring is the spot, we are informed, where stood the inn of Rahab the harlot. From here a magnificent view is to be had of the mountains of Gilead and Moab. It was here that David's servants were by Hanun, son of Nahash. ... Hanun took David's servants and shaved them. ... Then there went certain, and told David

make their arrangements to attend, which it is to be hoped they will do. The meeting is not intended for officials only, but other members of the church are invited.

Davis City is situated on the Chariton branch of the C. B. & Q. railroad, on which a freight and accomodation train arrives at 11 o'clock A. M. from Chariton, and the regular passenger train from Chariton arrives at 2 o'clock P. M. The regular passenger train from St. Joseph, Mo., arrives at 2.30 P. M., and the freight train from St. Joseph at 8 P. M. These are the only regular trains which pass our place.

---o---

CAIAPHAS' REPORT.

In this issue will be found the report of Caiaphas the high priest, who condemned our Savior to death, as published by the Rev. Mr. Mahan, in his Book entitled, "Archæological writings of the Sanhedrin and Talmuds."

This report, he says, was found among the ancient writings preserved in the Archives of the Mosque of Omer, in Constantinople.

It is reasonable to believe that the high priest should make a report to the Sanhedrin, the great council of the Jews who had charge of the ecclesiastical and civil affairs of the Jewish nation, of an event of such a wonderful character as the crucifixion and resurrection of Christ. This report is of thrilling interest, as are other articles in Mr. Mahan's book.

---o---

THE MISFORTUNE WHICH has come upon the farmers of the town of Germania causes intense excitement all over Southern New Jersey. Over forty families are now homeless. Sheriff Johnson of Atlantic county has sold within the last 2 days over 200 farms to satisfy mortgages which have been foreclosed. One of the farmers, George Ling, was evicted. His misfortune made him crazy, and he set fire to his home and burned it to the ground, dying himself in the flames. Another farmer, Fred Wersbo, barricaded himself in his house and announces his intention to keep possession or die.

The above is only the beginning of the end.—*Ed.*

---o---

ITEMS OF PERSONAL HISTORY OF THE EDITOR.

BAPTISM FOR THE DEAD INTRODUCED.

Spiritual wives privately spoken of in 1841.

No. 14.

Continued from page 262.

In the last number of Personal History I gave an extended account of the mission to Cincinnati, getting the Book of Mormon stereotyped, in 1840.

While there became personally acquainted with General Wm. H. Harrison, who was then Whig candidate for the presidency of the United States, and who was duly elected that fall.

He was a plain, affable gentleman, of the old school, sociable and friendly with all, being entirely devoid of any appearance of aristocracy; very courteous and easy in his manner, making a stranger feel at home in his presence.

I gave him a detailed account of our persecutions in Missouri, to which he replied that, when he was governor of the Territory of Indiana, a persecution arose against the Quakers, and complaint was made to him, when he investigated the matter, and had no difficulty in bringing about a reconciliation. I believe him to have been a good man. He lived only about one month after he was inaugurated President.

Our present President is his grandson, and evidently inherits many of his excellent traits of character.

I had not been in Cincinnati but a few weeks until I learned there was a family that belonged to our church, by the name of Ware, that kept a boarding house on 5th Street Market Place. I changed my boarding place and boarded with them the remainder of the time I was in Cincinnati.

Early in August, Elders Orson Hyde, and John E. Page, came to Cincinnati and commenced holding meetings, and in a short time a number of persons were baptized and a branch of the church organized there.

These Elders had started on a mission to Jerusalem, in Palestine, and were preaching by the way. After a few weeks Elder Hyde proceeded on his mission, but Elder Page remained preaching in Cincinnati and vicinity, and failed to go with Elder Hyde, who prosecuted the mission alone, of which we may speak hereafter.

On the 14th of September, 1840, Joseph Smith, Senior, father of President Joseph Smith, jr., died in Nauvoo, at an advanced age. He was Patriarch of the Church at the time of his death. Hyrum Smith was subsequently appointed Patriarch, to succeed him. I shall hereafter speak of President Joseph Smith without adding the junior, as heretofore.

This year, 1840, may be considered an eventful year to the church, as during the summer, Dr. John C. Bennett, a man of considerable note, being at the time Quarter Master General of the state of Illinois, came to Nauvoo, and joined the church.

He was a man of rather pleasing address, calculated to make a favorable impression upon the minds of most people. He soon gained the confidence of President Joseph Smith, but time developed the unpleasant truth that instead of his being a spiritually minded man, he was clearly a man of the world in more than one particular.

He immediately commenced taking an active part in the affairs of the church, and also writing articles for the church paper, the first of which appeared in the Sept. No. of the *Times and Seasons*, from which is taken the following extracts.

"For the *Times & Seasons*.

Burglary! TREASON!! ARSON!!!

MURDER!!!

Lt. Col. Smith:—

I feel disposed to address you a few lines in relation to one of the darkest events that ever blackened the history of man in his most savage and barbarous state. The history of the Goths and Vandals, the cruel Arabs, or the Savage Indians, does not contain a parallel —the heart sickens at the thought, and turnes from the contemplation of it with loathing and disgust.

* * * * * *

Missouri has hewn down the innocent and defenceless; it is true, but she is entirely destitute of military knowledge or prowess. The Poet truly describes her citizens when he says—

"Their power to hurt, each little creature feels,
Bulls aim their horns, and asses lift their heels;"

but the blood of the slain is crying from the ground for condign vengeance, and should she continue to pursue her present murderous policy, the day of righteous retribution and the avenging of blood will not be procrastinated—for her plains shall be bleached with the bones of the slain, and her rivers flow with blood, before another massacre will be suffered. More anon.

Yours, Respectfully,
JOAB,
General in Israel."

In the latter part of Sept. I left Cincinnati for Nauvoo, arriving there about the 2nd day of October. On the morning of the 3rd the semi-annual general conference of the church convened in Nauvoo, on which occasion I saw, for the first time, Dr. J. C. Bennett as he came upon the stand. I confess a feeling of disappointment arose in my heart, for I could not feel that he was what he professed to be, a man of God.

The following is the record of the proceedings of said conference, had on Sunday, Oct. 4, as found on page 186 of the October No. of the *Times and Seasons*:

"Sunday morning. Conference met pursuant to adjournment, and was opened by prayer by Elder Babbit.

The clerk was then called upon to read the report of the presidency, in relation to the city plot, after which the president made some observations on the situation of the debts on

THE RETURN.

city plot and advised that a committee be appointed to raise funds to liquidate the same.

On motion. Resolved, that William Marks and Hyrum Smith compose said committee.

On motion. Resolved, that a committee be appointed to draught a bill for the incorporating of the town of Nauvoo, and other purposes.

Resolved, that Joseph Smith Jr. Dr. J. C. Bennett and R. B. Thompson, compose said committee.

Resolved that Dr. J. C. Bennett, be appointed delegate to Springfield, to urge the passage of said bill through the legislature.

President Hyrum Smith then rose and gave some general intruction to the church.

Conference adjourned for one hour.

One o'clock, P. M. Conference met pursuant to adjournment and was opened by prayer by Elder J. P. Green.

President Joseph Smith jr. then arose and delivered a discourse on the subject of baptism for the dead, which was listened to with considerable interest, by the vast multitude assembled.

Dr. Bennett, from the committee, to draught a charter for the city, and for other purposes, reported the outlines of the same.

Resolved that the same be adopted.

Dr. Bennett then, made some very appropriate remarks on the duty of the saints in regard to those, who had, under circumstances of affliction, held out the hand of friendship, and that it was their duty to uphold such men and give them their suffrages, and support.

Elder E. Robinson then arose, and gave an account of the printing of another edition of the Book of Mormon, and stated, that it was now nearly completed and that arrangements had been made for the printing of the hymn book, book of doctrine and covenants, &c.

Conference adjourned to Monday morning.''

On this occasion was the first time I ever heard the subjec of baptism for the dead mentioned in public.

In December, 1840, our business had increased to such an extent we thought it advisable to divide it, which we did by Don Carlos Smith taking the *Times and Seasons* and handbill job printing, and myself the book and fancy job printing, the stereotype foundry and book-bindery. We divided the material and dissolved partnership by mutual consent.

Dr. J. C. Bennett went to Springfield and attended the legislature, where he exerted all the influence he could bring to bear, to secure the passage of the Nauvoo City Charter, and other bills which he had prepared, and remained until they were all passed, viz:

A charter for "The City of Nauvoo," the "Nauvoo Legion," the "University of the City of Nauvoo," and the "Nauvoo Agricultural Association."

The city charter confered upon the Mayor and board of Aldermen extraordinary powers, including the authority to issue writes of *habras corpus*, which privilege. it was claimed, no other city in the state enjoyed.

After these charters were granted the First Presidency of the church issued a "*Proclamation to the saints scattered abroad,*" in which they set forth the favorable circumstances attending the church, and spoke very highly of the Legislature of the state, and also of many individuals who had extended acts of kindness, from which is taken the following extract, as found on page 275 of the *Times and Seasons* for Jan. 15, 1875.

"Not only has the Lord given us favor in the eyes of the community, who are happy to see us in the enjoyment of all the rights and privileges of free-men, but we are happy to state that several of the principal men of Illinois, who have listened to the doctrines we promulge, have become obedient to the faith and are rejoicing in the same, among whom is John C. Bennett, M. D., Quarter Master General of Illinois. We mention this gentleman first, because, that during our persecutions in Missouri, he became acquainted with the violence we were suffering, while in that State, on account of our religion—his sympathies for us were aroused, and his indignation kindled against our persecutors for the cruelties practised upon us, and their flagrant violation of both the law and the constitution. Amidst their heated zeal to put down the truth, he addressed us a letter tendering to us his assistance in delivering us out of the hands of our enemies, and restoring us again to our privileges, and only required at our hands to point out the way, and he would be forthcoming, with all the forces he could raise for that purpose—He has been one of the principal instruments in effecting our safety and deliverance from the unjust persecutions and demands of the authorities of Missouri, and also in procuring the city charter—He is a man of enterprize, extensive acquirements, and of independant mind, and is calculated to be a great blessing to our community."

Heretofore the church had strenuously opposed secret societies, such as Free-Masons, Knights of Pithias, and all that class of secret societies, not considering the "Order of Enoch" or "Danites" of that class; but after Dr. Bennett came into the church a great change of sentiment seemed to take place, and application was made to the Grand Lodge of Free Masons of the state of Illinois for a charter for a Lodge to be organized at Nauvoo, under dispensation, which was granted, and a Masonic Lodge was organized with Hyrum Smith, one of the First Presidents of the church as master. Large numbers of the brethren united with it, including Joseph Smith, Don Carlos Smith, and other prominent members of the church. After the Lodge had been in operation some months, the writer united with it. It increased in numbers until, in 1843, they built a large brick Masonic Hall, the lower story of which was fitted up for a theatre.

In the spring of 1841, the doctrine of "spiritual wives" began to be secretly talked about. In June, 1841, Don Carlos Smith and myself left Nauvoo for Cincinnati, to settle with Mr. Shepherd, and also to lay in a stock of paper and other printing material for our office in Nauvoo.

We went to Keokuk to take a larger class of steamboat than passed over the rapids in a low stage of water, and while there, waiting for a steamer, we conversed upon the subject of that new doctrine, when Don Carlos Smith said: "*Any man who will teach and practice the doctrine of spiritual wifery will go to hell. I don't care if it is my brother Joseph.*" This was the light in which he viewed that matter at that early day.

TO BE CONTINUED.

:0:

EXTRACTS FROM LETTERS.

A brother in the west writes:

BROTHER E. ROBINSON: *Dear Sir:* The RETURN not coming to hand makes me think that you are on the sick list, and as either of us is likely to lay down this body of clay at any time, and as I hope and believe that we will meet each other in the same glory, makes me have a desire to let you know that I have no hard feelings towards you, but that I love you as a brother in Christ. I thought, when you refused to publish my letter, that you done wrong, but I admitted at the same time, that you had the right to decide in that matter. * * *

With so little encouragement as you have had, I admire and approve your work in the RETURN, for I do not believe there is another man in the church that would have acted with more wisdom than you have, and I hope you may be spared to complete this volume. * * *

I do not mean to write on church matters, I only wanted you to know that I have nothing but warm feelings towards you, and hope that if we cannot be the means of saving others, that we will save ourselves. Love to all the faithful.

From your brother in the gospel.

———o———

From a friend in the west.

May the 18th, 1890.

DEAR BROTHER I have had some correspondence, and learned that there is a branch of the true church in the world, and as I have been looking for it for the last thirty-eight years I hope and trust in God that I have found it, and I have been assured through the spirit of Christ it is so.

PUBLISHED MONTHLY AT $1,00 A YEAR.

Entered at the Post Office at Davis City, Iowa, as second class matter.

Report of Caiaphas to the Sanhedrin Concerning the resurrection of Jesus.

Sanhedrin, 89. By Siphri II, 7.:

TO YOU, MASTERS OF ISRAEL:—As I have made a former defense to you, and you have approved the same, I feel in duty bound to communicate to you some facts that have come to my knowledge since the former communication. A few days after the execution of Jesus of Nazareth the report of his resurrection from the dead became so prominent I found it was necessary to investigate it, because the excitement was raging more heavy than before, and my own life as well as that of Pilate was in danger, and it seemed worse than if he had not been apprehended at all. I sent for Malkus, captain of the royal city guard, who informed me he knew nothing personally as he had placed Isham in command of the guard, but from what he could learn of the soldiers the scene was perfectly overwhelming, and it was so generally believed that it was no use to deny it. He thought my only chance was to suppress it among the soldiers, and have John and Peter banished to Crete, or have them arrested and locked up in prison, and if they would not be quiet to treat them as I had treated Jesus. He said all the soldiers he had conversed with were convinced that he was either resurrected by supernatural power, or he was not dead, or that and the angels, and the dead that came out of their graves, all went to prove that it was something that had never occured on earth before. He said that John and Peter were spreading it all over the country, and if it should be so that Jesus should appear at the head of a host, and declare for the king of the Jews, he believed all the Jewish soldiers would fight for him. I sent for the lieutenant, who gave a lengthy detail of the occurence there that morning, all of which I suppose you have heard, and will investigate the subject by a committee. From this I am convinced that there was something above the laws of nature transacted there that morning that can't be accounted for upon natural principles, and I find it is of no use to try to get any of the soldiers to deny it, for they are so excited over it that there is no doing anything with them. I am now sorry that I had the soldiers placed at the tomb, for the very things that they were to prevent they have established.

After investigating the soldiers and officers to my satisfaction, my mind being so disturbed that I could neither eat nor sleep, I sent for John and Peter. They came, and brought Mary and Joanna. These are the women that went to embalm his body the morning of the resurrection, as it is called. They are very interesting, as they relate the circumstances. Mary says when they went it was just getting light. They met the soldiers returning from the sepulcher, and they thought nothing strange until they came to the tomb, and found that Jesus was gone. The stone that covered the sepulcher was

...emselves to go up to Jerusalem to rob ...e Jews, and will unite their mighty ...mies under Gog, from the north quar... ...r and go to Jerusalem, where they will ...eet with their final doom, and the Lord ...sus will come according to the follow... ...g scripture:

"Behold, the day of the Lord com... ...h, and thy spoil shall be divided ... the midst of thee. For I will gath... ...all nations against Jerusalem to ...ttle; and the city shall be taken, ...d the houses rifled, and the wo... ...en ravished; and half of the city ...all go forth into captivity, and ...e residue of the people shall not ...cut off from the city. Then shall ...e Lord go forth, and fight against ...ose nations, as when he fought in ...e day of battle. And his feet ...all stand in that day upon the ...ount of Olives, which is before ...rusalem on the east, and the ...ount of Olives shall cleave in the ...dst thereof toward the east and ...ward the west, and there shall be a ...ry great valley; and half of the ...ountain shall remove toward the ...rth, and half of it toward the ...uth. And ye shall flee to the val... ...of the mountains; for the valley ...the mountains shall reach unto A... ...; yea, ye shall flee, like as ye fled ...om before the earthquake in the ...ys of Uzziah king of Judah: and ...e Lord my God shall come, and all ...e saints with thee. And it shall ...me to pass in that day, that the ...ht shall not be clear, nor dark; ...t it shall be one day which shall ...known to the Lord, not day, nor ...ght: but it shall come to pass, that ...evening time it shall be light. ...d it shall be in that day, that ...ing waters shall go out from Jeru... ...em; half of them toward the form... ...sea, and half of them toward the ...der sea: in summer and in winter ...ll it be. And the Lord shall be ...g over all the earth: in that day ...ll there be one Lord, and his ...me one."—Zech.—14: 1-9.

Ye have learned from the foregoing ...ptures there is a great work to be ac- complished before the second coming of Christ, therefore we need not be alarmed when men tell us the Lord will come on a given day, before the things spoken of above have come to pass, as we may know assuredly they are false witnesses, and know not whereof they affirm.

Jesus will come, however, but it will be in the exact time appointed of the Father. The signs spoken of by Jesus and the prophets, and the gathering of the great and mighty army against Jerusalem, all are given as tokens of his appearing. "But of that day and hour knoweth no man, no, not the angels of heaven, but my Father only."

ITEMS OF PERSONAL HISTORY OF THE EDITOR.

No. 15.

Continued from page 287.

On the 19th of January, 1841, Joseph Smith received a lengthy revelation, from which is taken the following extract:

"And build an house to my name, for the Most High to dwell therein; for there is not a place found on earth that he may come and restore again that which was lost unto you, or, which he hath taken away, even the fullness of the priesthood; for a baptismal font there is not upon the earth; that they, my saints, may be baptized for those who are dead; for this ordinance belongeth to my house, and can not be acceptable to me, only in the days of your poverty, wherein ye are not able to build an house unto me. But I command you, all ye my saints, to build an house unto me; and I grant unto you a sufficient time to build an house unto me, and during this time your baptisms shall be acceptable unto me.

But, behold, at the end of this appointment, your baptisms for your dead shall not be acceptable unto me; and if you do not these things at the end of the appointment, ye shall be rejected as a church with your dead, saith the Lord your God."—D. & C. 107, part of 10 and 11.

I do not purpose here, to speak of the merits or demerits of the revelation, but to relate that, with such a wonderful incentive as the fear of being *rejected* with *their dead*, the brethren went to work with their mights, to accomplish the building of the temple within the time appointed. In the mean time large numbers were baptized in the Mississippi river for their dead friends. On one occasion it was reported that 400 were baptized in one day.

The excavation was made for the basement of the temple, and four suitable stones were prepared for the corner stones, to be laid on the sixth of April.

The officers of the Nauvoo Legion procured beautiful and costly uniforms, and had the Legion drill preparatory to taking a prominent part in the ceremony of laying the corner stones, as will be seen by the following quotation from the 2nd vol. of *Times and Seasons*, commencing on page 880.

"For some days prior to the sixth, the accession of strangers to our city was great, and on the wide spread prairie, which bounds our city, might be seen various kinds of vehicles wending their way from different points of the compass to the city of Nauvoo, while the ferry boats on the Mississippi, were constantly employed in wafting travellers across its rolling and extensive bosom.

Among the citizens, all was bustle and preparation, anxious to accomodate their friends who flock in from distant parts, and who they expected to share with them the festivity of the day, and the pleasures of the scene.

At length, the long expected morn arrived, and before the king of day had tipped the eastern horrizon with his rays, were preparations for the celebration of the day going on. Shortly after sun rise, the loud peals from the artillery were heard, calling the various companies of the legion to the field, who were appointed to take a conspicuous part in the days proceedings.

The citizens from the vicinity, now began to pour in from all quarters, a continuous train, for about three hours and continued to swell the vast assembly.

At eight o'clock A. M. Major General Bennett left his quarters to organize and prepare the Legion for the duties of the day, which consisted of about fourteen companies, several in uniform, besides several companies from Iowa, and other parts of the county, which joined them on the occasion.

At half past nine Lieut. General Smith was informed that the Legion was organized and ready for review, and immediately accompanied by the staff, consisting of four Aids-de-camp, and twelve guards, nearly all in splendid uniforms, took his march to the parade ground. On their approach they were met by the Band, beautifully equipped, who received them with a flourish of trumpets and a regular salute, and then struck up a lively air, marching in front of the Lieut. General. On his approach to the parade ground the artillery was again fired, and the Legion gave an appropriate salute while passing. This was indeed a glorious sight, such as we never saw, nor did we ever expect to see such a one in the west. The several companies, presented a beautiful and interesting spectacle, several of them being uniformed and equipped, while the rich and costly dresses of the officers, would have become a Bonaparte or Washington.

After the arrival of Lieut. General Smith, the ladies who had made a beautiful silk flag, drove up in a carriage to present it to the Legion. Maj. General Bennet, very politely attended on them, and conducted them in front of Lieut. General Smith, who immediately alighted from his charger, and walked up to the ladies, who presented the flag, making an appropriate address. Lieut. General Smith, acknowledged the honor conferred upon the Legion, stated that as long as he had the command, it should never be disgraced; and then politely bowing to the ladies gave it into the hands of Maj. General Bennett, who placed it in the possession of Cornet Robinson, and it was soon seen gracefully waving in front of the Legion. During the time of presentation, the Band struck up a lively air, and another salute was fired from the artillery.

After the presentation of the flag, Lieut. General Smith, accompanied by his suit, reviewed the Legion, which presented a very imposing appearance, the different officers saluting as he passed. Lieut. General Smith then took his former stand and the whole Legion by companies passed before him in review.

THE PROCESSION.

Immediately after the review, Gen. Bennett organized the procession, to march to the foundation of the Temple, in the following order; to wit:

Lieut. Gen. Smith,
Brig. Generals Law & Smith,
Aids-de-Camp, & conspicuous strangers,
General Staff,
Band,
2nd Cohort, (foot troops,)
Ladies eight abreast,
Gentlemen, eight abreast,
1st Cohort, (horse troops.)

Owing to the vast numbers who joined in the procession, it was a considerable length of time before the whole could be organized.

The procession then began to move forward in order, and on their arrival at the Temple block, the Generals with their staffs and the distinguished strangers present, took their position inside of the foundation, the ladies formed on the outside immediately next the walls, the gentlemen and infantry behind, and the cavalry in the rear.

The assembly being stationed, the chorister, under the superintendance of B. S. Wilber, sung an appropriate hymn.

Prest. Rigdon, then ascended the platform, which had been prepared for the purpose, and delivered a suitable

ORATION,

which was listened to with the most profound attention by the assembly." * * *

"The first Presidency superintended the laying of the

CHIEF CORNER STONE

on the south east corner of the building, which done, Prest. J. Smith, arose and said, that the first corner stone of the Temple of Almighty God was laid, and prayed that the building might soon be completed, that the saints might have an habitation to worship the God of their fathers.

Prest. D. C. Smith and his counsellors, of the high priest's quorum, then repaired to the south west corner, and laid the corner stone thereof.

The High Council, representing the Twelve laid the north west corner stone.

The Bishops with their counsellors laid the north east corner stone with due solemnities.

The ceremony of laying the corner stones being over, the Legion marched to the parade ground, and formed a hollow square for an address. Maj. General Bennett addressed the Legion at some length, applauding them for their soldier like appearance, and for the attention which both officers and men had given to the orders.

Lieut. General Smith, likewise expressed his entire approbation of the conduct of the Legion and all present.

The assembly then seperated with cheerful hearts, and thanking God for the great blessings of peace and prosperity by which they were surrounded, and hearts burning with affection for their favorite and adopted state."

Thus the corner stones of the house of the Lord, or what was claimed to be the house of the Lord, were laid amid the roar of cannon, and by the hands of men wearing the garments, and bearing the implements of war and of blood.

Lieut. General Joseph Smith, who superintended laying the chief corner stone, and Brig. Gen'l. Don Carlos Smith, President of the High Priests' Quorum, who superintended laying the second corner stone, were both clothed in their military garments, and wearing their swords at the time.

Although I took part in the procession and ceremonies, yet I took no part in the military portion of it, as I never mustered a *single day or time* in the Legion, always believing the church of Christ had no use for such an organization, and really feeling that that part of the charter business was of the devil. The officers of the Legion threatened to court-martial and fine me. I told them to fine as often, and as much as they pleased, I never would train with them, neither would pay one cent of fine. And I never did.

While upon the subject, will give a brief outline of the history of the temple. It was commenced to be built within two years from the time the church were driven from Missouri; and as such great and stupendous results depended upon its completion, according to the revelation, the members of the church strained every nerve to build it. We doubt if ever there were a people who more readily obeyed the counsel of their leaders, than did that people. They were ready to make every sacrifice to accomplish an object so dear to their heart, but the conduct of some of the members of the church was such, and the City Council, with Joseph Smith at their head as Mayor, ordered the City Marshall to destroy the *Nauvoo Expositor* printing press, type and material, which he did with his posse. These acts so exasperated the people of Illinois, who so recently were the friends of the church so that before the walls of the temple were much more than half way up, Joseph and Hyrum Smith were both brutally murdered in Carthage jail, on the 27th day of June, 1844, and threats were made to drive the church from the state.

Notwithstanding all this the work on the temple was pushed with all possible dispatch, until it was completed so they began to use it for the purpose it was intended, in which they gave what they called the keys of the Priesthood, and the endowments with the signs, grips, tokens and garments, such as were given in the Holy Order in Joseph Smith's life time.

But they were not permitted to enjoy the use of the temple long, as by some means it took fire and was partially burned, and besides, the church was compelled to leave the state. The first company, with Brigham Young and the twelve, at its head left Nauvoo for the Rocky Mountains in February, 1846, in less than five years from the time the corner stones were laid.

A brother who was living in Nauvoo at the time, and who received in the temple what was called his endowment, with the signs, grips, tokens and pass words, and peculiar garment or protection robe, informs me that two or three nights before Brigham and his party left for the west, they had a dancing party in the temple, and occupied nearly or quite the whole night long in music and dancing.

I speak of these things not because I take pleasure in dwelling upon them, but because I feel it my bounden duty to present these truths of history, so that those who come after may shun the shoals and rocks upon which that people made shipwreck; for know assuredly, that these things could not be of the Lord.

After the church had left, a French Icarian Society purchased and undertook to repair the building, and when engaged in that work one pleasant May day, there suddenly arose a whirlwind, as such stormes were then called, and blew down the north wall, and so shattered the remainder of the building that its further repair was abandoned. It has since been entirely torn down, and the foundation stones quarried out and burned into lime, and the place where it stood, levelled up, and set out to grape vines, thus showing

...ly to my mind, the displeasure of the Almighty in its construction.

I am fully persuaded, after these years of experience, that the church and military organizations, or church and state, cannot be united and enjoy spiritual prosperity. "Ye cannot serve God and mammon."

Let the history and downfall of Nauvoo be a solemn warning to the members of the church of Christ, and let us be content with the simple and plain teachings and gospel of the Lord Jesus Christ.

But to return to my narrative. In the spring of 1841, I had a building erected suitable for a printing office, stereotype foundry, book bindery and dwelling combined, where those different branches were successfully carried on under my personal supervision. Commenced stereotyping the book of Doctrine and Covenants and hymn book.

On the 7th of August, 1841, Don Carlos Smith died, after only a few days illness. He was buried with military honors, greatly beloved and mourned by all who knew him. From a close and intimate acquaintance with him from May 1835 unto the day of his death, I do think he was one of the most perfect men I ever knew. He was a bitter opposer of the "spiritual wife" doctrine, which was being talked quite freely, in private circles, in his lifetime.

Elder Robert B. Thompson, who was assistant editor of the *Times and Seasons*, also died on the 27th day of August. He too, was a man greatly beloved by those who knew him. He was esteemed as an exceptionally good, christian man.

Brother Don Carlos Smith died in the 5th year of his age, and Bro. Thompson in his 30th year. Thus in the very prime of life those two noble men of God, as I have every assurance they were, laid down their armor, and passed into the beyond, where they "may rest from their labors and their works do follow them."

After the death of Brother Smith, his widow, Sister Agnes M. Smith, wished to dispose of her entire interest in the *Times and Seasons*; and I purchased the entire establishment, and combined it with my other business.

(*To be continued.*)

CORRESPONDENCE.

Hillsdale, Ia., June 19th 1890.

DEAR BRO. ROBINSON:—I have been thinking for some time to write a short article for the RETURN, to let the children of God know that I, for one, am firm in the church of Christ. I have been in two factions before I united with the church of Christ, and I can look back now and see that I had a zeal without knowledge. I looked for men to teach me instead of the pure words of Christ, my redeemer, the true shepherd, who gave his life for his sheep. He said I am the true shepherd, follow me. He also laid down the plan of salvation, whereupon mankind can have eternal life.

I find in the book of Mormon, the same teaching, and gospel, was taught on this land to the children of Joseph, as we can plainly see that these Indians, according to that history, are remnants, and must be brought to a knowledge of their fore fathers and also their Redeemer, as well as the Jews have to be brought to the knowledge of Christ and the new testament. Ezekiel speaks of these two sticks, 37th chap. 16th verse, which I believe is the new testament and book of Mormon. Lehi saw the rod of iron that led to the tree of life, which is the word of God. Christ says: "this gospel of the kingdom must be preached to all the world, and then shall the end come." Mathew 24:14.

Now I would advise all to search the words of God for themselves, and then live according as they teach.

Adieu ye proud, ye rich, ye gay.
I'll seek the broken hearted:
For which the mighty Savior came
And heavenly truths imparted.

For this religion thrives again,
  In it Christ's power is given;
May all mankind, through it regain
  On earth, the gifts of heaven.
    Your Sister in Christ,
        LUCY M. THOMAS.

---:0:---

A friend in Kansas City writes:

Mr. ROMIXSON:—*Sir:*—We enclose one dollar for the RETURN for the year 1890. We are pleased with it, and believe it will be the means of bringing many to a knowledge of the truth as it is in Christ, and will lead many to investigate, and know for themselves what is truth and what is error.

Trusting God will bless you in your efforts for good, and guide you by his spirit in love and truth.

With regards to yourself and family, I remain as ever, &c.

---(:-:)---

Capsicum as a Counter-irritant.

Dr. Henry J. Buck, writing to the Lancet, says: "I have used this drug for more than twenty years—I may almost say daily—and many of my patients will not travel without a bottle of the 'magic lotion,' as they call it. I find the simplest and most efficacious way of applying it is to soak a large handful of the crushed pods in half a pint of hot water for an hour, then strain, and bottle for use. A teaspoonful of eau-de-cologne added will help to keep the solution, or it can be well boiled after preparing. I then have it applied to the affected parts on a piece of linen folded three or four times, or on lint, and covered with gutta percha tissue or a dry flannel. In this way the lotion may be kept on for hours without vesicating, and in many cases the skin is hardly reddened. The stinging and burning sensation produced by the capsicum lotion is, after a few minutes, welcomed by the sufferer, so magically does it often remove the rheumatic or neuralgic pain for which it is being applied. In acute torticollis a cure is often speedily obtained by covering the side affected with the application. In any form of neuralgia, rheumatism, subacute gout, pleurodynia, and such like, it will be found most useful, and may be reapplied over and over again during the the day and night without any fear of vesication." (blistering.)-Scientific American.

---o---

The Supreme Court of the United States declared that a state has the constitutional right to prohibit the importation of cattle that are liable to spread disease, or are suspected of containing poison or disease lurking under their fair skin, and behind their horns. That Iowa and Illinois had such rights. Yet the same court decides that liquors may be imported from one state to another, no matter if each barrel has in 1½ more of disease and damage than was ever contained in a trail of Texas cattle 500 miles long. We fear that temperance people have not yet learned as to the time of the day to have their cases called, and that they forgot that one bar aims to protect another.—Ex.

---o---

Palestine.

The long projected railway from Jaffa to Jerusalem is at last being laid. A French company is constructing the line, with the permission and promised protection of the Sultan. Though only a single line will at present be laid, such stuctural arrangements will be made as will facilitate the laying of a second line in the course of time.—*Selected.*

One of the movements for the spread of the Gospel in the Holy Land is the "English Deaconess House" in that city. Here young Christian women are studying the Arabic language in order to teach the native women.—*Selected.*

ELDER DAVID WHITMER'S "Address to all believers in Christ" can be had by sending a 2 cent stamp to D. Whitmer, Richmond, Mo., or to this office.

THE RETURN.

"Truth, crushed to earth, shall rise again; The eternal years of God are hers."

Vol. 2. No. 7.   DAVIS CITY, IOWA, JULY, 1890.   Whole No. 19.

The Return.

PUBLISHED MONTHLY AT $1.00 A YEAR.
Entered at the Post Office at Davis City, Iowa, as second class matter.

BY THE FALL OF ISRAEL SALVATION CAME TO THE GENTILES.

(*Continued from page 278.*)

Now the gentiles are as dark in regard to understanding the scriptures, as Israel were when Christ preached to them; for they see, but see not the light as it is in Christ Jesus our Lord. They are fulfilling the prophecy of God's servants in denying the power of God, and teaching for doctrine, the commandments of men, for they will not preach the gospel and promise the Holy Ghost with signs following them that believe.

But when the servants of Christ are sent out, they are commanded to cry repentance, and to promise the Holy Ghost to all those who will repent and be baptized; then, through the laying on of hands, the Holy Ghost will be given to those that come in with a broken heart and a contrite spirit, and the signs shall follow them that do believe all things whatsoever is taught or promised by the apostles of Christ as found in the new Testament or Book of Mormon. For the Testament part of both books is the same as to the doctrine of Christ, and the promise is to those who believe, for the words of Christ are yea, and amen, for heaven and earth may pass away, but Christ's words shall never fail, and by his words shall all be judged of our works whether good or bad.

Let us turn to Revelations 12th chapter, 1-2-3 verses. "And there appeared a great wonder in heaven; a woman clothed with the sun, and the moon under her feet, and upon her head a crown of twelve stars: and she being with child cried, travailing in birth, and pained to be delivered. And there appeared another wonder in heaven; and behold a great red dragon having seven heads and ten horns, and seven crowns upon his heads." 5th and 6th verses. "And she brought forth a man child who was to rule all nations with a rod of iron: and her child was caught up unto God and to his throne. And the woman fled into the wilderness, where she hath a place prepared of God, that they should feed her there a thousand and two hundred and three score days."

This woman was the true church of Christ with the twelve apostles as the crowning power, which is the crown upon the head of the church, for the twelve did rule at the head, and will at the day of judgment; and this is why they are represented as the crown of twelve stars.

And the woman clothed with the sun, nothing more than showing the power and the excellency of light of the Son of God, that he bestowed upon the church, with twelve apostles at the head, which this woman represented with the moon under her feet. This moon is the lesser light, as was under the law which Christ fulfilled and put under the feet of the church, for the Mosaic law ended in Christ. He fulfilled the law, and restored the gospel of salvation, with the authority to build up the church of Christ, clothed with the greater light, even that of the Holy Ghost.

Tuesday 29. At 10 a. m. the brethren and sisters met at Brother E. Robinson's and held a prayer and sacrament meeting in which every member present took part, and bore their testimony. It was a meeting long to be remembered by those present, as the Lord manifested his loving kindness, pouring out upon us his peaceful and Holy Spirit, causing our hearts to burn with joy within us. We felt it was truly good to wait upon the Lord.

At this meeting Brother Burns was ordained an Elder by Elder E. Robinson, assisted by Elder J. C. Whitmer.

Soon after dinner, the brethren and sisters gave each other the parting hand, and those from abroad left for their respective homes, (except Elder D. E. McCartey, who intends to remain here for a season,) all expressing joy and thankfulness for the precious blessings received from our heavenly Father at our meetings.

ITEMS OF PERSONAL HISTORY OF THE EDITOR.

No. 16.

Continued from page 302.

In what is termed, the temple revelation, given on the 19th of January, 1841, the commandment was given to build a boarding house, to be called the "Nauvoo House," as will be seen by the following extract from the revelation:

"And now, I say unto you, as pertaining to my boarding house, which I have commanded you to build, for the boarding of strangers, let it be built unto my name, and let my name be named upon it, and let my servant Joseph and his house have place therein, from generation to generation; for this anointing have I put upon his head, that his blessing shall also be put upon the head of his posterity after him; and as I said unto Abraham, concerning the kindreds of the earth, even so I say unto my servant Joseph, in thee, and in thy seed, shall the kindred of the earth be blessed. Therefore, let my servant Joseph, and his seed after him, have place in that house, from generation to generation, forever and ever, saith the Lord, and let the name of that house be called the Nauvoo House: and let it be a delightful habitation for man and a resting place for the weary traveler, that he may contemplate the glory of Zion, and the glory of this the corner-stone thereof; that he may receive, also, the council from those whom I have set to be its plants of renown, and as watchmen upon her walls.

Behold, verily I say unto you, let my servant Geo. Miller, and my servant Lyman Wight, and my servant John Snyder, and my servant Peter Haws, organize themselves, and appoint one of them to be a president over their quorum for the purpose of building that house. And they shall form a constitution whereby they may receive stock for the building of that house.

Verily I say unto you let my servant, Joseph, pay stock into their hands for the building of that house, as seemeth him good; but my servant, Joseph, can not pay over fifteen thousand dollars stock in that house, nor under fifty dollars; neither can any other man saith the Lord." D. C. 107: 18, 19, 21.

The persons named in the revelation, as the building committee, organized according to the instruction therein given, and opened stock books, and commenced operations immediately. The foundation was prepared, and the ceremony of laying the corner stone was attended to on the 2nd day of October, 1841. One thing transpired on that occasion worthy of note.

After the brethren had assembled at the south east corner of the foundation, where the corner stone was to be laid, President Joseph Smith said: "Wait, brethren, I have a document I wish to put in that stone," and started for his house, which was only a few rods away, across Main Street. I went with him to the house, and also one or two other brethren. He got a manuscript copy of the Book of Mormon, and brought it into the room where we were standing, and said: "I will examine to see if it is all here," and as he did so I stood near him, at his left side, and saw distinctly the writing, as he turned up the pages until he hastily went through the book and satisfied himself that it was all there, when he said: "I have had trouble enough with this thing,", which remark struck me with amusement, as I looked upon it as a sacred treasure.

It was written on foolscap paper, and formed a package, as the sheets lay flat, of about two, or two and a half inches thick, I should judge. It was written mostly in Oliver Cowdery's hand writing, with which I was intimately acquainted, having set many pages of type from his hand writing, in the church printing office at Kirtland, Ohio. Some parts of it were written in other hand writing.

He took the manuscript and deposited it in the corner stone of the Nauvoo House, together with other papers and things, including different pieces of United States' coin. I put in some copies of the *Times and Seasons*; all were carefully encased in sheet lead to protect the contents from moisture, and a stone had been cut to closely fit into the cavity which had been made in the corner stone to receive these things, which stone was fitted in its place and cemented, when it was thought the papers and other articles would be preserved without decay or injury for ages, if not disturbed.

From this circumstance we know there must have been at least two manuscript copies of the Book of Mormon, which necessarily must have been the case, as the printer who printed the first edition of the book had to have a copy, as they would not put the original copy into his hands for fear of it being altered. This accounts for David Whitmer having a copy and Joseph Smith having one. They were both mostly written in Oliver Cowdery's hand writing, as I have seen both. He was scribe for Joseph most of the time he was translating the Book of Mormon.

The Nauvoo House was never completed. It was in the shape of an L, with one wing facing west on Main Street, and the other wing facing south on the Mississippi river. It was located on the east side of, and at the foot of Main Street, directly on the bank of the river. The basement story was built of fine cut lime stone, and but one story of brick built up when the church were compelled to leave Nauvoo. It remained in this unfinished state for perhaps 20 years, or more, when Major Bideman, who had married Joseph Smith's widow, wishing to utilize the walls, had a roof put upon the west wing, fronting on Main Street. While this work was being done, Alexander Hale Smith, one of Joseph Smith's Sons met with a serious accident which greatly endangered his life. A new beam which had been placed for the joists to rest upon, suddenly broke, and striking him upon the head cut a gash said to be near four inches in length, as I was informed.

Knowing that manuscript copy of the Book of Mormon was deposited in that corner stone, and supposing it to be the original copy written by Oliver Cowdery, and others, as dictated to them by Joseph Smith, as he translated from the plates, and not knowing that David Whitmer had a manuscript copy, and being satisfied the Nauvoo House would never be completed, I had an intense desire to ultimately become possessor of that manuscript, as a sacred treasure; consequently, whenever being at Nauvoo in after years, would visit the Nauvoo House to see if the corner stone had been disturbed.

When there the last time, I staid all night with Major Bidamon, and occupied one of the rooms in the wes' wing of the Nauvoo House, that part of the building which had been prepared for occupancy, at which time I saw that a portion of the east wing had been taken down, and the hewn stone window caps and sills were being used in a fence near by, but the south-east portion of the wall, and the corner stone, were in place undisturbed.

Believing I was the only person in the country who had a knowledge of the contents of that stone, concluded not to make a request to open it out, but keep the secret in my own breast until some future time, when the walls would be more nearly taken down.

A few years since, President Joseph Smith, of Lamoni, asked me if I knew "what was put into the corner stone of the Nauvoo House?" Still wishing to retain the secret, as I supposed, hesitated to reply, until allusion was made to the manuscript of the Book of Mormon, when I told him I had some recollection it was put in that corner stone. He then informed me Major Bidamon had taken down the wall and opened the stone, and found the manuscript ruined. It had gathered moisture, and much of it had become a mass of pulp, and only small portions of it were legible. That Mr. Bidamon had sent him portions of it.

Since being at Nauvoo, I learned David Whitmer had preserved a manuscript copy of that book; which he guarded with sacred fidelity. A cyclone passed through the city of Richmond, where he lived, and tore away a portion of his house, but the room where the manuscript was kept, was marvellously preserved uninjured.

Thus a manuscript copy of that sacred book has been preserved by David Whitmer, the *faithful witness*, who prized it far above gold, or the treasures of earth, as was clearly demonstrated when Orson Pratt and Joseph F. Smith came from Utah, to Richmond, Mo., and offered him a large sum of money for it. When he declined accepting their offer, Orson Pratt said to him: "Name your price; we have the money." His reply was: "Gentlemen, you have not got money enough to buy that manuscript." I am told that one of the Richmond bankers afterwords stated that he could have taken *one hundred thousand dollars*, or more, for that manuscript, to his knowledge. But no, he would not sell it. He prized the truth above rubies.

He was the only one to whom the angel of the Lord spoke, when he brought the gold plates from which the Book of Mormon was translated, and showed them to the three witnesses, whose testimony is published with the Book of Mormon.

The angel said: "DAVID, BLESSED ARE THEY WHO KEEP THE COMMANDMENTS." He kept the commandments, and lived to a ripe old age, and died in his own home, with his family and friends around him, to whom he bore this testimony:

"Now, you must all be faithful in Christ. I want to say to you all, the Bible and the Record of the Nephites are true; so you can say that you heard me bear my testimony on my death bed. All be faithful in Christ and your reward will be according to your works. God bless you all. My trust is in Christ forever, world without end. Amen."

The next morning after giving this testimony, he had an open vision, in which, among other things, he said: "I see Jesus." Thus died this good and true man, an account of whose happy death was given in the first number of THE RETURN. May the Lord help us to so live that our end may be as his.

TO BE CONTINUED.

:o:

FROM the Deseret Semi-weekly *News*, Utah, for July 8th, we publish the following taken from the Press dispatches:

THE INDIAN CLAIM

OF HAVING SEEN THE MESSIAH AND RECEIVED HIS TEACHINGS.

"The following have appeared in the public journals in the form of press dispatches:

Fort Custer, Mont., July 3.—Early this morning a small squad of Cheyenne Indians appeared on the hill back of Fort Custer and sent word they wanted to come in. It was Porcupine, the apostle of the new Christ, and a few followers and believers in the new Messiah.

Porcupine's arrest had been ordered by General Brisbin, but a respite had been obtained for him by Major Carroll and he now came to explain his religion and personal conduct.

All the officers in the field, including Major Carroll, had given Porcupine letters of recommendation. At

forth his hands, prayed in silence for nearly five minutes. Suddenly his face lit up and he seemed filled with the Holy Spirit. He began speaking in low, modulated tones, which grew louder and faster as he proceeded until they reached a tempest of Indian eloquence.

He claimed Christ was on the earth and in the flesh, at Walker Lake, Nevada, and that he had seen him and talked with him face to face, and that Christ had sent him abroad to preach His gospel to all who would hear.

The man he had seen told him he had been on earth before, hundreds of years ago, when the people had treated him badly and killed him. He showed scars on his hands and feet where he said the people had driven spikes, nailing him to a cross. He also had a bad wound in his side, where he said the spear had pierced his flesh.

He said he lived in heaven with his Father and had a mother who was a holy spirit. His Father had made the earth and everything that was upon it.

Porcupine is a splendid specimen of the Indian, over six feet tall, straight as an arrow, with a fine face and head. He is about 35 years old, and his large black eyes glow with the earnestness of his convictions.

He is modest and graceful as an orator. He refuses to bring the new Christ where the soldiers' can capture him. This new religion is breeding trouble among the Cheyennes and gives the military much uneasiness.

Fort Custer, Mont., July 5.—The Indians on all the reservations in this section are in a state of excitement bordering on frenzy over the related his story with additional details. He spoke to the officers and ladies of the post for over an hour, and fully explained his religion, which closely resembles the Christian religion of the whites, except that Porcupine claims positively that Christ has come back to earth and was seen in the flesh near Walker Lake, Nevada. Porcupine did not know anything about the first Christ, but he says this Christ told him he had been on earth hundreds of years ago, when he appeared to the white people, who used him roughly, and even killed him. Porcupine says he saw marks on the hands of the Christ, who said he had been nailed to a tree by the hands, and that spikes had also been driven through his feet and his side had been cut open.

The Christ did not show the scars on his feet as he did on his hands, nor did he show the wound in his side, but all knew what he told them was true. Porcupine said he did not believe in the Christ when he first heard of him, but no sooner did he see him than all doubt vanished from his mind and he knew that he was looking at God. He had never seen such a man before and never would unless he saw this man again, which he meant to do. It was evening when Christ came walking into the camp, and they all knew who he was without being told.

He described Christ as a large man with a noble carriage and face. Christ did not speak the first day Porcupine saw him, but commenced talking the next day soon after sunrise and did not cease until the sun was near the western horizon.

Hundreds of Indians, representatives from scores of tribes, heard him. He did not speak in Cheyenne, but Porcupine understood him

THE RETURN.

"Truth, crushed to earth, shall rise again; The eternal years of God are hers."

Vol. 2. No. 8.   DAVIS CITY, IOWA, AUGUST, 1890.   Whole No. 20.

The Return.

PUBLISHED MONTHLY AT $1,00 A YEAR.

Entered at the Post Office at Davis City, Iowa, as second class matter.

THE AMERICAN INDIAN.

THE LORD'S BATTLE-AXE.

What is best to do with the Indians? and what will be their final destiny? are questions which have agitated the minds of our statesmen, and thinking men for years.

One thing is certain, they are here in our midst. They were found on this land when Columbus discovered America. They were the rightful owners of the soil so far as man can acquire a right to the soil. This right has been recognized by our general government, in the fact that the government have purchased from the Indians large scopes of the country, from time to time, until the white man has obtained, what he pretends to claim a legal ownership and possession of, almost the entire area of the United States. But one remarkable peculiarity in this whole affair is, that the Indians have retained small reservations here and there, in almost every state and territory in the Union. This had to be in order to fulfill prophecy, of which will be spoken further on.

The means employed, and the policy pursued by the whites, which induced the Indian to finally consent to sell his land, may be worthy of a passing notice.

Generally the purchases have been made after the whites have made encroachments upon the Indians' land, and made up their mind to have it at all hazard. These professed purchases have one feature about them differing from purchases made from other nations, in this, that the whites usually set their own price, and dictate the terms of sale, and influences are brought to bear that the Indian feels compelled to yield; but in several instances would not give possession until compelled to do so by force of arms.

In a word, they have been driven back, and from place to place, until they are reduced to a very small number, having but small reservations, altogether insufficient to furnish game for their support, and some of them are in an actual state of starvation. The whole country is filled with villages and cities from the Atlantic to the Pacific; and the entire land traversed by railroads from the north to the south, and from the east to the west, and the poor Indian, it is thought by some, will become exterminated.

Those who anticipate such a fate to befall the red man will be sadly disappointed; for a wonderful destiny yet awaits the Indian. He will become an important factor in the overthrow of this great and mighty nation.

There are many elements at work to bring about the destruction of our beloved country; among which are the many secret combinations and trusts which are forming all over our land. The intense feeling, and it may be said hatred, that is being engendered and cultivated, between the laboring classes and the capitalists of our country, are assuming dangerous proportions, although, at the present, there seems to be a lull in the storm. Possibly this apparent calm may be partially owing to the advice which appeared in the public prints some time since, advising the Brotherhood to keep quiet, and carefully refrain from any overt act for at least two years yet, but to continue their organizations, and increase their numbers as much as possible, so that when they do strike, it will be effectual.

The Return.

PUBLISHED MONTHLY AT $1,00 A YEAR.

Entered at the Post Office at Davis City, Iowa, as second class matter.

ITEMS OF PERSONAL HISTORY OF THE EDITOR.

No. 17.

Continued from page 316.

The question has frequently been asked, by virtue of what principle could Joseph Smith hold control over as many people as he did?

The answer, as I understand it, is briefly this: He was the instrument in the hands of the Lord, of translating the Book of Mormon, and introducing the fullness of the gospel of our Lord and Savior, Jesus Christ, in its simplicity and purity, which all the colleges of the universe never could have done. And when he, and Oliver Cowdery, (who had been ordained to the same priesthood, and invested with the same power and authority to administer the ordinances of the gospel equal with him,) began to administer the ordinances of that gospel, in meekness and humility before the Lord, the persons so administered to, received the gift and power of the Holy Ghost, by which they were enabled to enjoy and exercise the gifts and blessings of the gospel, promised by our Savior in the last chapter of Mark. These gifts and blessings were enjoyed in the church in an early day, to my certain knowledge,. And, thanks be to our heavenly Father, they continue with the faithful humble soul, to this day.

Persons receiving such precious heavenly blessings under the administration of Joseph Smith, very naturally looked upon him as more than an ordinary man; and when with him, felt they were in the presence of a superior personage. This feeling, instead of being checked, was intensified, when, on the occasion of the church of Christ being *legally* organized according to the *laws of the land*, a revelation was received through him, commanding the church to receive his word as from the *mouth of God*, as will be seen by the following extract: "For his word shall ye receive, as if from mine own mouth, in all patience and faith; for by doing these things the gates of hell shall not prevail against you." Under these circumstances, the feeling prevailed that his word should be received as law.

The Lord, evidently foreseeing this, had given him a solemn charge that whatever he should do should be done with an eye single to the glory of God, and not for any worldly gain or agrandizement. And that: "Although a man may have many revelations, and have power to do many mighty works, yet, if he boasts in his own strength, and sets at nought the counsels of God, and follows the dictates of his own will and carnal desires, he must fall and incur the vengeance of a just God upon him." — Doc. and Cov. 2:2.

Notwithstanding the strictness of the charge, and the wonderful admonition given above, the following quotations from his history partially show the manner in which he exercised the unbounded influence and control he had over the people, not only in spiritual but temporal matters.

EXTRACT FROM JOSEPH SMITH'S HISTORY.

"Sunday, Oct. 31st, 1841. Attended a Council with the Twelve Apostles. * *
I instructed the Council on many principles pertaing to the gathering

of the nations, the wickedness and downfall of this generation, &c.

After having received the following minutes—"A Conference was held at Kirtland, Ohio, Oct. 2, 1841. Almon W. Babbitt, President, and William W. Phelps, Clerk. Resolved, That Thomas Burdick, Bishop of Kirtland, and his Counsellors, be constituted a company to establish a press in Kirtland, and publish a religious paper, entitled *The Olive Leaf*, and that the Saints adjacent be solicited to carry the above resolution into effect"—my brother Hyrum wrote to the brethren in Kirtland, of which the following is an extract—

All the Saints that dwell in the land are commanded to come away, for this is "Thus saith the Lord;" therefore pay out no monies, nor properties for houses, nor lands in that country, for if you do you will lose them, for the time shall come, that you shall not possess them in peace, but shall be scourged with a sore scourge; yet your children may possess them, but not until many years shall pass away; and as to the organization of that Branch of the Church, it is not according to the spirit and will of God; and as to the designs of the leading members of that Branch relative to the printing press, and the ordaining of Elders, and sending out Elders to beg for the poor, are not according to the will of God; and in these things they shall not prosper, for they have neglected the House of the Lord, the baptismal font, in this place, wherein their dead may be redeemed, and the key of knowledge that unfolds the dispensation of the fulness of times may be turned, and the mysteries of God be unfolded, upon which their salvation, and the salvation of the world, and the redemption of their dead depends: for "Thus saith the Lord," "there shall not be a general assembly for a general Conference assembled together until the House of the Lord shall be finished, and the baptismal font, and if we are not dilligent the Church shall be rejected, and their dead also saith the Lord." Therefore, dear brethren, any proceedings otherwise than to put forth their hands with their might to do this work, is not according to the will of God, and shall not prosper; therefore, tarry not in any place whatever, but come forth unto this place from all the world, until it is filled up, and polished, and sanctified according to my word, saith the Lord. Come ye forth from the ends of the earth, that I may hide you from mine indignation that shall scourge the wicked, and then I will send forth and build up Kirtland, and it shall be polished and refined according to my word; therefore your doings and your organizations and designs in printing, or any of your Councils, are not of me, saith the Lord, even so. Amen.

HYRUM SMITH.
Patriarch for the whole Church.
—*Page 742, 18th Vol. Mil'n'l Star.*

The church at Kirtland obeyed the orders here given, thus entirely changing their temporal affairs. Although the letter was in Hyrum's name, the revelations were Joseph's.

(One of the charges against Oliver Cowdery in Far West, Mo. was, that he refused to be dictated to in his temporal business.)

In the following discourse, taken from Joseph Smith's history, are some most remarkable items of doctrine, which I never could endorse, but give them here that the reader may have a sample of the peculiar doctrine he began to introduce, and the dictatorial spirit manifested.

DISCOURSE BY JOSEPH SMITH.

"Sunday, November 7th. Elder William O. Clark preached about two hours, reproving the Saints for a lack of sanctity, and a want of holy living enjoining sanctity, solemnity, and temperance in the extreme, in the rigid sectarian style.

I reproved him as Pharisaical and hypocritical, and not edifying the people; and showed the Saints what temperance, faith, virtue, charity, and truth were. I charged the Saints not to follow the example of the adversary in accusing the brethren, and said, "If you do not accuse each other, God will not accuse you. If you have no accuser you will enter heaven, and if you will follow the revelations and instructions which God gives you through me, I will take you into heaven as my back load. If you will not accuse me, I will not accuse you. If you will throw a cloak of charity over my sins, I will over yours—for charity covereth a multitude of sins. What many people call sin is not sin; I do many things to break down superstition, and I will break it down;" I referred to the curse of Ham for laughing at Noah, while in his wine, but doing no harm. Noah was a righteous man, and yet he drank wine and became intoxicated; the Lord did not forsake him in consequence thereof, for he retained all the power of his Priesthood, and when he was accused by Cainaan, he cursed him by the Priesthood which he held, and the Lord had respect to his word, and the Priesthood which he held, notwithstanding he was drunk, and the curse remains upon the posterity of Cainaan until the present day." * * *

The foregoing, and kindred doctrine, coming from such a source, could not fail to bear evil fruit, as is evidenced by the subsequent course pursued by the church. It began to be frequently talked by the people, that what we formerly considered sin was not sin. This had a direct tendency to lower the standard of vital piety, which the masses of the people were endeavoring to maintain.

The temple revelation, and also Hyrum Smith's letter, speak of a baptismal font to be in the temple, in which to baptize for the dead. Therefore, before the temple was built, as soon as the basement walls were up, a baptismal font was made in the basement, and dedicated, as will be seen by the following quotation from the same history:

DEDICATION OF THE BAPT

"Monday, 8th. At fi m., I attended the dedi baptismal font in the L President Brigham spokesman.

The baptismal font is the centre of the baseme der the main hall of the is constructed of pine put together of staves grooved, oval shaped, long east and west, and wide, seven feet high fi dation, the basin four f moulding of the cap a formed of beautiful car antique style. The side with panel work. A fli in the north and south up and down into the b by side railing.

The font stands upon four on each side, and end, their head, should legs projecting out fro font; they are carved plank, glued together, after the most beautiful steer that could be f country, and they are striking likeness of the horns were geometricall ter the most perfect ho be procured.

The oxen and ornam ings of the font were c der Elijah Fordham, f of New York, which o months of time. The f closed by a temporary f sided up with split oa with a roof of the same was so low that the timb story were laid above i was supplied from a w deep in the east end of This font was built tisms for the dead unti should be finished, whe able one will supply its

While these things we in the church, I labored al ly, day and night, to ke

THE RETURN.

...e printing office, stereotype foundery and book bindery, in successful operation. Took a personal supervision of the Editorial, and each department of the business. Kept my own books. Knew from whence every shilling came, and where every dime was paid. Made up my own mail, and also attended a small stationery store, which I opened in the front room. To successfully accomplish all this labor, *twelve* and *one* o'clock at night often found me hard at work. The result was, success crowned my efforts.

I felt that the blessing of the Lord rested upon my labors, as I was endeavoring with all my heart, to try and help establish righteousness and truth in the earth, and at the same time build up a permanent business for myself and family, little dreaming what was in store for me.

It did not enter my mind for a single moment, that the brethren who were partaking freely of our hospitality, were becoming envious of my success, and coveting my business, but such seemed to be the case, as the sequel will show.

Brigham Young, President of the quorum of the twelve apostles, and Heber C. Kimball, also one of the twelve, used to come and spend a considerable time with me in the office. I enjoyed their visits, as I believed we were all laboring for the same great end, the building up the kingdom of God for the last time. I looked upon them as zealous, spiritually minded men, who had endured much privation and suffering for the gospel's sake, and could not realize that they would do the least thing that would militate to our injury. But one day in December, President Joseph Smith came to me and said he wished to give me a word of "warning." He said: "The twelve are wanting to get the *Times and Seasons* from you, and I thought I would tell you, for I am sorry to see any feelings of difference arise between you brethren who have borne the burthen in the heat of the day."

I confess I was astonished, as no one of the twelve, or any one else, had ever intimated such a thing to me before; I therefore took it as an act of kindness on the part of brother Joseph to give me the timely warning. I pondered it in my heart, but said nothing about it.

I now allude to another subject.
REVELATION TO NANCY MARINDA HYDE.

On the second of December President Joseph Smith received the following revelation, which is copied from his history, as found on page 805. of the 18th vol. Millenial Star. The revelation explains itself.

"Thursday, Dec. 2. I received the following revelation to Nancy Marinda Hyde—

Verily thus saith the Lord unto you my servant Joseph, that inasmuch as you have called upon me to know my will concerning my handmaid Nancy Marinda Hyde; behold it is my will that she should have a better place prepared for her, than that in which she now lives, in order that her life may be spared unto her; therefore go and say unto my servant Ebenezer Robinson, and to my handmaid his wife—Let them open their doors, and take her and her children into their house, and take care of them faithfully and kindly until my servant Orson Hyde returns from his mission, or until some other provisions can be made for her welfare and safety. Let them do these things and spare not, and I the Lord will bless them and heal them, if they do it not grudgingly, saith the Lord God; and she shall be a blessing unto them; and let my handmaid Nancy Marinda Hyde hearken to the council of my servant Joseph in all things whatsoever he shall teach unto her, and it shall be a blessing upon her and upon her children after her, unto her justification, saith the Lord."

On receiving the above revelation, President Smith came and delivered the message to me, which we readily and ungrudgingly, obeyed. I immediately harnessed my horse to the buggy, and brought sister Hyde and her two little daughters to our home, where they remained until the twelve took possesion of the printing office, which was brought to pass on this wise.

THE RETURN. 325

Friday, January 28th, 1842, being in President Smith's office, Brigham Young Heber C. Kimball, Willard Richards, William Clayton and W. W. Phelps, being present. President Smith gave the following revelation, as found in his history on pages 38 and 39 vol. 10, Mil. Star.

"I received the follwing revelation to the Twelve concerning the *Times and Seasons*, given January 28, 1842—

Verily thus saith the Lord unto you, my servant Joseph, go and say unto the Twelve, that it is my will to have them take in hand the editorial department of the *Times and Seasons*, according to that manifestation which shall be given unto them by the power of my Holy Spirit in the midst of their council, saith the Lord. Amen."

I was greatly surprised on hearing the foregoing revelation, after the warning he had given me, but knowing it was useless to demur, replied, that they could have the *Times and Seasons*, but they must take the *whole establishment*, including the stereotype foundery, bookbindery, and the whole book concern.

Brigham Young asked President Smith if they should take the whole establishment? President Smith droped his face in his hands for a short time, when he replied, "Yes;" whereupon W. W. Phelps said to me: "Go home and make out your invoice." Which I did.

TO BE CONTINUED.

---:o:---

ON A MISSION TO THE LAND OF MY FATHERS.

REV. ISAAC LEVINSHON IN "THE JEWISH HERALD."

DOTHAN AND ESDRAELON.

"Let us go to Dothan," said Joseph's brethren, was the report of the wayfaring man to the dreamer. "Let us go to Dothan," said I to Ibrahim, "and view well the country that so attracted the Hebrew shepherds as a suitable place to pasture their flocks." Our request was at once granted by the good-natured dragoman, who delighted to chat very freely, whilst pathetically reciting to us the beautiful story of *Genesis xvii.*

Here we met a splendid flock gently following their shepherd, and as he played on a musical reed we could perfectly imagine Jacob's sons leading their flocks over the same fields. And we also thought of the Good Shepherd leading His flocks in beautiful pastures. Every now and then our dragoman would please us by singing Sankey's well known hymn, "We are marching on with shield," etc. Our horses and mules having carried us so well, we dismounted and led our weary animals leisurely until we arrived at the

RUINS OF DOTHAN,

where we sat down for a short time and rested. Our most pleasant companion, the Bible, not only interested but charmed and refreshed our minds as we read the story of Elisha —how he was pursued by the army of the King of Syria. Very realistic to us was the story of the army of Ben-hadad suddenly becoming blind. "And it was told him, saying, Behold, he *is* in Dothan. Therefore sent he hither horses, and chariots, and a great host: and they came by night, and compassed the city about. . . . And his servant said unto him, Alas, my master! how shall we do? And he answered, Fear not: . . . . Elisha prayed unto the Lord, and said, smite this people, I pray Thee, with blindness. And He smote them with blindness according to the word of Elisha." (2 *Kings vi.*)

Having rested under the shadow of a beautiful grove of trees, we again took to our saddles and hastened onwards. We descended a rocky and somewhat unpleasant, slippery path, and passed through the famous territory of the old robbers, and were glad to learn that the country has thus far improved that the robbers are no longer there.

ness which will be enjoyed at that time. Reader, may we be worthy to enjoy it.

---:o:---

ITEMS OF PERSONAL HISTORY OF THE EDITOR.

No. 18.

Continued from page 325.

I took an invoice of the printing establishment, including the stereotype foundery, book bindery and building, which amounted to *six thousand six hundred dollars*, which they agreed to pay, and I made and executed a deed accordingly. But instead of the transaction being made with the Twelve alone, I find by reference to my account book, which I kept at the time, and which is now before me, that Joseph Smith's name stands as principal, as will appear by the following quotation from said account book.

"1842, Feb. 4. Joseph Smith, per W. Richards, Dr.
To printing office, stereotype foundery, book bindery, house and lot 50 by 58 feet on the corner of Water and Bain streets, $6,600,00
Contra, Cr.
Feb. 4. By deed of *three fourths* of lot 4 on Main street, $1,000,00
" " By this amount put to my credit on the book of the Law of the Lord, for the temple, 800,00
" " By cash, 200,00
" " By 2 shares stock in N. H. 100,00
" " By live stock delivered to Wm. Marks, 296,00
" 22. By this amount due him on settlement, 1,035,91
" 25, By cash per B. Young, 80,00
Ap'l 6. By assumption of debt due D. G. Luse. 330,00
Afterwards I find him credited with goods at his store to am't of 871,87

The remainder was paid in small payments from time to time.

Joseph Smith in his history, on page 86 in the 10th vol. Millennial Star, speaking on this subject, says:

"Friday, Feb. 4, [1842.] Closed stereotype foundery, by proxy, namely Willard Richards, cost between 7 and 8000 dollars, and in the evening attended a debate."

As before stated, the actual price was $6,600. Perhaps his proxy might have reported between 7 and 8000 dollars.

Willard Richards, one of the Twelve, was to be the business manager, and Joseph Smith's name was published as Editor of the *Times and Seasons*, notwithstanding the Twelve were instructed by revelation to "take in hand the editorial department" of that paper, which shows conclusively the light in which they held the divinity of that revelation. John Taylor and Willford Woodruff, both members of the quorum of the Twelve, assisted in the different departments.

The transfer was made in the dead of winter, and the day I gave the deed was required to give possession. My log cabin was occupied by my father-in-law, Asa works, sen., and family, and was altogether too small for both our families. I made faithful search for a vacant house or room to move into, but could find none. Just before night I notified Willard Richards that they would need to give me a little more time to find a place to move to. He replied, "you must get out to-night or I will put you *in the street*."

'Bro. Aaron Johnson, who lived next door, in a two story brick house with four rooms, two below and two above, the two front rooms being occupied by Agnes M. Smith, Don Carlos Smith's widow, and family, leaving but two rooms for the use of his own family, knowing the situation, let me move into the upper room in the back part of his house, which we moved into at sunset.

That evening Willard Richards nailed down the windows, and fired off his revolver in the street after dark, and commenced lying with Mrs. Nancy Marinda Hyde, in the rooms we had vacated in the printing office building, where they liv-

One of the hands in the printing office having just been married, another hand in the office wrote, and put in type, a notice of the event, in which he incorporated several printers' phrases in such a way as to render it very inappropriate for a religious paper. Neither the Editor or his assistants being printers, it escaped their notice. Not seeing the proof sheet, I did not see the article until the papers were printed. The appearance of that article called forth from President Joseph Smith, the following notice:

"*Times and Seasons*. This paper commences my editorial career: I alone stand responsible for it, and shall do for all papers having my signature henceforward. I am not responsible for the publication or arrangement of the former paper; the matter did not come under my supervision. JOSEPH SMITH."

Thus Joseph Smith was the purchaser, and editor. Soon after this he took the benefit of the bankrupt law.

I have heretofore stated that Joseph Smith united with the Free Masons, but did not give the date, not having it before me at the time, but will give it here as copied from his history.

"Tuesday, 15th of March, 1842.

I officiated as grand chaplain at the installation of the Nauvoo lodge of Free Masons, at the Grove near the Temple. Grand Master Jonas of Columbus being present, a large number of people assembled on the occasion; the day was exceedingly fine, all things done in order, and universal satisfaction manifested. In the evening I received the first degree in Free Masonry in the Nauvoo Lodge assembled in my general business office."

"Wednesday, 16th. I was with the Masonic Lodge, and rose to the sublime degree."—Mil. Star, page 152, also 211.

The doctrine of spiritual wives was talked more freely in private circles, and Joseph Smith began to preach about keys are certain signs and words by which false spirits and personages may be detected from true, which cannot be revealed to the Elders till the Temple is completed. The rich can only get them in the Temple, the poor may get them on the mountain top as did Moses. The rich cannot be saved without charity, giving to feed the poor when and how God requires, as well as building. There are signs in heaven, earth, and hell; the Elders must know them all, to be endowed with power, to finish their work and prevent imposition. The devil knows many signs, but does not know the sign of the Son of Man, or Jesus. No one can truly say he knows God until he has handled something, and this can only be done in the Holiest of Holies."—Mil. Star, page 390.

This discourse was evidently given to help prepare the minds of the public for the introduction of the ceremony had in the secret chambers, where the signs and key words would be revealed to the Elders, although he said they "cannot be revealed till the temple is completed;" but we find *he could not wait*, for the very next Wednesday he commenced to reveal them to a chosen few, as will be seen by the following quotation from his history.

"Wednesday, 4th. I spent the day in the upper part of the Store, that is, in my private office (so called, because in that room I kept my sacred writings, translated ancient records, and received revelations) and in my general business office, or lodge room (that is, where the masonic fraternity met occasionally, for want of a better place) in council with General James Adams of Springfield, Patriarch Hyrum Smith, Bishops Newel K. Whitney, and George Miller, and Presidents Brigham Young, Heber C. Kimball, and

on to the highest order of Melchisedec Priesthood, setting forth the order pertaining to the Ancient of Days, and all those plans and principles by which any one is enabled to secure the fulness of those blessings which have been prepared for the Church of the First Born, and come up and abide in the presence of the Eloheim in the eternal worlds. In this Council was instituted the ancient order of things for the first time in these last days."—Mil. Star, page 391.

Here was instituted, undoubtedly the order of things which represented the scenes in the Garden of Eden, which was called in Nauvoo, the "Holy Order," a secret organization. The terrible oaths and covenants taken by those who entered there were known only to those who took them, as one of the members said to me, "I could tell you many things, but if I should, my life would pay the forfeiture."

In the spring built a small brick house on my own lot, into which we moved.

TO BE CONTINUED.

COMMUNICATIONS.

MODERN REVELATIONS.

EDITOR RETURN;

Dear Brother: I noticed in an issue of your paper the publication of the *Salem Revelation*, given Aug. 6, 1836.

It seems to me that anyone who reads that document carefully will notice the avarice and greed that inspired it, and unless the individual is steeped in bigotry and superstition, must also see that to prefix the name of the Lord God, to such a production, is but a travesty on divine revelation, a sacrilege against God! Yet Joseph Smith the "Choice Seer"

...act of the Legislature of Ohio. But not to be outdone by any state legislature on earth these men of God, "Choice Seer" included, come together and "annul the old constitution," and make a new one whereby the name of the institution is changed from "Kirtland Safety Society," to "Kirtland Safety Society Anti Banking Company." Just so, the law of "enlargement" here appears so beautiful. But to make the matter binding upon the minds of the poor honest saints the "Choice Seer" writes, "It is wisdom, and according to the mind of the Holy Spirit, that you should call at Kirtland and receive counsel and instruction upon those principles that are necessary to further the great work of the Lord etc; and further we invite the brethren from abroad, to call on us and take stock in our "Safety Society," and we would remind them also of the saying of Isaiah, contained in the 60th chapter, and more particularly the 9th and 17th verses, which are as follows: "Surely the isles shall wait for me, and the ships of Tarshish first, and to bring thy sons from far, their silver and their gold [not their bank notes,] with them, unto the name of the Lord thy God and to the Holy one of Israel, because he hath glorified thee."

A more contemptible perversion of scripture could scarcely be made. Here the "Choice Seer" injects the words ("not their bank notes") into the text, and by his willful perversions seeks to give life and beauty to an illegitimate child the "Kirtland Safety Society etc.," and seeks to make the faithful saints believe that it is the mind of the Holy Spirit that they should come with their "silver and their gold" and "take stock" in a *bastard* institution, one

guilty of such conduct, guilty of such *revealments*, Latter Day Saints everywhere would denounce him as an "impostor" and a "religious fraud!" This "Safety Society," issued bank notes, received money on deposit and did a *banking* business, while in *fact* according to their own constitution they were an "*anti Banking company*," and yet Joseph Smith and Sidney Rigdon, two chief captains of the bank and *exofficios* of the *Kingdom*, would prattle about "whoso keepeth the laws of God hath no need to break the laws of the land."

About June 30th, 1837, we find in Joseph's history the statement that, "sometime previous to this I resigned my office in the "Kirtland Safety Society," disposed of my interest therein, and withdrew from the institution; being fully aware, after so long an experiment, that no institution of the kind, established upon just and righteous principles, for a blessing not only to the Church, but the whole nation, would be suffered to continue its operations in such an age of darkness, speculation, and wickedness." Well, this is delightful—the "Choice Seer" running a bank, that is not a bank, but an "anti bank," and that too *without* a *charter*, therefore *unlawful*, yet claiming that he withdrew because his institution based upon "righteous principles" could not "continue its operations in such an age of darkness, speculation and wickedness!" And to add insult to injury, the "nation" whom this bankless bank without a charter or scarcely a dollar in cash, was intended to "bless" did not, and would not accept the "blessing" (?) Oh what ingratitude! that the state of Ohio *refused* to give foul business for folks less divine."

Again, just prior to the *Salem* business, i. e. on Feb. 14, 1835, Joseph Smith, called a meeting at Kirtland, Ohio, of those who had journeyed to Zion, and stated the meeting was called "because God had commanded it." Of those who had gone up to Zion &c. he said: "God had not designed all this for nothing, but he had it in rememberance yet; and those who went to Zion with a determination to lay down their lives, if necessary, it was the will of God that they should be ordained to the ministry, and go forth to prune the vineyard for the last time, or the coming of the Lord, which was nigh—even fifty-six years should wind up the scene."

From the foregoing it follows, 1st, that they who were willing to lay down their lives for Zion were the chosen. 2nd. They were to be ordained to the ministry of pruning the vineyard. 3rd. This "pruning the vineyard" was "for the last time" and the 'coming of the Lord' is here definitely fixed at *fifty-six years*, which brings it to Feb. 14, 1891. Less than a year remains for the fulfillment of this prediction, and many who read these lines will doubtless live to test the truth or falsity of the same. If Christ does not come at the time designated by the "Choice Seer," then he must go upon the record as a false prophet, like all others who have undertaken to tell the *time* of our Lord's coming.

Wm. Miller, *et al*, have tried it and failed; The Mother Shipton alleged prophecy fixed it thus—"In 1881, the world unto its end will come." But according to Joseph Smith, she missed it just ten years, being too previous.

The Return

PUBLISHED MONTHLY AT $1.00 A YEAR.

Entered at the Post Office at Davis City, Iowa, as second class matter.

DEATH—RESURRECTION.

The doctrine of the resurrection of the dead is one that is calculated to inspire with gratitude, and fill the heart of the child of God with joy and gladness. All living, both saint and sinner, are alike interested, as the resurrection will pass upon all.

"For as in Adam all die, even so in Christ shall all be made alive. But every man in his own order; Christ the first fruits; afterwards they that are Christ's at his coming."—1st Cor. 15:22,23.

It requires no argument to prove that we are all subject to death; but to have a just conception of our condition after death, is what fills the mind with anxiety.

"Secret things belong to the Lord our God; but those things which are revealed belong to us and to our children forever."—Deut. 29:29.

I feel exceeding thankful that sufficient has been revealed to give us a very clear conception of the condition of the spirit of man after it passes from the body after death.

"Then shall the dust return to the earth as it was: and the spirit shall return unto God who gave it."—Eccl. 12:7.

The edict had gone forth in the beginning with regard to the body of man:

"For dust thou art and unto dust shalt thou return,"—Gen. 3:19.

By these scriptures we learn the body of man at death goes back to its mother earth, and the spirit goes to God who gave it. For these revelations I am thankful.

Now if we can discern as clearly what disposition is made of the spirit of man after it returns to God who gave it, then we will have double reason to be thankful. To my mind it is very clear. They are evidently classified into at least two classes. The righteous are permitted to enter into a place of rest, a place of comfort and peace, which our Savior calls in one place, "Abraham's bosom." But the wicked have their portion appointed with the hypocrites, in a place of unrest, a place of torment, "where there is weeping and gnashing of teeth."—Mat. 24:51.

Our Savior, in the parable of the rich man and Lazarus, gives us a very clear delineation of the condition of the spirits of the two classes, the righteous and the wicked after death. Let no one say that because it was a parable it is not to be taken as real. Jesus dealt in stern realities. His teachings presented great and mighty truths, which are not to be trifled with by the children of men. He gave us the words of his Father; therefore when we are reading his words we should remember we are reading the words of our heavenly Father, who is full of grace and truth. Jesus says, speaking to his Father: "Thy word is truth."—John 17:17.

PARABLE OF THE RICH MAN AND LAZARUS.

"There was a certain rich man, which was clothed in purple and fine linen, and fared sumptuously every day. And there was a certain beggar named Lazarus, which was laid at his gate, full of sores, and desiring to be fed with the crumbs which fell from the rich man's table: moreover the dogs came and licked his sores. And it came to pass,

...g ready for the conflict. Every ...e the shrill whistle of these locomotives is heard on the plains of Palestine, let the gentile nations take warning, for the time of their utter overthrow draws near.

---:o:---

INDIAN EXCITEMENT.

From what I can gather from the various newspaper reports respecting the excitement among the Indians, I am inclined to look upon it as a false claim.

Whether false or true, there certainly exists a very great and wide spread excitement among them, but it does not seem to be universal. According to recent accounts the Sioux seem to be about equally divided between those who believe in the immediate coming of their Messiah, and those who disbelieve it. But those who profess to believe it seem to be terribly in earnest, and may commit some depredations, perhaps before these lines are printed, but I believe they will be subdued, so that practically it will undoubtedly serve to allay the fears of the whites when the fatal time does come.

---:o:---

Sitting Bull's new Messiah.

The report of Indian Agent James McLaughlin recently made to the department of the interior has attracted unusual attention from the fact that it gives authentic facts about what is known as the "Indian Millennium craze." Great excitement, the report says, has for some time prevailed among certain of the Sioux Indians. They look for the coming of a Messiah for the Indian. He is to appear next spring when the grass begins to grow. He is to be a mighty Messiah and all the whites are to be annihilated. The Indians are to be restored to their hunting grounds and the world is to be improved backward at a rapid rate. Sitting Bull, the toughest old Indian in the whole country, seems to be high priest and great apostle of the craze.—*State Register. Nov. 6.*

---o---

ITEMS OF PERSONAL HISTORY OF THE EDITOR.

No. 19.

Continued from page 348.

DR. JOHN C. BENNETT ATTEMPTS SUICIDE.

ELDER ORSON PRATT TEMPORARILY INSANE.

President Joseph Smith in his history, says a letter was received, soon after Dr. John C. Bennett came to Nauvoo, stating that he was a married man, and had a wife and children in Ohio, whereas he represented himself as a single man, but this letter was kept secret, Joseph says, thinking perhaps it was dictated by a spirit of persecution because Dr. Bennett had joined the church, therefore they kept the letter from him, but preserved it for future use if necessary. The public community did not know of its existence.

In the spring of 1841 Dr. Bennett had a small neat house built for Elder Orson Pratt's family, and commenced boarding with them. Elder Pratt was absent on a mission to England.

Sometime after this, Presidents Hyrum Smith and William Law went on a mission to the eastern states. (William Law was one of the three first Presidents of the church.) When passing through Ohio, a gentleman told them Dr. Bennett had a wife and children living, but she left him because of his adulterous practices. They wrote a letter to Joseph Smith giving him this statement, which letter, Joseph says in his history, was shown to Dr. Bennett, when he confessed he had a wife and children living.

Soon after this Dr. Bennett made an attempt to commit suicide by taking poison. It required quite an effort on the part of the physicians to save his life, as he strenuously resisted their efforts to save him.

When Elder Pratt returned home from his mission, and learned of the secret teachings of the spiritual wife—doctrine, and the true situation of things, it was too much for him, and his mind temporarily gave way, and he wandered away no one knew where. I remember well the excitement which existed at the time, as a large number of the citizens turned out to go in search for him, fearing lest he had committed suicide. He was found some 5 miles below Nauvoo, setting on a rock, on the bank of the Mississippi river, without a hat. He recovered from his insanity, but at the next conference, when the vote was called to sustain Joseph Smith as President of the church, he alone voted, No. He could not at that time conscienciously sustain him in that position.

In the spring of 1842, Dr. John C. Bennett having been detected in very immoral conduct, public sentiment and feeling bore down so heavily upon him, that on the 19th day of May he resigned the office of Mayor of Nauvoo, and on the 25th he was notified that "the First Presidency, Twelve, and Bishops, had withdrawn fellowship from him." Also on the 16th of June notice was given that he was expelled from the Masonic lodge of Nauvoo, and on the 30th cashiered by the Legion. Not long after this he left Nauvoo and commenced publishing against the church.

On the 7th of May there was a grand parade and sham battle fought by the Nauvoo Legion, which was witnessed by Judge Stephen A. Douglass with several prominent lawyers, and a large concourse of citizens. At the close of the parade, Lieutenant General Joseph Smith delivered an animating address, in which he remarked "that his soul was never better satisfied than on this occasion." He had a sumptious dinner prepared, of which the consolidated staff of the Legion, with their ladies, and the distinguished guests partook.

On the 14th of May, it was reported in Nauvoo, "that Ex-Gov. Boggs of Missouri had been shot." And on "the 15th the report was confirmed, and mentioned on the stand." See Joseph Smith's history, in 19th vol. Mil. Star, page 408.

Bennett's disaffection, and his desperate effort to create a feeling and excitement against the church, taken together with the Bogg's affair, caused quite a feeling of apprehension with the citizens of Nauvoo.

On the 8th of August, Joseph Smith was arrested as accessorary before the fact, and O. P. Rockwell as principal, in the Bogg's shooting affair, when the Municipal court of Nauvoo, issued a writ of Habeas Corpus, and the sheriff left them in charge of the city marshall, without leaving the original writ, without which they could not be legally held, therefore they went about their business. But as a re-arrest might be made, it was thought advisable for Joseph Smith to leave the city, or secrete himself for a season, which he did until the 29th day of August, when he came upon the stand and addressed the audience which had assembled as a special conference, because of the emergency of the occasion. From this address I take the following extract:

JOSEPH SMITH'S ADDRESS.

"I had been in Nauvoo all the while, and outwitted Bennett's associates, and attended to my own business in the city all the time. We want to whip the world mentally, and they will whip themselves physically. The brethren cannot have the tricks played upon them that were done at Kirtland and Far West. They have seen enough of the tricks of their enemies, and know better. Orson Pratt has attempted to destroy himself, and caused almost all the city to go in search of him. Is it not enough to put down all the infernal influences of the Devil, what we have felt and seen, handled and evidenced, of this work of God? But the Devil had influence among the Jews, after all the great things they had witnessed, to cause the death of Jesus Christ, by hanging him between heaven and earth. They would deliver me up, Judas like; but a small band of us shall overcome.

We don't want or mean to fight with the sword of the flesh, but we will fight with the broad sword of the Spirit. Our enemies say our Charter and writs of Habeas Corpus are worth nothing. We say they came from the highest authority in the State, and we will hold to them. They cannot be disannuled or taken away.

port the character of the Prophet, the Lord's anointed; and if all who go will support my character, I prophesy in the name of the Lord Jesus, whose servant I am, that you will prosper in your missions. <u>I have the whole plan of the kingdom before me, and no other person has. As to all that Orson Pratt, Sidney Rigdon or George W. Robinson can do to prevent me, I can kick them off my heels as many as you can name; I know what will become of them.</u> I concluded my remarks by saying I have the best of feelings towards my brethren, since this trouble begun; but to the apostates and enemies, <u>I will give a lashing every opportunity, and I will curse them.</u>"—Mil. Star. vol. 19, page 775.

This address speaks for itself.

The masses of the people did not know what was passing in the secret chambers. They were a faithful, industrious people, who gathered to Nauvoo, in obedience to the command of the Lord, as they believed, and came with the firm conviction they were "gathering home to Zion," as the elders taught them when they embraced the faith. <u>If they had been told, at the time many things took place, spoken of in Joseph Smith's history, I am sure they would not have believed such a state of things existed.</u> They looked upon him as the mouth piece of the Lord, and all persons who presumed to speak against him or his teachings were called apostates, and treated as such.

TO BE CONTINUED.

COMMUNICATIONS.

Magnolia, Iowa, October 12, 1890.

EDITOR RETURN, *Dear Sir:*—I enclose you some verses written by Mrs. Elmira M. Streeter, (an old time Latter Day Saint,) on the death of her sister Lucinda. She asked me to right them up a little and send them to the Herald or Return. As I wished to write you a few lines any way, I send them to you; but knowing that poor rhymes nearly amount to a nuisance some-

ket.

I enclose $1 to pay for the RETURN in advance for the year 1891.

Now about something else:—I have a copy of two letters never in print, written by W. E. McLellen in 1877 from Independence, Mo., to my brother-in-law, Mr. Thomas Fuller, of Chester Center, Poweshiek Co., Ia. These letters give something of a history of his connection with Mormonism, and give some of his reasons for believing the Book of Mormon true, and give some account of the driving from Jackson Co., and from Mo., also give some things of interest concerning the doings of the church leaders. For instance he says:—"<u>I found that Smith did not always tell the truth.</u> He would drink to excess. He and others of the Presidency went to New York and *run* in debt Forty thousand dollars, (which was never paid.) The leading men went into pride, fine dress for themselves and their women. Took expensive rides, costing them hundreds of dollars, while the poor among them were suffering for the necessaries of life. <u>He materially altered his own revelations before they were ever printed.</u>"

I also have a copy of an "Epistle" of Wm. Marks dated June 15, 1853, which, though it was printed in the July No. of Charles B. Thompson's "Zion's Harbinger and Baneemy's Organ" for that year, you may never have seen. <u>This "Epistle" gives a history of his connection with the old church, and also gives a more particular account of the same things touching Joseph and polygamy that he relates in his letter written six years later, and published in the first No. of the Saint's Herald.</u> It also tells some of the questionable doings of the leaders. For instance he says:—"<u>I was also witness of the introduction (secretly) of a kingly</u>

Since you started the RETURN, I have been thinking of placing copies of these letters in your hands, that perhaps they might be of use to you. But I have been led to use and embody them in a long article of over a hundred pages of manuscript on the subject of "The Heresies in Mormonism—Who is Responsible for Them?" (The article being an enlargement of a long letter that I wrote some months ago to ―――― ――――. He requested that I would not send these things to any other publisher until he and I should have some correspondence in regard to them. Since then I have not heard from him, but have been employing some of my spare moments (which have been few) in rewriting and enlarging on the theme that I had taken in hand. The writing begins with Wm. Marks' Epistle and ends with the McLellin letters.

The tone and spirit in which the manuscript is written, is hardly in accord with the love and patience manifested in the RETURN, in dealing with the errors and misdeeds of others; for I have while writing, felt much indignation over the way the honest, faithful and too trusting and confiding saints,—who believed they were divinely commanded to take and obey the words and commandments of Joseph Smith, and consequently of those on whom his mouth of authority was supposed to have fallen, as from God's own mouth, have been treated by their leaders; being led into the darkest and grossest errors and doctrines of any priest-ridden paganism that has ever cursed the earth since the first murderer, Cain, entered into Gadianton robber and Masonic-like league with the devil and slew the first (Irad) "For the oath's sake;" (*Gen. 5:36,) and being ground down financially and held in poverty, to build costly all borrowed from masonry and its founder the devil—"For he is the foundation of all these things."—2nd Nephi 11:14, Book of Mormon.) to bind the saints fast, body and soul, in the most abject and servile bondage, to a corrupt and depraved Priesthood, more ambitious for the material power and gain and pleasure of the present world than for the spiritual and eternal good of the laity or the honor and service of God. Yours respectfully,

CHAS. W. LAMB,
Magnolia, Iowa.

* Inspired translation.

MISCELLANEOUS.

JEWS.

The New York "Evangelist" says: "It may be said that there is still another factor in this interesting problem of the future—the Jews. The ruthless expulsion of them by Russia and several other countries of Europe is accelerating their return, to some extent, to Palestine, despite Mohamedan jealousy. We should hope that England and the Protestant world generally would not remain silent should Russia some day undertake to repeat her outrages against them in the land of their fathers. The strategic advantages of Palestine make it a coveted country now, as of old. Thus the possession of Palestine is emerging as one of the questions of the near future."

Thus it may be seen, that the thoughts of men are already comprehending the possibility of a great struggle for the possession of Palestine. Russia's cruelty combined with the loved and revered traditions of their race, is taking Jews to Palestine by thousands. England and

The Return.

PUBLISHED MONTHLY AT $1,00 A YEAR.

Entered at the Post Office at Davis City, Iowa, as second class matter.

DEATH—RESURRECTION.

Continued from pag. 340.

In the former article it was shown that at death the spirit of man goes to God who gave it, and the body returns to dust from whence it came; and that the spirit, the inner man, which goes to God who gave it, is in a conscious state, and will here say, each retain their identity, else the rich man would not have known Lazarus when he saw him "afar off."

It was also shown from the old testament scriptures, that the dead would be resurrected, and their bodies brought forth and redeemed from the grave.

Also, from the new testament it was clearly shown that Christ was the first fruits of the resurrection, and that he came forth from the tomb with his body composed of flesh and bones, but not flesh and blood. His blood, which is the natural life of man, had been shed and withdrawn when upon the cross, until, from the wound of the spear there came forth blood and water; and with that body he went to heaven in the sight of his disciples, and Stephen testified he saw him standing at the right hand of God.

It was also shown that when the saints come forth they will be like him, thus fully establishing the truth that flesh and bones will inherit the kingdom of God, while flesh and blood cannot.

It will now be shown from the new testament scriptures, that the dead will be raised, and the power by which this great work is accomplished. Jesus says

"For as the Father hath life in himself, so hath he given to the Son to have life in himself. And hath given him authority to execute judgment also, because he is the Son of man. Marvel not at this; for the hour is coming, in the which all that are in the graves shall hear his voice, And shall come forth; they that have done good, unto the resurrection of life; and they that have done evil, unto the resurrection of damnation."—John 5:26-29.

Here we have revealed unto us the true source of all life, and from whence sprang all animate existance. That "as the Father had life in himself" so also he gave unto the Son to have life in himself, and that by him and through him and for him were all things created and made.

With this great truth revealed unto us, we have a perfect assurance that the same creative power can re-create our bodies from the dust of the earth, and bring them together from the elements into which they dissolve after death, and bring them forth in a glorified form, freed from blood, but the place thereof supplied by the quickening, everliving principle and presence of the Spirit of God, which spirit of life never tasted death, or ever slumbered or slept.

Jesus also says: "Marvel not at this, for the hour is coming in the which all that are in the graves shall hear his voice, and shall come forth; they that have done good, unto the resurrection of life and they that have done evil, unto the resurrection of damnation."

Here we have the two classes clearly set forth, and, that too by him who will bring to pass the resurrection by virtue of the power and authority conferred upon him by the Father, and who will also be the Judge before whom all men will

carried over 450 miles, whereas now letters weighing one ounce are carried to any part of the United States and Canada for two cents.

The P. O. Money order system has attained such perfection that money in sums from 1 cent to $100, can be sent to any part of the world with perfect safety, and its annual business amounts to nearly $250,000,000.

The postal establishment of the United States has arisen from a condition of insignificance to the largest of all the nations of the world. Instead of one little room, which, in 1789, was sufficient to accommodate the entire central force of the post-office department, a building four stories high, and covering an entire block in Washington, is now inadequate to say nothing of the great postoffice structures all over the land. Instead of the postboy on his lazy horse, coming and going at will between straggling villages along a single line of post-routes, with here and there a diversion to a cross road, as was the way in Osgood's time, the mails are now transported almost with the speed of thought, according to fixed schedules of arrival and departure, over such innumerable routes as to make their aggregate journeys every working day, equivalent to forty-one times the circuit of the earth. From a total business of perhaps a thousand letters a day, which is but a trifle less than the estimate of the post master general in 1789, letters and other pieces of mail matter are steadily dropping into the numberless receptacles of the postal system at the rate of nearly 8,000 a minute. This marvelous system employs more than 150,000 agents.

☞ We respectfully request our friends to make an effort to not only get new subscribers, but also to secure subscribers for as many sets of the back numbers as they can, as each set disposed of will not only increase the circulation, but also aid in defraying the cost of the future numbers of THE RETURN.

ITEMS OF PERSONAL HISTORY OF THE EDITOR.

No. 20.

Continued from page 304.

As stated in my last No. of Personal History, the masses of the people in Nauvoo were honest, faithful and industrious; very zealous in their religious devotions; anxiously laboring for the up-building of the principles of truth and righteousness, in view of the permanent establishing of the Zion of our God; firmly believing that Nauvoo was to be the corner stone thereof, as set forth in what is called the "temple revelation," given by Joseph Smith on Jan. 19, 1841. See 107, Doc. and Cov., Plano edition:

In addition to the regular Sunday meetings, prayer meetings were held on week day evenings, at which the gifts of the gospel were enjoyed and exercised by different members of the church. I attended these meetings.

Several of these prayer meetings were held at Brother Sessions, at one of which sister Sessions spake in tongues, in which she very feelingly warned the sisters to beware lest they be overtaken in sin, as a spirit of adultery would be poured out upon the people.

Soon after this the brethren and sisters who attended these meetings, were notified to desist from speaking in tongues, for soon the sisters would get to commanding the elders. This had the desired effect, and the exercise of the gift of tongues ceased for a time.

The work on the temple was pushed forward as fast as possible, so as to have it finished within the appointed time according to the revelation heretofore referred to.

The brethren seemed to vie with each other in their diligence in the labor upon it, as many of them felt that it was more than a matter of life and death, for if they failed to have the work accomplished by the time appointed, they lost not only their own soul's salvation, but also that of their dead friends for whom they had been baptized; as it is positively stat-

ell in the revelation that if the work was not completed within the time appointed, "the church should be *rejected with their dead.*"

I confess that was too strong meat for me. I could not believe our heavenly Father would make our dead friends responsible for the performance, or non performance of any duty assigned the living. If our being baptized for them did them any good whatever, that good was permanent as I believed. Neither could I believe he would reject the innocent for the acts of the guilty, therefore I came to the conclusion that the Lord did not give that revelation.

When speaking of that revelation on one occasion, since I united with the Reorganized church, in conversation with elder Zenas H. Gurley, Sen. I told him I did not believe it. His reply was: "*Don't tell it.*" But I have repeatedly told it, as it was, and is the settled conviction of my mind.

Notwithstanding Bishops had been appointed by revelation, whose duty it was to receive and handle all the church property, look after the poor, etc. And notwithstanding the Lord told Joseph in July, 1839, (D. C. 20:4,) that "in temporal labors thou *shalt not have strength*, for this is not thy calling," yet he set at nought the counsel of the Lord, and in addition to his other temporal business had himself appointed "sole Trustee in Trust for the whole church," which placed in his hands, and gave him full and entire control of *all* the properties of the church, of which mention may be made more fully hereafter.

In addition to his office of Trustee in Trust, Editor of the *Times and Seasons*, and all the other varied business relations with which he was connected, on the 5th of March, 1842, he was appointed Registrar of Deeds for the city of Nauvoo, as will appear by the following quo-

Deeds for Nauvoo, and *prophesied* in the name of the Lord God, that Judge Douglas, and no other Judge of the Circuit Court, will ever set aside a law of the City Council establishing a registry of Deeds in the City of Nauvoo."—Mil. Star, Vol. 19, page 87.

"Saturday, March 5th. Attended the City Council, and spoke at considerable length on the powers and privileges of our City Charter; among other business of importance, the Office of Registrar of Deeds was established in the City of Nauvoo, and I was chosen Registrar by the City Council."—Mil. Star, Vol. 19, page 135.

This office of Registrar of Deeds for the City of Nauvoo, proved a mistake, as I have been credibly informed the courts did not recognize those records, as the statute of Illinois provides only for a Registrar of Deeds for each county in the state, and not for cities. Thus that prophecy failed.

In addition to the small brick house which I had built for our residence, also had a brick row of eleven tenements built, the rents from which helped liquidate my indebtedness, and also assist in meeting current expenses.

In 1841 I was elected a justice of the peace; and also appointed and commissioned by Gov. Carlin, a Notary Public. The duties of said offices I endeavored to fill to the best of my ability.

To be continued.

Macedonian Cry.

The following letters are inserted that our readers may know the state of feeling that is steadily obtaining among the careful, prayerful, considerate people, who feel that their own souls' interest is

THE RETURN.

"Truth, crushed to earth, shall rise again; The eternal years of God are hers."

Vol. 3. No. 1.   DAVIS CITY, IOWA, JANUARY, 1891.   Whole No. 25.

The Return.

PUBLISHED MONTHLY AT $1.00 A YEAR.

Entered at the Post Office at Davis City, Iowa, as second class matter.

SECRET SOCIETIES.

ARE NOT FROM THE LORD.

By Chas. W. Lanb.

Number 1.

"Truth crushed to earth shall rise again; The eternal years of God are hers."

EDITOR RETURN—*Dear Sir:* I see that the above is the motto of THE RETURN. It is a good one; for "Truth is mighty and will prevail," and is therefore the safest to tie to. and THE RETURN has been true to its motto. It has been trying to point to the truth in doctrine and practice as found in the gospel, and according to "the former covenant, even the Book of Mormon;" for a departure from which the whole church came under condemnation. Yes, laboring in the good work of clearing out the safe paths of peace—the good old way of light and truth; and endeavoring to revive and restore the true doctrines of Christ, by sweeping out the rubbish, and brushing down the cobwebs of fiction, and sifting out the false doctrines and abominable and ruinous heresies, that, like a fungus growth, have attached themselves to the truth, thus lifting the crushing weight that has been hung to the neck of truth, like a mill stone, by priestcraft, and assisting it to rise.

In order to do this, it has been necessary to show how, when and where, and by whom and what means the heresies in Mormonism were brought in. For that heresies have been added to the true doctrine of the church, is a fact admitted by many.

This work of clearing away the rubbish from the old foundation, and showing how, and by whom the evils were brought into original Mormonism—and, remember that all that does not agree with the Book of Mormon, is not truly Mormonism —has been a disagreeable, but necessary work. For the false was brought in "privily," as Paul says, and the effort was made to engraft it into the true with as much plausible sophistry and consumate cunning as was ever exhibited by crafty priests in any age of the world.

THE RETURN has been true to its motto, by bringing to light and recording truths and facts that some have sought to suppress. To obstruct truth, and to seek to make that which is evil and false in character or principle appear good and true, is the part of all that is sinful and satanical. Much of the warfare between light and darkness has always been on this ground. For there has always been a desperate effort made by all evil powers, associations, and individuals to hide from investigation behind falsehood, and to suppress the truth. For truth and investigation would drag to the light things distateful, and before which they might not be able to stand; for the latter would tear off their cloak of false colors and false claims, and show them up in their true color and native meanness.

Satan, early in the world's history, originated oath-bound secret socie-

Their visit was the first knowledge Elder Rigdon ever had of the Book of Mormon. The copy they took was the first he had ever seen of that sacred record. Elder Rigdon was then living in Mentor, about two miles from Kirtland, (near the place General Garfield afterwards resided.) He had charge of an interesting congregation of disciples or Campbellites. He kindly let the brethren have the use of his church to hold meetings in, and informed them he "would read the book of Mormon, give it a full investigation, and then frankly tell them his mind and feelings on the subject."

After two weeks of careful and prayerful examination of the book, "he was fully convinced of the truth of the work, by a revelation from Jesus Christ, which was made known to him in a remarkable manner, so that he could exclaim, "flesh and blood hath not revealed it unto me, but my Father which is in heaven.".

The result was, himself and wife and about twenty others of his church embraced the faith.

TO BE CONTINUED.

ITEMS OF PERSONAL HISTORY OF THE EDITOR.

No. 21.

Continued from page 13.

Inasmuch as we are not our own keepers, and our heavenly Father has so wisely hid from us the time of our departure, and my present feebleness of health admonishes me that it is wise to hasten with the personal history, noticing only some of the leading events, leaving many items to be noticed, should my life and health be spared, and feel it to be my duty to do so, hereafter.

From what has been stated heretofore it is to be seen that great effort was made to counteract the influence that was brought to bear against the church through the disaffection of Dr. J. C. Bennett.

In October, 1842, a statement was written out, and signed by a large number of the brethren and sisters, including myself and wife, setting forth the fact that we knew of no other form of marriage ceremony in the church except the one published in the book of Doctrine and Covenants, which statement was true at *that time*, as we had no *knowledge* of such a ceremony, or that "spiritual wifery," or "polygamy," was taught by the *heads* of the church, as *they* had not up to that time taught it to us.

We knew it was talked of in secret, and had been for more than a year, as I have heretofore stated, that Don Carlos Smith, in his life time, in June, 1841, had said to me, that "Any man who will teach and practice 'spiritual wifery' will go to hell, no matter if it is my brother Joseph."

These secret rumors could not constitute a knowledge that certain persons taught such things when they had not taught them to us.

Dr. Bennett had published the statement that Joseph Smith taught the doctrine of "Spiritual wifery," and had instituted a certain marriage ceremony connected therewith, of which we had no knowledge, and the certificate was given to counteract Bennett's statement.

Remember this was in October, 1842. In December, 1843, more than a year later, Hyrum Smith, one of the first Presidents, and also Partriarch of the church, came to my house in Nauvoo, and taught the doctrine of "spiritual wifery," (which I here say, is polygamy,) to myself and wife, which, we both certified to in her life time, which certificate has already been published to the world. Therefore, those who have made the statement that this last certificate of ours contradicts the first, make a great mistake, as the last certificate speaks of what Hyrum Smith taught us more than a year after the first certificate was given.

At a special conference held in Nauvoo on the 10th day of April, 1843, I was appointed to take a mission to preach the gospel in St. Lawrence Co., N. Y.

In those days the Elders, when appointed on a mission, were compelled to depend upon their own resources for means to travel with, or start out on foot without purse or script, as Jesus sent out his disciples, in his day. They had no idea of calling on the Bishop for money to travel with, as it was not used for such a purpose.

During the fore part of the summer of 1843, continued tending to my temporal affairs, and making arrangements to take the mission assigned me. In the mean time the spiritual wife doctrine was pressed so closely that I felt the time was at hand when I must determine whether to accept it or not. I knew I had not so learned Christ, and for about three days it seemed that I must almost go distracted, so great was the struggle.

I prayed almost constantly to my heavenly Father to know what *I should do*. I did not trouble myself about others, what they should do, but the burden of my soul, and the intense agony of my heart, was, to know what my individual duty was in this matter. I did not wish to embrace anything that was not of the Lord, nor reject anything that was from him. About ten o'clock, on the morning of the *third day* my heavenly Father, in his loving kindness, answered my prayer. As I was walking by myself, down Parley street, just before entering Main street, he spake to me, clear and distinct, and said: "I have not placed you to set in order the affairs of my church, stand still and see the result of all things, but *keep yourself unspotted from the world.*"

'AMEN, FATHER,' was my glad and earnest response. I knew from that day to this, that if others could have more wives than one, and have the spirit of the Lord, I could not, and there I let the matter rest. It troubled me no more.

Nauvoo was denominated a stake of Zion, with three Presidents, and a High Council. Wm. Marks was President, with Austin Cowles and Amasa Lyman as his counsellors, which constituted the three Presidents over the stake and High Council.

Presidents Marks and Cowles were among the good and solid men of the age. Both were opposed to polygamy, but Brother Cowles was far more outspoken, and energetic in his opposition to that doctrine than almost any other man in Nauvoo. In fact, I think his opposition excelled all others. Hyrum opposed it at first, but afterwards became its warm advocate, to my certain knowledge.

One day, in July, before I got ready to start on my mission to New York state, I met Bro. Cowles on Main Street, when he said to me: "Brother Robinson, how can you go out on a mission under these circumstances, with things as they are?" I replied: "I can go readily, for I would preach the gospel of our Lord and Savior, Jesus Christ." "Yes" said he, "And when people have obeyed that, have them come here to this sink of iniquity." I replied, "that was no part of my mission, that when they obeyed the gospel I left them in the hands of their heavenly Father, before him they must stand or fall."

On the 12th of this July it is claimed the revelation on polygamy was given through Joseph Smith. I did not see the revelation, but was told a few days after, and before leaving Nauvoo, that such a revelation had been given.

I started on that mission on the last day of July, 1843, accompanied by my wife, Gen. Wilson Law and wife, who were going to Pennsylvania, and my wife to stop in Ohio visiting our relatives there, while I should prosecute the mission in the state of New York.

Gen. Law and myself employed President Wm. Marks to take us in his family carriage to Chicago, Ill., where we took a steamer for Ohio and Penn. On our way to Chicago the subject of spiritual wives, or polygamy, was freely discussed, when President Marks also told us that a revelation had been received on the subject, or, to use his own words, "They have got a revelation on the subject."

From Bro. Marks' testimony and what I had been told in Nauvoo, before leaving home, as firmly believed that Joseph Smith had given a revelation on polygamy as that he had ever given one on any subject, in his life.

Notwithstanding the revelation every member of our party were opposed to the doctrine.

We returned home from that mission the latter part of November, 1843. Soon after our return, I was told that when we were gone, the revelation on polygamy was presented to, and read in the High Council in Nauvoo, three of the members of which refused to accept it as from the Lord, viz, Presidents Marks and Cowles, and counsellor Leonard Soby. At that time and place, and on that occasion, President Austin Cowles resigned his position as one of the Presidents of the High Council, which necessarily included his presidency of the church at Nauvoo. After that he was looked upon as a seceder, and no longer held a prominent place in the church, although morally and religiously speaking, he was one of the best men in the place.

My Missionary labor was mostly in St. Lawrence and Jefferson counties, New York, where I met with reasonable success, and baptized several persons.

With regard to the gospel, I had, as heretofore stated, received a testimony which amounted to a certainty to me of its truth, and I rejoiced, and was greatly blest of my heavenly Father when presenting its glorious truths to my fellow men. I am certain that those who receive and obey it, and endure in faith to the end, will be lifted up at the last day, and inherit eternal life in the celestial Kingdom of our God.

I may have occasion to refer to some things connected with that mission hereafter.

TO BE CONTINUED.

CORRESPONDENCE.

Davis City, Iowa, Feb. 19th, 1891.
To The Church of Christ.

Brethren, and co-workers in the vineyard of our Lord and Master, Jesus Christ, inasmuch as the Lord has called us to help prune his vineyard for the last time, I feel to address you by letter, and as to what I may say, may the spirit of God direct me, that I may speak in the fear of the Lord; for by his counsel should we be directed in all things.

My prayer to God is, that all those who have taken upon them the name of Christ, may hold firm to the pure principles of Christ; and that we may never quench the spirit that will guide us into all truth; and may we let our light so shine, that others may see our good works, and glorify our Father who art in heaven; and come and walk in the light of the gospel.

May the day hasten, when all honest in heart will have the gospel presented to them with the convincing power of God, in its purity. And I pray that we may all be united, as members of one household; that strife and contention may never be found in our midst, but love and unity; for in union there is strength.

And may God bless all his servants with power and wisdom from on high, that they may proclaim his word in mighty power. Let us pray to our heavenly Father to increase our faith, for without faith we are nothing. In the 14th chapter of Romans, and 22-23, verses, it reads like this: "Hast thou faith? have it to thyself before God. Happy is he that condemneth not himself in that thing which he alloweth. And, he that doubteth is damned if he eat, because he eateth not of faith: for whatsoever is not of faith is sin."

In the .... chapter of Hebrews, and first verse, it says: "Now faith is the substance of things hoped for, the evidence of things not seen." And as it is for the children of God, to have all the blessings of God, if we walk upright and just. I pray that the day may soon come, when the members of the church of Christ, will all enjoy the blessings of God, in full; and that the spirit of God will be with us all to the end of our journey. May the blessings and peace of heaven, be with you all, is my prayer, Amen.

Your Brother in Christ,
S. F. LaPoint.

Hillsdale, Iowa, Feb. 19, 1891.

DEAR BROTHER ROBINSON: It is with pleasure that I write to you. I have been very sick for about three weeks, and now I am nearly well. They did not expect me to live, and the neighbors asked what doctor we had; we told them God was our doctor. Then they asked me if I did not want a doctor; I told them that I leaned upon my Maker, and if he would not heal me the doctor could not, and if it was my time to die, I would die; but if it was the Lord's will, I wanted to live to help my aged mother, who is not able to do all the work.

The Lord has greatly blest me in my illness, and also my little brother, who was very sick, but is now able to go to school. The Lord has blest us more than we can realize or thank him for; but I hope that we can do a great deal for him, for he has done so much for us. I want to please him in every thing. O how kind a Father we have; when I was in great pain, and would call upon his name in the name of his Son, he would relieve my pain. O may we be more humble before our Go than we have been in the past. I hope to do so myself.

It was sad news to hear of the death of Bro. George Adams; he seemed so mild and humble in his talk. I think he will hear the pleasing words saying, "come up ye blessed of my Father, to inherit eternal life," and to meet his wife who had gone before him. My prayer is that we may meet them in heaven, where our loved ones have gone before us.

Your sister in Christ,
PHEBE R. THOMAS.

Drum Creek Feb. 14th, 1891.

DEAR BROTHERS AND SISTERS:

We see by the heading of these lines that another year is now bearing us all onward to that great eternity. Let us pause and ask ourselves these questions, are we striving to be prepared? are we keeping our lamps trimmed and brightly burning? ready at any moment the Master may call us? for we know not whether he may call us at midnight, or in the morning; but we feel certain, how joyful the summons to us, if we are ready. Let us never grow weary in well d ing.

This is a blessed gospel we live in, and I know if faithful, it will be a blessed time to me; yea, blessed beyond description, to die firm in he faith of the gospel Christ has taught us.

My son and self spent a few days, also the first Sabbath of the month, at Brother W. P. Brown's, of Newton, Kansas. We held Fellowship and Sacrament meeting at his house, and as each one rose and bore their testimony, I felt by the power of the spirit present, how good it is to be a child of God; and how our Heavenly Father delighteth to bless his children, if we will but live humble and meek before him.

A few days before our arrival, Brother Brown had Baptized Brother Robert Garrard, of Little River, Rice Co. Kansas. And thus they come, as it were, one out of a town and two out of a city. We know the work of the Lord will roll on until he has accomplished all his purposes.

My earnest desire, and prayer to God is, that we may be wise, in this the day of our probation, and that we may each be counted worthy of a part in the first resurrection.

Ever your sister in the new and everlasting covenant,
MRS. CHARLOTTE DOOP.

MISCELLANEOUS.

DAMASCUS, one of the oldest cities in the world, still retains the peculiarities it held in the time of Christ. A writer, just returned from there after a three years' residence, describes the city as a "diamond set in the dark green of fruitful gardens,"

THE RETURN.

"Truth, crushed to earth, shall rise again; The eternal years of God are hers."

Vol. 3. No. 2.   DAVIS CITY, IOWA, FEBRUARY, 1891.   Whole No. 26.

The Return.

PUBLISHED MONTHLY AT $1.00 A YEAR.

Entered at the Post Office at Davis City. Iowa, as second class matter.

COMMUNICATIONS.

The writers of all articles under this head are solely responsible for the views expressed therein. The Editor disclaims all responsibility.

The Law All Fulfilled In Christ.

BY W. S. ROBERTS

Dear Reader:—By writing upon this subject, I wish to show that those who go back to the law of Moses, and Abraham, to substantiate any particular office or doctrine, do greatly err, by so doing. I shall quote from Christ's own words, as recorded in the New Covenant Scriptures; in both the Bible and Book of Mormon, and also from his Disciples; believing they taught the same doctrine that Christ taught to them, and sent them into the world to teach.

I shall now quote from Book of Mormon, pages 445 and 446, par. 9 to 11, 5th chap.; I will not quote all of these paragraphs for want of space, just enough to give the meaning. Christ, speaking, said:

"Verily, verily, I say unto you, that this is my doctrine, and whoso buildeth upon this buildeth upon my Rock, and the gates of hell shall not prevail against them. And whoso shall declare more or less than this, and establish it for my doctrine, the same cometh of evil, and is not built upon my Rock, but he buildeth upon a sandy foundation, and the gates of hell standeth open to receive such, when the floods come and the winds beat upon them."

Oh; how careful we should be that we are not found teaching some other doctrine which Christ never taught; please bear this in mind.

We now turn to last of 9th par. "Think not that I am come to destroy the law or the prophets. I am not come to destroy but to fulfill; for verily I say unto you, one jot nor one tittle hath not passed away from the law, but in me it hath all been fulfilled." No; Christ did not destroy the law, for if he had it would not be found in existence to day. The law exists to day, but it is of no force, because it has all been fulfilled in Christ, and a new and better covenant established in its stead; a spiritual and everlasting covenant.

We find these words in 10th par. "Behold ye have the commandments before you, and the law is fulfilled; therefore come unto me and be ye saved; for verily I say unto you, that except ye shall keep my commandments, which I have commanded you at this time, ye shall in no case enter into the Kingdom of heaven." In 11th par. he says: "Old things are done away, and all things have become new."

Again, page 451 found in 1st par. 7 chap. "And it came to pass that when Jesus had said these words, he perceived that there were some among them who marveled, and wondered what he would concerning the law of Moses; for they understood not the saying that old things had passed away, and all things had become new. And he said unto them, Marvel not that I said unto you, that old things had passed away and that all things had become new. Behold I say unto you that the law is fulfilled that was given unto Moses. Behold I am he that covenanted with my people Israel; therefore the law in me is fulfilled, for I have come to fulfill the law, therefore it hath an end. Behold I do not destroy the prophets, for as many as have not been fulfilled in me verily I say unto you shall all be fulfilled. And because I said unto you that old things hath passed away, I do not destroy that which hath been spoken concerning things which are to come; for behold the covenant which I have made with my people is not all fulfilled, but the law which was given unto Moses hath an end in me. Behold I am the law, and the light, look unto me and endure to the end and ye shall live, for unto him that endureth to the end, will I give eternal life. Behold, I have given unto you the commandments, therefore keep my commandments. And this is the law and the prophets, for they truly testified of me."

Oh what a glorious thought contained in the above scripture. But the thought we wish to notice is, that Christ is the law, and the light, hence we need not look for another law-giver. Christ has fulfilled the old law, and has given a new law, and made a new covenant, the old one having become old, and like an old garment, decayed, which passeth away. Also if we keep his commandments, we shall have eternal life,

He also says in the 6th chap. 6th par., Page 450: "Therefore, whoso heareth these sayings of mine, and doeth them, I will liken him unto a wise man, who built his house upon a rock, and the rain descended, and the floods came, and the winds blew, and beat upon that house, and it fell not; for it was founded upon a rock." Now what sayings did Christ mean when he said, these sayings of mine, did he mean his sayings which should some time in the future come through a man, and be called a revelation to his people like some of the revelations in the Doctrine and Covenants which requires us to comply with some other law in order to be saved? Oh, no, I think not; I think he meant what he said: "*These* sayings of *mine*,' They were the sayings which He had been teaching them in that day. Yes his everlasting gospel, which he has brought forth to us in its fullness, in these last days.

Brethren I believe we have both seen and heard those sayings of his, for they are recorded in both the new covenant scriptures of the bible and book of Mormon; and if we do them we will be likened unto that wise man, and will surely be in a safe condition when the gates of hell cannot prevail agains us. Remember that the sayings of his at that time, spoken by his own mouth, (and not through another,) was to come down to us as the fullness of his gospel to us.

Some would claim that only the carnal part of the old law was done away, according to Christ's words, when he said it was all fulfilled, and had an end in him. The law of Moses must have been all carnal. But be that as it may, if there ever was a spiritual law given before Christ, it would never be done away, for that which is spirit liveth forever, hence it would have to be grafted into the new covenant; which covenant is a spiritual covenant, for says Christ: "My words are Spirit and life."

I believe Christ set up a spiritual kingdom when he set up the church, he himself being the King or head; and consequently that spiritual kingdom must have a spiritual head, and be governed by a spirtual law, (an everlasting law.) And if a spiritual kingdom takes upon it a carnal head, (all men are fallible, liable to carnality,) and introduce carnal laws to govern it, it is then that it becomes carnal, and Christ cannot be its head, for he is a spiritual being.

Now the law was given to Moses, but grace and truth came by Jesus Christ. I prefer that grace and truth to govern the church of Christ, rather than the law of Moses, or Abraham, or any part thereof. On account of the hard heartedness and stiff necks of the children of Israel, they were given a law that was not good, and that law was called a law of carnal commandments. And although this law was carnal, it was full of types and shadows of the real, and everlasting law, which Christ should come in person, and by his own mouth, instigate; which was a perfect law of liberty, which would make men free; and enable them to become sons of God; yes, heirs of God, and joint heirs with Jesus Christ, which comes by the power of the Holy Ghost; the new covenant made with Israel; the law written in their hearts. Yes, the Holy Ghost, so every one could know God for themselves, and not for another.

In the book of Doctrine and Covenants, there are laws and revelations just as carnal as any found in the law of Moses. Any law governing property or money, (compulsory,) are temporal, and carnal. Who is so blind as to think that the law of tithing is any less carnal than the law of circumcision, or the law governing the feast of the passover, or to bring an offering to be offered upon an altar for remission of sins? Is money any more spiritual than rams, or he goats, or incense? I think not.

Christ taught freewill offerings which were not compulsory, instead of a law of tithing, (one tenth,) with a penalty of being burned if you do not observe it. In Christ's plan of salvation, he does not say we must pay our tithing in order to be saved. But according to the revelation on tithing, our salvation now rests as to whether we have paid our tithing or not. Paul says, 2nd Cor., 3rd chap. 11th verse: "For if that which is done away was glorious, much more that which remaineth is glorious." And again he saith, Gal. 3rd chap , 19th to 25th verses: "Wherefore then serveth the law; it was added because of transgression, till the seed should come to whom the promise was made; and it was ordained by Angels in the hand of a Mediator. But the scriptures hath concluded all under sin, that the promise by faith of Jesus Christ might be given to them that believe. But before faith came, we were kept under the law, shut up unto the faith which should afterwards be revealed." (Not revealed at that time:) "Wherefore the law was our school master to bring us unto Christ, that we might be justified by faith. But after that faith is come we are no longer under a school master." And again, Heb. 7th and 12th verse: "For the Priesthood being changed, there is made of necessity a change also of the law."

But, says one, did they not have the new covenant scriptures before Christ? I answer, yes, to a certain extent; although according to Paul they, in his day, knew nothing of it. And I find nothing in the Bible to prove that they did, and it was undoubtedly on account of their unbelief, and lack of faith, that they did not know of it, and when it would be preached first by Christ himself, and afterwards by his servants; and after it was sealed by the death of the testator, (Christ,) it would be in full force, (and not before,) as Paul says, Heb. 9th, 16-17 verses: "For where a testament is, there must also of necessity be the death of the testator. For a testament is of force after men are dead; otherwise it is of no strength at all while the testator liveth." So we see that in order for the new testament to be in full force, Christ had to come into the world and seal it with his death, and by so doing ...... the old law.

We find that the Jews were a faithless and perverse people: and by the absence of that living faith, which they should have had, they knew not of these things before hand. And if they had been more obedient to the law, (their school master,) they would have been better prepared to accept of this New Covenant when it did come, as Paul says: "They were shut up under the law until faith came." There must be a living faith in God, before a people can know of things to come in the future.

Paul says: "The law and the prophets were until John, afterwards the kingdom of God was preached."

John began to preach repentance as a forerunner to Christ, to get the hearts of the people better prepared to accept of the one that was mightier than he, that should baptize them with fire and the Holy Ghost. I deem it needless to quote any more scripture to show that the old law was all fulfilled in Christ, for the Son of God had spoken it. It should suffice.

As I have just been speaking of a faithless people, I now turn to a people with faith, viz. the Nephites. We learn that they knew of Christ and his Mission, and at least a good portion of the great plan of salvation, before Christ came; question: How was it possible? we answer, by reason of their great faith. Some had such great faith that they could not be kept from within the vail. We also find that this knowledge profited them greatly. These things were made known to them that they might look forward for a remission of their sins, by the Son of God, the great mediator, through the atonement which he should make. Remember, the atonement was not made yet, consequently the new covenant was not yet in full force.

Nephi says, in his second book page 95, last of 6th and first of 7th 11th chap.. "For we labor diligently to write to persuade our children and also our brethren, to believe in Christ, and to be reconciled to God; for we know that it is by grace that we are saved, after all we can do.

And notwithstanding we believe in Christ, we keep the law of Moses, and look forward with steadfastness unto Christ, until the law shall be fulfilled; for, for this end was the law given; wherefore, the law hath become dead unto us, and we are made alive in Christ, because of our faith; yet we keep the law because of the commandments, and we talk of Christ; and we rejoice in Christ, we preach of Christ; we prophesy of Christ; and we write according to our Prophecies; that our children may know to what source they may look for a remission of their sins. Wherefore, we speak concerning the law, that our children may know the deadness of the law; and they, by knowing the deadness of the law, may look forward unto that life which is in Christ, and know for what end the law was given. And after the law is fulfilled in Christ, that they need not harden their hears against him, when the law ought to be done away."

We see by this scripture that it was by faith that they received these things, and that they taught these to their children that they might be the better prepared to accept of Christ when he did come; and that they might know that the law was not life; and to know where to look for a remission of their sins. They were under the law of Moses then, and still would be until it was done away. (Men are only under the law that exists in their day.)

An old law must first be repealed before a new one can be in full force. Now the question, how could they be under the law and yet above it? when that faith came that Paul speaks of, it gave them a greater knowledge than their schoolmaster (the law) could give them, and of course they were above it, yet they had to be subject to the law they were under (viz,) the law of Moses.

Let us illustrate this matter: suppose you were going to school to a common school teacher, (or school master,) and you became a better scholar than your teacher, would you not be above your teacher in learning? consequently your teacher would be dead to you. He could no longer teach you, for you know more than your teacher. Nevertheless you would be under his control and jurisdiction and his government as long as you went to his school.

Now another question arises, what benefit was there in those people keeping the New Covenant which they received before Christ came and sealed it with his death, which of course would make it binding and in full force! we learn by reading the History of those people that they were greatly blessed by observing it. Now let us illustrate this matter also, there is a certain man by the name of Edward Bellamy, who has written a book called Looking Backward, in the which he portrays a system of government, (a great commonwealth plan) which far excels our present system of government (or at least the way our government is being run at present.) Now there are 2 or 3 different colonies in this country trying to carry out Bellamy's plan of government; and although they may receive a great benefit by it, nevertheless they have got to be subject to the powers that be, (viz,) the statute laws and regulations of the government of which they are citizens. Their form of government cannot fully and practically be carried out, as long as they are under some other different mode of government; another evidence that the New Covenant was not in full force before Christ is this, that all those that were baptized before Christ, had to be baptized over again.

Yours in the freedom of Christ.

W. S. ROBERTS.

SECRET SOCIETIES.

Joseph Starts the Temple endowments.

By Chas. W. Lamb.

Number 2.

"Truth crushed to earth shall rise again; The eternal years of God are hers."

MR. EDITOR:—As your paper the RETURN, for Oct., 1890, shows from Joseph Smith's own writings in the 19th Vol. of the Millenial Star, page 390 and 91, the fact that he introduced a secret "order of the priesthood," on the 4th day of May, 1842; in a secret "Council" held with the other leading men in the church, and with some of the highest Free Masons in that part of the land; and held in what was then used as the masonic lodge; and which order his writings also show was intended to be given to the Elders in *the temple as an endowment*, when that building should be "completed." Joseph says that "in this council was instituted the ancient order of things for the first time in these last days."

Joseph's preparatory discourse on the first of May, shows what kind of a snare was being "prepared for the church of the first born." We can see that his new "ancient order of things," which he says pertained "to the Ancient of Days"—who, according to the book of Doctrine and Covenants, Sec. 26, par. 2, is Michael or Adam—had "certain *keys* and *words*," which he calls "the *keys of the kingdom*." By these keys and the "plans and principles" of this secret "order of the priesthood," Joseph says, "any one is enabled to secure the fullness of those blessings which have been prepared for the church of the First Born, and come up and abide in the presence of the Eloheim in the eternal worlds." He says: "The keys are certain signs and words by which false spirits and personages may be detected from true which cannot be revealed to the Elders *till the temple is completed.* * * There are signs in heaven, earth, and hell; the Elders must know them all, *to be endowed* with power, to finish their work and prevent imposition."

After all that is said in the Book of Mormon in condemnation of secret societies with their oaths and penalties and grips and "signs and words," which were and are the keys by which the members thereof know each other and can detect the "false spirits and personages" from the true members, and "prevent imposition:" After all, I say, it turns out, according to Joseph's showing, that the kingdom of God, and the church of Christ, when it is to attain to "the *fullness* of those blessings which have been prepared" for it, is run on the same plan and principle' as these condemned secret combinations; in which the Book of Mormon tells us. "*The Lord worketh not,*" and which it also says '*are built up by the devil,* who is the father of all lies.' See Ether 3rd 12, 13, Book of Mormon.

Now let us notice a few of the *parallels* between this order started by Joseph, and the Nauvoo and Utah endowments:

1st. This "Eloheim" also figures as the highest or Head God in the endowments.

2nd. The endowment was also, like this, an "ancient order," and also "pertained to the Ancient of Days," For it went back to Adam, and its ceremonies represented the creation of the earth and Adam and Eve, and the scenes in the Garden of Eden.

3rd, The so called Brighamite endowment was also an "order of the priesthood."

4th, And it also had "certain signs and words."

5th, And Joseph's words in the Millennial Star concerning his secret order, will also apply to and describe the secret endowments to perfection; for the secret grips and signs and words of the latter institution were also "keys pertaining to the Aaronic Priesthood, and so to the highest order of the Melchisedec Priesthood."

6th, And the key words, etc. of the priesthood communicated in the endowments were also to entitle those possessing them,—or to enable them "to secure the fullness of those blessings which have been prepared for the church of the First Born, and to come up and abide in the presence of Eloheim in the eternal world."

In order to show more of the points of similarity existing between the two, I will have to quote more of Joseph's words concerning his secret order.

"Wednesday, (May) 4th. *I spent the day* in the upper part of the store (Masonic lodge room,) in council with General James Adams of Springfield, Patriarch Hyrum Smith, Bishops Newel K. Whitney, and George Miller, and Brigham Young, Heber C. Kimball and Willard Richards, *instructing them in the principles* and order of the Priesthood, attending to *washings, anointings, endowments,* and the *communication of Keys* pertaining to the Aaronic Priesthood, and so on to the highest order of the Melchisedec Priesthood, setting forth the order pertaining to the Ancient of days, and all those plans and priciples by which any one is enabled to secure the fullness of those blessings which have been prepared for the church of the First Born, and come up and abide in the presence of the Eloheim in the eternal worlds."

This General James Adams of Springfield, which Joseph mentions first in this council, was the Masonic Deputy *Grand Master* of the State of Illinois. Hyrum Smith was then' or at least was only 13 days later, acting as master *Pro-tem* of the Nauvoo lodge of Free and Accepted *Ancient* York Masons. For this, see his affidavit at the trial of John C. Bennett, in Vol. 3 of Mil'um. Star, page 140. George Miller, and her person in this council, that instituted "for the first time" the Masonic-like temple endowments, was "Master of Nauvoo lodge, under dispensation." See same Star, P. 105.

Notice that in the above quotation Joseph says he "*spent the day*," in the work of going through with the various performances and administering the ceremonies, consisting of lectures "setting forth the order," and giving instructions on its plans and principles, and the communication of key words and signs, etc. Those who went through the ceremonies and took the secret covenants administered in the Nauvoo temple and Utah endowment house, began early in the day and also nearly "spent the day" in going through the endowment ceremonies. This gives the parallel between the two.

8th, Part of Joseph's time on that day was occupied in giving lectures of instruction on the principles of his secret order. It was the same in the secret endowments.

9th. Joseph speaks of "*washings*" as part of the performances in his ceremonies designed for the temple. And in the endowment ceremonies given in the temple and in Utah, the candidate was stripped and washed all over, with a running comment or blessing, by the one officiating, to the effect that he or she was washed clean from the blood of this generation.

10th. Joseph tells of "*anointings*" as being part of the ceremonies in his secret temple order. And in the Utah endowments, after being washed, every part and organ of the body of the initiate, from head to foot, was anointed, a blessing at the same time being pronounced upon each part. For instance, the mouth was anointed that he might with wisdom speak the words of eternal life.

11th. Part of Joseph's time on that memorable day was occupied in the "communication of keys" pertaining to the Aaronic and Melchisedec Priesthoods, consisting of "signs and words." And in the Utah endowment ceremonies there were numerous signs and words communicated, pertaining to those two priesthoods; and the words were the key words of the priesthood.

12th. Joseph gives away the fact that "*endowments*" of some sort were pretended to be administered in his order that he designed for the secret temple ceremony, when that building should be "completed." And so pretended endowments were also administered in the ceremonies in the Nauvoo temple when a suitable number of rooms had been finished and prepared. And so these secret ceremonies finally came naturally enough to be termed "Endowments."

13th. As Joseph's key words, etc., were the "Keys of the Kingdom," and pertained to the priesthood which were its rulers, and by which the initiate was pretended to be fully born or inducted into the Kingdom, and the possession of which entitled him to a "fullness of the blessings prepared," and finally to "come up and abide in the presence of the Eloheim." So also with the Utah endowment key words, etc. They were the keys of the kingdom, because they were keys of the priesthood, by which authority the kingdom was run; and by his initiation which gives him these keys the candidate is pretended to be fully ushered into the kingdom, ready to receive the "fullness" of its blessings, and their possession to entitle him to finally enter the presence of the same Eloheim, where he shall give these holy secret-pass words or key words at the door of the Holiest of Holies in the eternal worlds.

14th. I might mention as another pointer, that Joseph's secret order, started on the 4th of May, 1842, was by him *designed as the temple ceremony, and was to be given to the El-*

ders in the temple, or in the "Holiest of Holies" therein, when the temple should be "completed."

15th. And I might also add as a separate and final pointer, that by Joseph's temple secret order the Elders were "to be *endowed* with power," when the temple was completed. Therefore *it was designed as an endowment*. And with these facts before us, that it was for an *endowment* and to be given *in the temple*, how can we avoid the conclusion that it was beyond question, *designed* by him to be the *Temple Endowment?* And that it was the same that was afterwards given in the temple as an endowment by "Brigham and associates," with whom he had "spent the day," and perhaps many other days afterwards, in instructing in its "plans and principles." For we have seen that the two run parallel all the way through, and that the evidence is undeniable, *that the two are one and the same*. And thus "Brigham and associates" were truly, as they always claimed," carrying out Joseph's measures," in finishing the temple and giving the kind of endowment they did. In fact I believe they have been "carrying out the measures of our martyred prophet" all the time, and in every other particular. The Reorganized church claims to be carrying out Joseph's measures also. And so they are in many things. But why is not Joseph's secret combination of the priesthood or his temple endowment, found in that church?

Endowments Then, and Now.

God's people of old, who had truly believed,
On Penticost day by His Spirit received
Endowments with power, *coming down from the Lord*,
Through His gifts inspiring to utter His word.
But "in these last days" sadly changed in the view!
"Endowments" were given that came *from below;*
And given in secret, with oaths to obey,
And put trust in men, who soon led us astray.

So iniquity's myst'ry did greatly abound,
But the "keys" of the latter day priestcraft are found.
And we'll handle these "keys" with the righteous intent,
The like "*imposition*" henceforth to "*prevent.*"

CHAS. W. LAMB.

IS THE MANUSCRIPT DIVINE?

A regular reader of the Republic residing at Richmond, Missouri, furnishes the editor of this department the following note concerning the original manuscript copy of the Book of Mormon, which belonged to the late David Whitmer, one of the three witnesses to the divine authenticity of the book. June 1st, 1878, the city of Richmond, Missouri, was visited by a terrible cyclone. The residence of David Whitmer, the possessor of the manuscript of the Book of Mormon, was directly in the storm's path. Although the house was almost totally demolished, one room, that in which the book was deposited—being an extention of a porch, consequently not as substantial as the other parts of the house—was left uninjured in the least degree; not a shingle was removed or a single crack made in the plastering, says the St. Louis *Republic*. Like the Athenian watch tower it stood, piled up with wrecks on all sides, itself unwrecked. When the citizens of the afflicted city learned of the above facts they formed a committee and made a report on the miraculous preservation of the single room and its highly valued treasure. The written report of the committee is now in possession of one of the prominent attorneys of the city in which the events related occured.—*St. Paul Daily.*

CONTINUED HEALTH.—It was the celebrated Dr. Abernethy, I believe, who left at his death a sealed envelope, said to contain the secret of his success as a physician. Upon being opened, it was found to contain simply the following prescription: "To insure continued health and a ripe old age, keep the head cool, the system open, and the feet warm."-Ex.

The Return.

PUBLISHED MONTHLY AT $1.00 A YEAR.

E. ROBINSON, EDITOR AND PROPRIETOR.

DAVIS CITY, IOWA, FEB. 1891.

TO CORRESPONDENTS.

We respectfully request our friends and correspondents, when writing articles for THE RETURN, and making quotations from the Bible and Book of Mormon, to be particular and give the quotations correctly, including all the punctuation marks, as they occur in the book from which they make the quotation. If they will do this, it will save much trouble and time in preparing the articles for the press.

An otherwise well written article has been reviewed, on which nearly or quite a whole day's time has been devoted in comparing the quotations, and preparing it for the press. In one of the quotations one whole line was left out, greatly marring the sense, and apparently no regard taken to the commas, periods, or other punctuation marks.

If correspondents would be particular and write the quotations correctly, and give all the punctuation marks as they write, it would save the Editor much valuable time.

Write for our Paper.

Several persons write and express a wish to have THE RETURN a semi monthly, and some say a weekly. Very few persons realize the labor it takes to prepare the copy for even a monthly, when it is mostly original matter, as is the case with our paper. It is made up of solid reading matter, not filled with advertisements heretofore, therefore the first and second volumes furnish a large amount of reading matter for the size of the paper.

All wish it to be as interesting as possible. The way to have it so, is for all the friends to take an interest in its welfare, and each write a short article on some good religious spiritual subject, and write often. Make it a subject of prayer, and ask your heavenly Father to aid you by his Holy Spirit, and I sure you that you will feel greatly blessed in so doing.

Please avoid doubtful or personal questions, calculated in their nature to stir up animosity and strife. The gospel, with its numerous Christian graces, the gathering of Israel, and the great work of the Father to be accomplished in these last days, together with many other beautiful, spiritual subjects, all furnish food for contemplation and thought, and are worthy to be written upon, and stir up our pure minds by way of remembrance of these things.

ELDER THOMAS' VISIT.

Elder Solomon Thomas, came and made us a visit of several days duration.

He had been called here to assist in attending to the business connected with the Estate of Elder Geo. Adams, deceased.

Elder Adams made a will, bequeathing his property to the Church of Christ, and appointed John C. Whitmer, Solomon Thomas, and Ebenezer Robinson, Executors of his will; which was probated on the 19th of January, 1891, in the District court of Decatur co., Iowa, and Letters Testamentary issued to the said Executors, by order of the court.

Elder Thomas came on the 26th and remained until Monday, the second inst.

His visit was appreciated very much by all our members here. He took active part with us in our sacrament meeting.

On Sunday evening, when here, he received a telegram that his daughter Phebe, who is fifteen years old, was dangerously ill, and urged his immediate return. He took the first train for home, where he found his daughter as represented, but through the kindness of our heavenly Father, she has recovered, as will be seen by a letter from her under the head of correspondents.

February 14, 1891.

The 14th day of February is past, and the "winding up scene," or "second coming of Christ," which I understand to be synonimous terms, has not taken place, therefore another prediction of Joseph Smith, jr., has entirely failed, showing clearly that his prophecy on this subject is as false as that of William Miller, and others, who have prophesied concerning the time of that event.

"Joseph Goodal was recently found dead at his door in Dunlap, from heart disease, it is supposed. He was a disciple of Joseph Smith and helped build the Mormon temple at Nauvoo, Ill."

The above item was published in the *Lamoni Journal* of a recent date. The Joseph Goodal there spoken of, I believe to be Joseph D. Goodale, who made us a visit last June. If it be the same, he was of the old stock of Latter Day Saints, but held to some peculiar ideas, differing from other members of the church.

From my acquaintance with him I believe him to have been not only a good citizen, but an upright christian gentleman.

☞ VICK'S FLORAL GUIDE, FOR 1891, has been received. It contains 100 richly embelished pages, including several beautiful colored plates.

Vick is evidently the leading seedsman of our country, having as I understand, some 1,500 acres of land devoted to raising seeds and nursery stock. Customers ordering seeds from him may feel sure of getting good fresh seeds. Address, James Vick, seedman, 343, East Avenue, Rochester, N. Y.

—BROTHER JAMES COMPTON, of Attica, Wisconsin, has kindly sent us a copy of a hymn Book, entitled "spiritual songs and sacred hymns, published by Russel Huntley for the Church of Christ." It is a neatly printed, well bound book, of 278 pages, containing a choice collection of 219 hymns.

Bro. Compton will please accept our thanks for this token of his regard.

TESTIMONY.

From the tenor of some letters received it seems necessary that I should repeat what has so often been stated in THE RETURN, that I still bear the same positive testimony of the truth of the glorious gospel of our Lord and Saviour Jesus Christ, as revealed in the new Testament and book of Mormon, as I ever did.

Because I feel that I have been called upon to show the Latter Day Saints *some* of the gross errors which have been introduced into the church, therefore it is stated by some that I have denied the faith. To such, and to all the world, I will say in all calmness and sincerity, that the statement is a great mistake. I as firmly believe the divine authenticity of the book of Mormon, as of any other truth extant. The evidences of its truthfulness are accumulating almost daily.

Some who, in years past, heard me bear my testimony in favor of the gospel and book of Mormon, seemed to understand that those testimonies included the Reorganised church, when I intended no such thought. I never did believe the Reorganized church was right in all things, but lived in hopes it would ultimately see its errors, and renounce them; but after the positive stand taken on the subject of tithing, adding it to the gospel, and the review in the *Saints' Herald* of Elder David Whitmer, my eyes were opened more clearly to see the true position occupied by the church, when I abandoned all hope of ever seeing it restored to the primitive order of church government and standing, such as I believe the Lord will have when Jesus comes to take to himself the "Bride, the Lamb's wife."

May the Lord bless the honest in heart to see clearly the truth as it is in Christ Jesus, and enable one and all to obey it in its simplicity and purity, is my earnest prayer.

I trust no one will think, because I bear testimony to the truth of the gospel and book of Mormon, that thereby I testify to the unity and harmony of all the members of the church of Christ, for I do not wish to be so understood.—ED.

CHURCH HISTORY.

NUMBER TWO.

In the former article it was shown, according to the records, that the church of Christ was established in 1829, but on the 6th of April, 1830, it was organized *agreeable to the laws of our country*, in order, as Elder David Whitmer testifies to comply with the laws of the land.

Some things transpired on that day which will bear a careful examination, as great, and in many respects, fearful results have been brought to pass there from.

It was on that day the revelation came through Joseph Smith, instructing the church as follows:

"Behold, there shall be a record kept among you, and in it thou, [Joseph Smith,] shalt be called a Seer, a translator, a Prophet, and Apostle of Jesus Christ, and Elder of the church through the will of God the Father, and the grace of our Lord Jesus Christ;"

Also, in the same revelation the following direct and positive command was given to the church:

"Wherefore, meaning the church, thou shalt give heed unto all his words and commandments which he shall give unto you as he receiveth them, walking in all holiness before me; for his word ye shall receive as if from mine own mouth, in all patience and faith; for by doing these things the gates of hell shall not prevail against you;"—D. & C. 19:1,2.

Here we find in this early stage of the history of the church, this remarkable doctrine was given by *commandment* that the church should give heed unto "*all his words* and commandments," &c., with a promise that, "by doing these things the gates of hell shall not prevail against you."

Upon this foundation the church was built, after the sixth of April, 1830, as its history clearly shows. Thus early were the brethren taught to look to *one man* as their spiritual adviser, and that he was the *head* of the church, through whom they should learn the will of the Lord concerning themselves.

During the summer and fall of 1830, the Elders continued preaching and baptizing those who believed their testimony. The officers of the church being elders, priests and teachers. No mention being made of high priests or high counsellors, notwithstanding the church was led by direct revelation, through its prophet.

In September a revelation came through Joseph Smith, directed to Oliver Cowdery, from which the following extract is taken:

"Verily, Verily I say unto thee, no one shall be appointed to receive commandments and revelations in this church, excepting Joseph Smith, Jr., for he receiveth them like Moses; and thou, [Oliver] shall be obedient unto the things which I shall give unto him, even as Aaron, to declare faithfully the commandments and the revelations with power and authority unto the church."—D. and C. 27:2.

By this revelation we find that notwithstanding the angel had restored the everlasting gospel, and the church was under a gospel dispensation, yet, at one step the Mosiac order was introduced, and Oliver Cowdery *commanded* to be *obedient* thereto.

In the Book of Mormon, which had so recently been translated and printed, the statement is made that the Lamanites should be converted and build a city in this land, to be called the New Jerusalem, to be assisted in this work by the believing gentiles. This statement led the brethren to understand that a work was to be done among the Lamanites, and evidently believing the time had come for that work, four Elders were appointed by revelation to go on that mission, viz, Oliver Cowdery, Peter Whitmer, Parley P. Pratt and Ziba Peterson.

These Elders made preparation and started on their mission to the Lamanites, in October, 1830, preaching in the villages through which they passed, until they came to "Kirtland, Ohio, where they tarried some time, there being quite a number there who believed their testimony and obeyed the gospel. Among the number was Elder Sidney Rigdon, and a large portion of the church over which he presided."

Their visit was the first knowledge Elder Rigdon ever had of the Book of Mormon. The copy they took was the first he had ever seen of that sacred record.

Elder Rigdon was then living in Mentor, about two miles from Kirtland, (near the place General Garfield afterwards resided.) He had charge of an interesting congregation of disciples or Campbellites. He kindly let the brethren have the use of his church to hold meetings in, and informed them he "would read the book of Mormon, give it a full investigation, and then frankly tell them his mind and feelings on the subject."

After two weeks of careful and prayerful examination of the book, "he was fully convinced of the truth of the work, by a revelation from Jesus Christ, which was made known to him in a remarkable manner, so that he could exclaim, 'flesh and blood hath not revealed it unto me, but my Father which is in heaven."

The result was, himself and wife and about twenty others of his church embraced the faith.

TO BE CONTINUED.

ITEMS OF PERSONAL HISTORY OF THE EDITOR.

No. 21.

Continued from page 13.

Inasmuch as we are not our own keepers, and our heavenly Father has so wisely hid from us the time of our departure, and my present feebleness of health admonishes me that it is wise to hasten with the personal history, noticing only some of the leading events, leaving many items to be noticed, should my life and health be spared, and feel it to be my duty to do so, hereafter.

From what has been stated heretofore it is to be seen that great effort was made to counteract the influence that was brought to bear against the church through the disaffection of Dr. J. C. Bennett.

In October, 1842, a statement was written out, and signed by a large number of the brethren and sisters, including myself and wife, setting forth the fact that we knew of no other form of marriage ceremony in the church except the one published in the book of Doctrine and Covenants, which statement was true at that time, as we had no knowledge of such a ceremony, or that "spiritual wifery;" or "polygamy," was taught by the heads of the church, as they had not up to that time taught it to us.

We knew it was talked of in secret, and had been for more than a year, as I have heretofore stated, that Don Carlos Smith, in his life time, in June, 1841, had said to me, that "Any man who will teach and practice 'spiritual wifery' will go to hell, no matter if it is my brother Joseph."

These secret rumors could not constitute a knowledge that certain persons taught such things when they had not taught them to us.

Dr. Bennett had published the statement that Joseph Smith taught the doctrine of "Spiritual wifery," and had instituted a certain marriage ceremony connected therewith, of which we had no knowledge, and the certificate was given to counteract Bennett's statement.

Remember this was in October, 1842. In December, 1843, more than a year later, Hyrum Smith, one of the first Presidents, and also Patriarch of the church, came to my house in Nauvoo, and taught the doctrine of "spiritual wifery," (which I here say, is polygamy,) to myself and wife, which, we both certified to in her life time, which certificate has already been published to the world. Therefore, those who have made the statement that this last certificate of ours contradicts the first, make a great mistake, as the last certificate speaks of what Hyrum Smith taught us more than a year after the first certificate was given.

At a special conference held in Nauvoo on the 10th day of April, 1843, I was appointed to take a mission to preach the gospel in St. Lawrence Co., N. Y.

In those days the Elders, when appointed on a mission, were compelled to depend upon their own resources for means to travel with, or start out on foot without purse or script, as Jesus sent out his disciples, in his day. They had no idea of calling on the Bishop for money to travel with, as it was not used for such a purpose.

During the fore part of the summer of 1843, continued tending to my temporal affairs, and making arrangements to take the mission assigned me. In the mean time the spiritual wife doctrine was pressed so closely that I felt the time was at hand when I must determine whether to accept it or not. I knew I had not so learned Christ, and for about three days it seemed that I must almost go distracted, so great was the struggle.

I prayed almost constantly to my heavenly Father to know what *I should do*. I did not trouble myself about others, what they should do, but the burden of my soul, and the intense agony of my heart, was, to know what my individual duty was in this matter. I did not wish to embrace anything that was not of the Lord, nor reject anything that was from him. About ten o'clock, on the morning of the *third day* my heavenly Father, in his loving kindness, answered my prayer. As I was walking by myself, down Parley street, just before entering Main street, he spake to me, clear and distinct, and said: "I have not placed you to set in order the affairs of my church, stand still and see the result of all things, *but keep yourself unspotted from the world.*"

'AMEN, FATHER,' was my glad and earnest response. I knew from that day to this, that if others could have more wives than one, and have the spirit of the Lord, I could not, and there I let the matter rest. It troubled me no more.

Nauvoo was denominated a stake of Zion, with three Presidents, and a High Council. Wm. Marks was President, with Austin Cowles and Amasa Lyman as his counsellors, which constituted the three Presidents over the stake and High Council.

Presidents Marks and Cowles were among the good and solid men of the age. Both were opposed to polygamy, but Brother Cowles was far more outspoken, and energetic in his opposition to that doctrine than almost any other man in Nauvoo. In fact, I think his opposition excelled all others. Hyrum opposed it at first, but afterwards became its warm advocate, to my certain knowledge.

One day, in July, before I got ready to start on my mission to New York state, I met Bro. Cowles on Main Street, when he said to me: "Brother Robinson, how can you go out on a mission under these circumstances, with things as they are?" I replied: "I can go readily, for I would preach the gospel of our Lord and Savior, Jesus Christ." "Yes" said he. "And when people have obeyed that, have them come here to this sink of iniquity." I replied, "that was no part of my mission," that when they obeyed the gospel I left them in the hands of their heavenly Father, before him they must stand or fall."

On the 12th of this July it is claimed the revelation on polygamy was given through Joseph Smith. I did not see the revelation, but was told a few days after, and before leaving Nauvoo, that such a revelation had been given.

I started on that mission on the last day of July, 1843, accompanied by my wife, Gen. Wilson Law and wife, who were going to Pennsylvania, and my wife to stop in Ohio visiting our relatives there, while I should prosecute the mission in the state of New York.

Gen. Law and myself employed President Wm. Marks to take us in his family carriage to Chicago, Ill., where we took a steamer for Ohio and Penn. On our way to Chicago the subject of spiritual wives, or polygamy, was freely discussed, when President Marks also told us that a revelation had been received on the subject, or, to use his own words, "They have got a revelation on the subject."

From Bro. Marks' testimony and what I had been told in Nauvoo, before leaving home, as firmly believed that Joseph Smith had given a revelation on polygamy as that he had ever given one on any subject in his life.

Notwithstanding the revelation every member of our party were opposed to the doctrine.

We returned home from that mission the latter part of November, 1843. Soon after our return, I was told that when we were gone, the revelation on polygamy was presented to, and read in the High Council in Nauvoo, three of the members of which refused to accept it as from the Lord, viz, Presidents Marks and Cowles, and counsellor Leonard Soby. At that time and place, and on that occasion, President Austin Cowles resigned his position as one of the Presidents of the High Council, which necessarily included his presidency of the church at Nauvoo. After that he was looked upon as a seceder, and no longer held a prominent place in the church, although morally and religiously speaking, he was one of the best men in the place.

My Missionary labor was mostly in St. Lawrence and Jefferson counties, New York, where I met with reasonable success, and baptized several persons.

With regard to the gospel, I had, as heretofore stated, received a testimony which amounted to a certainty to me of its truth, and I rejoiced, and was greatly blest of my heavenly Father when presenting its glorious truths to my fellow men. I am certain that those who receive and obey it, and endure in faith to the end, will be lifted up at the last day, and inherit eternal life in the celestial Kingdom of our God.

I may have occasion to refer to some things connected with that mission hereafter.

TO BE CONTINUED.

CORRESPONDENCE.

Davis City, Iowa, Feb. 19th, 1891.
To The Church Of Christ.

Brethren, and co-workers in the vineyard of our Lord and Master, Jesus Christ, inasmuch as the Lord has called us to help prune his vineyard for the last time, I feel to address you by letter, and as to what I may say, may the spirit of God direct me, that I may speak in the fear of the Lord; for by his counsel should we be directed in all things.

My prayer to God is, that all those who have taken upon them the name of Christ, may hold firm to the pure principles of Christ; and that we may never quench the spirit that will guide us into all truth; and may we let our light so shine, that others may see our good works, and glorify our Father who art in heaven; and come and walk in the light of the gospel.

May the day hasten, when all honest in heart will have the gospel presented to them with the convincing power of God, in its purity. And I pray that we may all be united, as members of one household; that strife and contention may never be found in our midst, but love and unity; for in union there is strength.

And may God bless all his servants with power and wisdom from on high, that they may proclaim his word in mighty power. Let us pray to our heavenly Father to increase our faith, for without faith we are nothing. In the 14th chapter of Romans, and 22-23, verses, it reads like this: "Hast thou faith? have it to thyself before God. Happy is he that condemneth not himself in that thing which he alloweth. And he that doubteth is damned if he eat, because he eateth not of faith: for whatsoever is not of faith is sin."

In the fifth chapter of Hebrews, and first verse, it says: "Now faith is the substance of things hoped for, the evidence of things not seen." And as it is for the children of God, to have all the blessings of God, if we walk upright and just. I pray that the day may soon come, when the members of the church of Christ, will all enjoy the blessings of God, in full; and that the spirit of God will be with us all to the end of our journey. May the blessings and peace of heaven, be with you all, is my prayer, Amen.

Your Brother in Christ,
S. F. LaPoint.

Hillsdale, Iowa, Feb. 19, 1891.
DEAR BROTHER ROBINSON: It is with pleasure that I write to you. I have been very sick for about three weeks, and now I am nearly well. They did not expect me to live, and the neighbors asked what doctor we had; we told them God was our doctor. Then they asked me if I did not want a doctor; I told them that I leaned upon my Maker, and if he would not heal me the doctor could not, and if it was my time to die, I would die; but if it was the Lord's will, I wanted to live to help m aged mother, who is not able to do all the work.

The Lord has greatly blest me in my illness, and also my little brother, who was very sick, but is now able to go to school. The Lord has blest us more than we can realize or thank him for; but I hope that we can do a great deal for him, for he has done so much for us. I want to please him in every thing. O how kind a Father we have; when I was in great pain, and would call upon his name in the name of his Son, he would relieve my pain. O may we be more humble before our God than we have been in the past. I hope to do so myself.

It was sad news to hear of the death of Bro. George Adams; he seemed so mild and humble in his talk. I think he will hear the pleasing words saying, "come up ye blessed of my Father, to inherit eternal life," and to meet his wife who had gone before him. My prayer is that we may meet them in heaven, where our loved ones have gone before us.
Your sister in Christ,
PHEBE R. THOMAS.

Drum Creek Feb. 14th, 1891.
DEAR BROTHERS AND SISTERS:
We see by the heading of these lines that another year is now bearing us all onward to that great eternity. Let us pause and ask ourselves these questions, are we striving to be prepared? are we keeping our lamps trimmed and brightly burning? ready at any moment the Master may call us? for we know not whether he may call us at midnight, or in the morning; but we feel certain, how joyful the summons to us, if we are ready. Let us never grow weary in well doing.

This is a blessed gospel we live in, and I know if faithful, it will be a blessed time to me; yea, blessed beyond description, to die firm in the faith of the gospel Christ has taught us.

My son and self spent a few days, also the first Sabbath of the month, at Brother W. P. Brown's, of Newton, Kansas. We held Fellowship and Sacrament meeting at his house, and as each one rose and bore their testimony, I felt by the power of the spirit present, how good it is to be a child of God; and how our Heavenly Father delighteth to bless his children, if we will but live humble and meek before him.

A few days before our arrival, Brother Brown had Baptized Brother Robert Garrard, of Little River, Rice Co. Kansas. And thus they come, as it were, one out of a town and two out of a city. We know the work of the Lord will roll on until he has accomplished all his purposes.

My earnest desire, and prayer to God is, that we may be wise, in this the day of our probation, and that we may each be counted worthy of a part in the first resurrection.
Ever your sister in the new and everlasting covenant,
MRS. CHARLOTTE DOOP.

MISCELLANEOUS.

DAMASCUS, one of the oldest cities in the world, still retains the peculiarities it held in the time of Christ. A writer, just returned from there after a three years' residence, describes the city as a "diamond set in the dark green of fruitful gardens," which extend for miles round the city to the edge of the desert. The water-seller still walks through the city crying, "Ho, every one that thirsteth." The street called Straight is the same as that in which 1800 years ago, Ananias sought blind Saul of Tarsus. There is a church where they pretend the head of John the Baptist is preserved. And there, too, is the wall from which it is said Paul was let down in a basket. The city was, nearly thirty years ago, the scene of a terrible massacre of Christians on the part of the Arabs and others. Thousands were slain in a few hours, and the rest escaped only through the help afforded by Abdel-Koder, who, Muslim though he was, threatened to slay his co-religionists unless they desisted. To this day many Damascene Christians can tell of relatives whom they lost at that terrible time; yet Christianity still flourishes there, nearly all the gold and silver workers of the place being Christians.—*The Christian at Work.*

Note:—Damascus as a city in the days of Abraham, as he says: "The Steward of my house is this Eliezer of Damascus. —Gen. 15 2.

THE CHURCH WALKING WITH THE WORLD.

In our day when pure and undefiled religion, as defined in James 1:27, is so sadly lacking in many professed Christians, when there is so little difference between the church and the world, is it any wonder that a revival of religion is scarcely known in many places? We are told that in the last days perilous times shall come when men shall have a form of Godliness, but shall deny the power thereof; and is not this just what we are witnessing today? Sectarianism is wrong and a great hinderance to God's work. Christ prayed that His followers might be one, but how can they be when our churches are kept apart by sectarian bars and prejudices? Another terrible evil is that so many ministers and church members are connected with the secret lodge. These secret orders are sapping the very life from the church. Our prayer-meetings are neglected while the lodge rooms are well filled. Some professed Christians who are seldom seen in the prayer-meeting find it no trouble to go several miles in the worst travelling to meet with their lodge. They have plenty of money to pay their lodge dues but for Home Missions or for a much needed temperance lecture they can hardly afford to pay anything. Mr. Moody bears plain and emphatic testimony in regard to Christians joining any secret lodge. And if the ministers who have been led into them would set an example by renouncing and denouncing their sinfulness, we should soon see a change for the better. When our ministers and churches are willing to believe God's promises, and to accept Christ in His fullness, as a perfect supply for every need of soul and body, then we may expect to see multitudes coming to Christ. May God lead His children to take Christ as He is offered to us, our Saviour, Sanctifier, Healer and coming Lord. —*The Independent Christian.*

BACK NUMBERS

Of The Return constantly on hand, and for sale: will furnish post paid, a full set of the first vol., 12 numbers, for 50 cents. Or a full set of both the first and second volumes, 24 numbers, for $1.

ELDER DAVID WHITMER'S "Address to all believers in Christ" can be had by sending a 2 cent stamp to D. Whitmer, Richmond, Mo., or to this office.

THE RETURN is published monthly at $1 per year, payable in advance. Money can be sent by Bank draft, Post Office order on Davis City, Iowa, or Express order, at our risk. 1 cent and 2 cent P. O. stamps received in small amounts.
Address E. ROBINSON,
Davis City, Decatur Co., Iowa.

www.ingramcontent.com/pod-product-compliance
Lightning Source LLC
Chambersburg PA
CBHW030335170426
43202CB00010B/1135